1959

THE HUMANISM OF CICERO

THE
HUMANISM OF CICERO

by

H. A. K. HUNT

M.A. (Oxon), Litt.D. (Melb.)

Associate Professor of Classics
University of Melbourne

MELBOURNE UNIVERSITY PRESS

First published 1954

Melbourne University Press, Carlton, N.3, Victoria
London and New York: Cambridge University Press

Printed and bound in Australia by
Brown, Prior, Anderson Pty. Ltd.,
430 Little Bourke Street, Melbourne

Registered in Australia for transmission by post as a book

CONTENTS

PREFACE

THE purpose of this book is to offer an interpretation of Cicero's series of main philosophic works from the *Academica* to the *De Officiis*. Such a study seems to be needed because no comprehensive survey is readily available. Although there are valuable editions of single works, in each of them the editor has been preoccupied with his task of explaining the argument of the particular work in hand, grappling with textual problems or debating the sources, and has not endeavoured to link the argument with other works. In fact there has been a prejudice against seeking a coherent plan in the series because of a view commonly accepted that Cicero's purpose was merely to list the doctrines of the various schools on the several topics of philosophy. The result of this view has been that the works have been treated as if they lacked connection and might be read in any order. But by analysis such as is attempted in this book one may detect an orderly sequence in the series and a sustained argument. This does not mean that Cicero planned each step with lucidity and with nice appreciation of its bearing on the argument as a whole, for he admitted digressions and irrelevancies. But the broad development of the argument was coherent. Nor is the credit for this to be given to Cicero, for he was indebted to the Greeks, especially to the school of Antiochus of Ascalon. It was his investigation of Antiochus that suggested the order of topics to be treated and one of the tasks of the present work is to explain the significance in Cicero's programme of problems raised by his study of Antiochus.

From the general course of the argument it is possible to reconstruct the system which Cicero himself upheld. This is important in the history of philosophy because he now wins the credit not only for those services always ascribed to him as the chief source of information about the Hellenistic schools and the main Roman systematizer of their doctrines, but also for achieving himself a form of humanism unsurpassed in the pagan world for its comprehensiveness and enlightenment and thus establishing a personal position in a branch of philosophy whose importance is increasing in the modern world.

My main business being to explain the argument, I have not engaged on that other task which has occupied the energies of many scholars, the task of tracing Cicero to his sources. Yet the broad pattern of his indebtedness to the post-Aristotelian schools can be traced fairly well.

I have not felt that differences in text are serious enough to hamper the general interpretation of Cicero's works. Accordingly I have thought it reasonable to accept the texts of the editors who in the last generation performed the great work of reconstitution. The texts which have been used are listed in the bibliography.

A fair amount of translation from Cicero's Latin has been included in this work. Although some of the argument might have been summarized, it may be convenient for students to have readily accessible examples of those arguments where the Hellenistic schools displayed all their perverse ingenuity as in the contest between the dogmatists and sceptics on the distinguishability of appearances or the calculation of probabilities, or in the intricate Stoic defence of their categories of 'things preferred' but 'not good'. And again the various descriptions of the primary impulse as pleasure or self-preservation or of the chief good seem important to record for the understanding of the several schools. The translations are my own except for various short passages where for convenience I have followed the editors of the Loeb library, whose influence I also acknowledge in the longer passages. In those that come from the *Academica* I acknowledge a great debt to Reid: I have tried to be independent, not with any hope of improving upon his masterly rendering, but for the sake of self-discipline.

H.K.H.

Melbourne

CHAPTER I

CICERO'S PROGRAMME OF PHILOSOPHIC WORKS

In March 45 B.C. when he was over sixty years of age with the grief for his dear Tullia still heavy upon him and when the dominance of Caesar made him despair of effective political activity, Cicero started a period of almost continuous philosophic writing. He kept at it for the last year of Caesar's life and during the months of perplexity that followed the murder until, late in 44, he devoted himself entirely to the struggle against Antony. In this period of about twenty months he wrote eight main works and various minor ones. He started immediately after the death of Tullia with the *Consolatio* written in March 45. This was followed by the *Hortensius* in the spring of 45 (March-April). This work is almost entirely lost but we do possess two striking tributes to its effectiveness. From these and from the extant fragments we may conclude that Cicero intended the *Hortensius* to be a general introduction to the series of eight main works which followed. This series started with the *Academica,* quickly followed by the *De Finibus.* They were written from the spring to the first half of the summer of 45 (mid-April to July). Then in the second half of the summer of 45 (late July or August) he started the *Tusculan Disputations* and continued into the early summer of 44 with a group of theological and cosmological works—the translation of Plato's *Timaeus,* and the *De Natura Deorum, De Divinatione,* and *De Fato.* The murder of Caesar probably took place after the completion of the first book *De Divinatione* and before the completion of the second. The final work was the *De Officiis,* written from September to December 44. These eight works from the *Academica* to the *De Officiis* formed a coherent series written according to a planned programme, which it is the task of the present book to explain. In addition during 45 and 44 B.C. Cicero wrote several essays which may be described as works of philosophic sentiment not essential to the development of his argument, namely *De Senectute, De Amicitia,* and *De Gloria.*

Thus into a period of less than two years—a period of grave political anxiety—Cicero pressed a vast amount of philosophic

1

writing. His speed of writing was made possible partly because he proceeded for the most part not by original composition but by translation from Greek sources and partly by the nature of his plan for the eight main works. This plan was to examine certain salient issues in contemporary philosophy and Cicero was able to work quickly because he had been well trained as a student, had maintained his interest in philosophy throughout his life, had the main relevant Greek authorities readily available and knew enough about his subject to be able to write quickly himself in those parts where he found original composition necessary. Moreover, he had a warm interest in his work, as is shown in many references in his letters of 45 and 44. In September 45 he tells a friend that his devotion to philosophy grows day by day 'because the times are evil so that there is nothing else that can ease my mind of its annoyances' (*Ad. Fam.* iv. 4) : in the following January after describing the abandonment of constitutional procedure in Rome he says, 'there are countless cases of the same sort and I could not bear them if I had not taken refuge in the haven of philosophy (Ibid. vii. 30). But this was not just the refuge of an escapist, for there were issues in which he felt keen personal concern.

In order to understand the main issues with which Cicero was concerned it is necessary to know the general philosophic background of the half-century between the death of Carneades and Cicero's student days in Athens. Carneades was the last great figure of the Academy. He died in 129 B.C. His death marked the end of a period of two centuries in the course of which the passion for original inquiry had been blunted. Early in the third century the schools had been vigorous and the systems of the Academy, the Peripatetics and the Stoics were distinct. But with the decline of philosophic productivity men spent their time in turning over ground already worked and the natural result of oft-repeated debate was a tendency to concentrate on minor subtleties. Differences which seemed essential to the leaders of the great rival schools lost their significance. There was a general process of fusion or blending of philosophies whose points of distinction no longer seemed vital. In the Academy the importance of the doctrine of forms ceased to be understood; attention was paid more and more to the uncertainty of perception and less and less to the possibility of intellectual cognition. Hence the Academy, losing its original distinctive doctrine, became assimilated with the Peripatetics so that some went so far as to assert—as Cicero shows in the *Academica*—that both schools originally had one common body of doctrine.

But in this gradual fusion there was one point on which differences remained distinct and the debate vigorous. This was the question of validity of perception. It was a quarrel whose main lines were already clear two centuries before Cicero. Zeno the Stoic at the beginning of the third century with his definition of a 'grasping impression' ($\phi\alpha\nu\tau\alpha\sigma\iota\alpha$ $\kappa\alpha\tau\alpha\lambda\eta\pi\tau\iota\kappa\eta$) had set up perception as the standard of truth. Arcesilaus of the Academy, who was about a generation later, denied this. This Stoic doctrine of the 'cataleptic phantasm' meant that in the act of perception the external object was grasped immediately in its true nature without any subjective limitation. The mind was not allowed any modifying part. It was supposed to be completely passive under the influence of external objects and, in fact, to be non-existent prior to the reception of external impressions. By this means the Stoic sought to bridge the gulf between the object in thought and the object in nature and asserted their coextensiveness. But the Academy held that the thing in itself was incomprehensible because of subjective limitations: it did not, however, carry the examination of subjective limitations to the point to which it has been carried in modern scepticism: the Academy rested its case for incomprehensibility upon the impossibility of distinguishing the true perceptions from false ones. Pushed to its logical conclusion the scepticism of Arcesilaus, since he sought no other standard of truth, should impose suspension of judgment, which he called $\epsilon\pi o\chi\eta$. But the strong practical impulse of the age could not condone inactivity and Carneades, the next great figure of the Academy after Arcesilaus, expounded the doctrine of probability. By this he meant that, despite his subjective limitations, man may infer the nature of the objects of sensation from the evidence of his experience. Now Carneades died more than a century after Arcesilaus and since the dispute went on for the next fifty years we can see that the development and discussion of the rival views took up a large part of the period between Aristotle and Cicero.

The attempt of Carneades to pass beyond Arcesilaus and find a criterion was, as Zeller pointed out, the natural product both of scepticism and of the growing practical impulse of the age, to be intensified by the expanding influence of Rome. It is natural for the Sceptic to become dissatisfied with pure scepticism and to seek some criterion at all costs. The fact is that scepticism starts with a high definition of truth but, as that is destroyed in a period of philosophic degeneracy, scepticism goes with it by a 'natural and just diminution', as Hume said. The result is an attempt to formulate a criterion, although consistent scepticism could not support it.

Thus it came about that much of the argument of those who professed loyalty to the Academy in this period dealt with the doctrine of calculation of probability and, since the need for this doctrine sprang from their rejection of the Stoic theory of perception, they waged open war with the Stoics in the department of epistemology. But in the other departments of philosophy, physics and ethics, the differences were not so acute. This was the era of the Middle Stoa whose main men were Panaetius, who died about 110 B.C., and Posidonius (c. 135-51 B.C.) : of course the term 'Middle Stoa' must not be taken to imply the acceptance of a common body of doctrine since there were differences between these two men, which however are not the concern of the present work. In Cicero's time it was the theory of Posidonius that prevailed in contemporary Stoic physics. He upheld physical determinism and naturally came under vigorous attack from the Academy on this question. But in other respects he had so far relaxed orthodox Stoicism as to admit certain Academic doctrines with the result that much of his general scheme of the nature of the world was acceptable to the Academy, which accordingly aimed at the correction of details in his physical account rather than at the rejection of it in its entirety. In ethics the main contemporary issue was an attempted modification of the Stoic system. This was a challenge to the traditional absolutism of Stoic ethics and was advanced by Antiochus of Ascalon, who was probably developing a suggestion of Panaetius, and whose teaching had an important influence on Cicero early in his career. In this issue Cicero took so great an interest that he was to devote three works to it.

Now before he met Antiochus, Cicero felt the influence of the main contemporary exponent of the New Academy's doctrine of calculation of probability. This was Philo of Larissa who was head of the Academy after Clitomachus, the immediate successor of Carneades. Since he called his school the 'fourth' Academy, as if he had given a fresh direction to the tradition, it may be that he thought that he could advance beyond Carneades to a position between reasonable probability and absolute certainty.

As a young student Cicero was vividly impressed by Philo when he visited Rome in 88 B.C. not long before his death. Cicero had studied hitherto under Phaedrus the Epicurean and Diodotus the Stoic but now Philo seems to have won him to the New Academy: though their contact was not long its effects were lasting. But about ten years later, during his travels in the period 79-77, Cicero also sat in Athens at the feet of Antiochus. Antiochus claimed the headship of the New Academy after the death of Philo in 87 and did not die himself till 68 B.C. He responded to the practical impulse of the age and to the decline of the true spirit of scepticism with a resulting tendency to eclecticism. He thought that the Academy, the Peripatetics, and the Stoics were all part of a common tradition. He saw no essential difference between Plato and Aristotle, while Stoicism he considered to be a divergent form of the main tradition, itself containing some very desirable features. Thus he thought that by purging contemporary Stoicism of its errors he could establish a system which would represent the true development of the Academic and Peripatetic tradition. It might loosely be said that by his corrected version of Stoicism Antiochus was trying to re-establish an 'Academico-Peripatetic' system though he himself, as claimant to the leadership of the New Academy, probably would describe his system as a form of 'Stoicized' Academy. The fundamental difference between Antiochus and Philo's Academy was that Antiochus adopted whole-heartedly the Stoic doctrine of validity of perception and rejected the Academic doctrine of probability. The blurring of original distinctions allowed him to present the Stoic doctrine as the true development of the original Academic tradition and the contemporary scepticism as a perversion of that tradition. This Cicero could not accept, and in the *Academica,* drawing upon Philo, he stated the New Academy's objections. His contact with both men must have made him aware of the differences between them and what he set out to give was not an ancient story of old differences but an account of living issues fought out with some personal acrimony among his immediate seniors. Moreover, this was a topic on which he himself felt keenly. He desired to take his stand with the true sceptical tradition of the New Academy and to resist the attempt of Antiochus to graft this Stoic doctrine upon it.

But although he repudiated Antiochus here Cicero was deeply interested in his attempt to modify the Stoic ethics. He showed this by devoting the *De Finibus* and *Tusculan Disputations* to an examination of Antiochus' case and he reverted to the same question in his final work, the *De Officiis*. There were two main doctrines that Antiochus assailed: (a) the conception of the ethical end as moral worth (*honestum*), absolute and remote from the world of the senses, and (b) the doctrine that the pure state of virtue implies the complete excision of the emotions. On the first of these doctrines Antiochus maintained that the Stoics' ethical structure was inconsistent with their attitude in the department of dialectic in which he upheld their theory of the validity of perception. He found that, instead of seeking any connection between the starting point of facts validly grasped, on which they insisted so strongly, and the complete structure of perfect knowledge, at which they arrived, they abandoned epistemological inquiry and moved to the theory of the development of virtues from the impulses. Then, as they advanced higher up the scale, they suddenly made an abrupt transition to what they called moral worth, a conception of sole and absolute good. In comparison with this sole good none of the things of this world had any value at all. Antiochus' criticism of this aspect of Stoicism is given in the *De Finibus*. He felt that the abandonment of the world of the senses rendered pointless the previous insistence on the validity of perception. He himself set out to find a system which he could build up consistently from valid sense knowledge and the primary impulses to a complete knowledge of the system of reality and the perfect structure of the virtues. For support he gave his own interpretation of the old 'Academico-Peripatetic' tradition. According to this interpretation the tradition insisted that the things of this world did have reality and value and that the supreme good was not so entirely divorced from them that all objects of sense perception were deprived of all meaning whatever. Antiochus thought that by imposing this view upon the Stoic starting-point of valid perception he could avoid the Stoic error of the abrupt transition and could arrive at a complete knowledge of reality. This attempt does at least appear to be more logical than that of the Stoics: for he did try to build upon the basis of sense knowledge on which they insisted so strongly but ultimately used to so little purpose. Nor is it fair to think that Antiochus was exercising a haphazard eclecticism, jumping from one system to another. He did trace his own adherence back to the Academy and, though his understanding of it was distorted, he himself felt that he was making modifications in one coherent tradition. He did not feel that he was transferring allegiance although his present attempt aimed at a dogmatism more consistent than that of the Stoics and a final position completely opposite to the scepticism of the New Academy.

In the *De Finibus* the case for Antiochus rested on negative criticism of the Stoics, on a theory of the development of the structure of morality from man's primary impulses and on the implied assumption of man's attainment of complete understanding. Next he had to face the question whether this perfect understanding could function rationally in face of the forces which affect man from within himself and from without. He had to consider whether fears and emotions could prevent man from rational action. Here Antiochus differed from the second of the main Stoic doctrines distinguished above. Cicero studies their differences in the *Tusculan Disputations,* where we find the Stoic conception of pure reason, purged entirely of emotions, opposed by a modified doctrine of emotions as forces which must be present even in the Wise Man (*sapiens*), forces with which his reason must grapple and which it can overcome.

To sum up, Antiochus conceived a form of dogmatism which did not altogether abandon the world of the senses nor deny the influence of the emotions in the perfect morality. Man might attain this perfect morality by the continuous development of his own nature up to perfection, and it rested on the one hand on the assertion of validity of perception as the basis of complete knowledge and on the other hand upon the theory of the development of the perfect structure of the virtues from the primary ethical impulses. To Antiochus the most pernicious doctrine was that which placed moral worth in a realm apart from the senses. Against this he advanced his conception of the good as 'virtue together with the natural advantages'.

Now in his examination of this attempted modification of Stoicism Cicero stood outside the argument and was content to indicate briefly the Academic assessment of it by comments at the end of the *De Finibus* and *Tusculan Disputations*. It was not till *De Officiis* III that he gave the New Academy's verdict. This was that, since perception cannot be free from error in the first place, man cannot attain perfect morality but must be content with working standards of practical morality. But although he was thus forced to reject Antiochus' conclusion, Cicero had various grounds for sympathy with him. Antiochus' conception of wisdom, derived from sense experience and grappling with the emotions and overcoming them, must appeal to the New Academy because in the first place it too denied supra-sensual sources of information and must reject the Stoics' transcendental realm, and because in the second place the Antiochean case, making the attainment of morality a matter of man's own efforts, upheld human responsibility in ethics, which was what the Academy did in its doctrine of calculation of probability. Then again the Academy's was a limited form of scepticism since by fallibility it meant that false perceptions mingle with the true so that man cannot make positive assertion in particular cases. This did not prevent it from agreeing with Antiochus on what would be the nature of a true perception if only it could be distinguished.

Since the study of the Antiochean case in ethics raised the question of human responsibility it would naturally draw Cicero's attention to the problem of freedom involved in current physical theory and the spirit of the New Academy would inspire Cicero to attack the doctrines of detailed divine control and inexorable control by fate. For these doctrines, which denied human freedom, were in vogue in the Middle Stoa, their champion being Posidonius. Accordingly Cicero's purpose was to examine the Posidonian doctrines in his group of theological and cosmological works after stating in the *De Finibus* and *Tusculan Disputations* the problems in ethics raised by Antiochus and before giving his verdict in the *De Officiis*. Cicero's plan may now be summarized thus. In the first stage, the *Academica,* he intended to describe the direct contest between the New Academy and Antiochus over the problem of perception. In the *De Finibus* and *Tusculan Disputations* he would narrate the conflict of Antiochus against certain aspects of Stoic ethics, standing outside the dispute and coming in only towards the end of each work to hint his own view. In the cosmological and theological works he would attack the Middle Stoic physics for their denial of freedom. Then in the *De Officiis* he intended to revert to the ethical problem raised in the *De Finibus* and *Tusculan Disputations* and to end by his own statement of ethical standards for the ordinary man of imperfect understanding.

But this view that there is a coherent sequence in the works has not been supported by the traditional interpretation. Critics and editors have generally thought that Cicero's main purpose was to produce a sort of 'handbook of contemporary teaching', a review of the theories of the leading schools of philosophy in the various departments of thought. Consequently, his works have been printed in haphazard order in the various collections, as though it mattered not in what order they might be read. The neglect to seek a serious personal purpose in them has been encouraged by the suspicion and contempt which have befallen his reputation in various eras. In the first centuries of the Christian church he was regarded as the chief mouthpiece of the pagan literary culture, the upholder of beliefs that the early Church had to fight. Nothing more clearly reveals the hatred for poor Cicero than an anecdote of St Jerome, whose most frightful nightmare was a dream of Judgment Day: for, when his turn came, the stern voice assailed him: 'Thou art no Christian—thou art a Ciceronian.' Then in the disputes of the Sceptics and the dogmatists of the sixteenth and seventeenth centuries Cicero, as a Sceptic, fell under the heavy suspicion of the orthodox. More recently Cicero the philosopher has been judged for the supposed shortcomings of Cicero the politician, especially by German scholars who despised his indecision. The very frankness of his letters which exposed his emotionalism in private life and his vacillation in public affairs earned contempt. To them he stood as the type of liberal who listens to both sides and then does nothing. Various faults also have deprived these works of respect. The great orator who could plead a cause so that men would hang on his lips could not arrange a philosophic argument in an attractive form. In those opening passages where he tries to copy the conversational style of Plato he fails lamentably; in general he has an unattractive arrangement and an uninspired tone which make pleasurable reading impossible. The method of composition (by translating whole slabs of Greek originals), the awkward piecing together of the parts, the obvious fictions in characterization, all conspire to create works without the vitality of Plato. Cicero clutters up his books with countless digressions into the minor points which obscure men of the schools of the Hellenistic era disputed with the perverse subtlety of that unoriginal but contentious age. His method of translating caused him to insert arguments irrelevant to the particular theme on which he might be working: this is the explanation of many obscure and seemingly pointless passages. For example we shall find that the second half of *De Finibus* II is taken up by an unnecessary examination of aspects of Epicureanism which does not advance the argument. This was partly caused by his

B

readiness to flirt with the encyclopaedic role: where his main purpose called for an exposition of the Stoic and Antiochean views on some topic he would think it necessary to give the Epicurean views too and then to say what the other schools thought of the Epicureans. Now this was not without its uses, as we shall see, but it did impede clear and direct exposition. It is no wonder that Montaigne said of him: 'I want discourses which charge straight at the strongest part of the doubt: his languidly beat about the bush.' (*Essays*, ii. 10.)

And of course his extant works do not state clearly what he intended to do. Students are deterred from seeking his plan by the discouraging criticism of editors such as Hutchinson who in the introduction to the *De Finibus* said:

> He professed himself the interpreter and to some extent the critic of other thinkers, and nothing was farther from his purpose than to make independent contributions to the subject he treated. But even so limited, such a project called for a grasp of first principles, and a thorough mastery of authorities and a faculty of logical arrangement which Cicero was far from possessing.

Indeed the clumsiness of exposition and the faulty arrangement do show that Cicero had no clear grasp in advance of the details of his argument. But this did not prevent him from having a broad plan, which can be detected by analysis of the works. His experience as a student and later as a lifelong amateur of philosophy had made him aware of the issues. Since the Greeks had thoroughly debated these issues he had grounds for confidence that by drawing on them he could cover the whole field and state the opinion of the New Academy on most points of importance.

That he did start out with confidence is suggested by the little that we know about the lost *Hortensius*. We have two tributes by men who read it before it was lost which seem to show that it gave an inspiring statement of Cicero's attitude. The first of these tributes is by St Augustine. To the *Hortensius* he ascribes the commencement of his reform from a life of wantonness:

> In the ordinary course of study I had come across a certain book of Cicero, whose speech almost all admire, not so his heart. This book of his contains an exhortation to philosophy and is called *Hortensius*. But this book altered my attitude and turned my prayers to thyself, O Lord; and caused my

purposes and desires to change. Every vain hope at once became worthless to me; and with an incredible burning desire I thirsted for the immortality of wisdom, and began now to arise that I might return to thee. . . . Not to sharpen my tongue did I employ that book; nor did it impress upon me its style but its matter. (*Confessions*, iii. 4.)

A strong statement of the effect of the *Hortensius* upon the man 'who gave her new soul to Europe'![1]

The other tribute made six centuries later in the very dark days of Europe was that of a little crippled monk, Hermannus Contractus, who was saved from being pathetic and wretched by the force of spirit within him. He was so terribly deformed that he could neither stand nor walk nor lie at ease in bed. Great need had he of the comfort of intellectual activity; but despite his lasting pain he achieved versatility of accomplishment and a brightness of personality that made him generally loved and popular. He, who knew well the worth of intellectual comfort, described upon his death-bed the effect of the *Hortensius* upon him:

And under the strong inspiration of that reading, the whole of this present world and all that belongs to it—yes, this mortal life itself—has become mean and wearisome, and on the other hand, the world to come, that shall not pass, and that eternal life, have become so unspeakably desirable and dear that I hold all these passing things as light as thistledown.[2]

These passages suggest that there was a quality in the *Hortensius* which is not found in the other works. It would be going too far to assert that it contained a clear statement of Cicero's plan: it may be that it achieved no more than a strong utterance of his belief in the function of philosophy, an utterance which had a strong emotional appeal for St Augustine and Hermannus.

That Cicero had reason to be confident of the ample availability of Greek authorities is shown by the fact that he was obviously indebted to a great variety of sources. The actual identification of them is difficult and on many the discussions of scholars must remain inconclusive. As Reid said in his great edition of the *Academica,* 'few men ever had, and few ever will have the scholarship necessary for the critical investigation of his philosophical works and for the great task of relating them

1. Martindale, *What are Saints?*, p. 49.
2. Ibid., p. 54.

to the doctrines of the post-Aristotelian schools.' Now our task
in the present work is not to reconstruct the post-Aristotelian
schools but to interpret Cicero. We are more concerned with
the bearing of the arguments on his system than with their
affiliations. But I do think that the broad pattern is clear
enough. For the *Academica, De Finibus* and *De Officiis* there
can be little dispute and for the translation of the *Timaeus*
none at all. In the dialectical dispute of the *Academica* Cicero
stated the position of Antiochus from that man's own works and
the opposing views of the New Academy from the two main men
of the half-century after Carneades, namely Clitomachus and
Philo. In the *De Finibus,* where his main concern was to show
Antiochus' attack on the Stoic conception of moral worth, he
took the Stoic case probably from Diogenes Babylonius, who
preceded the era of the Middle Stoa, and opposed it by arguments again taken directly from Antiochus. The Epicurean part
of the *De Finibus,* having the purely ancillary role of throwing
the Stoic case into relief, was adequately represented by a statement founded on an epitome of Epicurus and answered on
orthodox Stoic lines, probably from a work of Antiochus. The
De Officiis is by its own confession based directly on Panaetius'
work *Concerning Duty* in its first two books, while the third
book, which is Cicero's own statement of practical morality, is
mainly composed by Cicero himself, but with the help of
arguments derived from Posidonius, Hecaton, Diogenes and
Antipater.

But with the *Tusculan Disputations* and the cosmological
group there is little certainty and much dispute about the
sources. The reason is that here Cicero's task was different. In
the *Academica* and partly in the *De Finibus* he was able to
follow a contemporary dispute. But in the cosmological discussions and the *Tusculan Disputations* there were manifold topics
that were relevant and very many sources from which argument
could be drawn. Here it was necessary to discuss various views
on immortality, the relation of reason and the emotions, the
nature of gods and of fate and other topics whose treatment was
not primarily a subject of contemporary debate but went right
back in the long tradition of philosophy. Here the eclecticism
of the age had its effect: an author who might be used to support
a case like that of Antiochus on one topic might be assailed
by Antiochus on another topic. In discussing these works our
main task will be to show why such and such an argument is
used at each stage. After that it is worth while, but not essential,

to show the consistency of the argument with a probable source. That is to say, with this group our argument does not stand or fall by the identification of sources: in fact it is not intended in the present work to become involved in the intricate disputes concerning the sources of these works.

However, I do think that the broad pattern can be traced. In the *Tusculan Disputations* the first book discusses the two views which can remove the fear of death, that the soul is immortal or that it perishes. The doctrine of immortality probably comes from Posidonius as one of the Platonic elements which he is reputed to have incorporated into his form of Middle Stoicism. The doctrine of the soul's destruction would probably come from some orthodox Stoic source deriving from Chrysippus:[3] it might even have been taken by Cicero from Panaetius, if, as Bréhier says, he denied immortality: the next task in the *Tusculan Disputations* was to refute the Stoic denial that pain is evil and we should expect Cicero to take this from a contemporary source such as Philo or Antiochus, who would agree with the New Academy in this. In fact this was one of the modifications of Stoicism which Antiochus desired to make. In Books II and III the central theme is the remediability of emotion conceived, according to the Stoic view, as 'wrong reason': an attempt is made to find a position intermediate between the Stoic view of the complete negligibility of emotions and the Peripatetic view of them as desirable 'mean states': the intermediate view is that of Antiochus. The task here being largely a matter of modifying Stoicism, and various Stoic arguments being useful for this purpose, Cicero's sources here are mainly Stoic. For example it is obviously from a Stoic such as Chrysippus that he draws the view that emotion is due to a mental decision and again it is a Stoic view that gives him the key to the remediability of emotion, namely that as reason pervades all parts of the soul, emotion may be corrected by an act of reason. And again the refutation of the Peripatetic doctrine of the mean state is made mainly with the aid of Stoic arguments. In all this Cicero must have had a great debt to Chrysippus or sources derived from him. Book V is Cicero's summing up of the dispute between Antiochus and the Stoics and here he relies mainly on original composition, reinforced by arguments from Chrysippus, Posidonius and Philo.

---

3. Chrysippus himself according to Diogenes Laertius vii, 156, said that only the souls of wise men last until the general conflagration.

The sources of the *De Natura Deorum* present less difficulty. Again we have some argument for and against the Epicureans intended once more to throw into relief the points at issue in the statement of the Stoic case which is to follow. There is a rather distorted description of the Stoic-Platonic theology, from some Epicurean such as Phaedrus and another Epicurean criticism of most other schools which may be ascribed with some certainty to Zeno the Epicurean. This is followed by a refutation of Epicureanism probably by somebody with New Academic tendencies, such as Clitomachus: but it may even be Posidonius. The central statement of the whole work, the Stoic-Platonic theology in Book II, is almost certainly from Posidonius. Against it we have in Book III a detailed argument from the New Academy which however seeks to modify it rather than to reject it *in toto*. This probably is based on arguments advanced in an earlier generation by Clitomachus.

In the *De Divinatione* and *De Fato* Cicero attempts that modification of the Posidonian theology which he suggested in *De Natura Deorum* III. The point at issue in the *De Divinatione* and *De Fato* is whether man is controlled by detailed divine intervention and by a complete nexus of physical causes, which is the orthodox Stoic view, or whether he has freedom of choice. The Stoic case for divination, which is regarded as evidence of divine interference, Cicero takes probably from Posidonius, with a section on man's origin based on Chrysippus. This would be quite consistent with the use of Posidonius as a source for the Stoic theology in *De Natura Deorum* II. The Academic refutation of divination could quite naturally come from the earlier writer Clitomachus, who was probably also the source of the general criticism of the Stoic theology in *De Natura Deorum* III. In the *De Fato* the case for freedom is upheld by an examination of the intricate but unsatisfactory attempt by Chrysippus to allow some element of choice within the general Stoic doctrine of control by fate. The implication is that one must go further than Chrysippus' system would allow him to go. The source which Yon suggests for the *De Fato* is Antiochus and, though I cannot feel certain of that, I have no doubt that the general lines of criticism of Stoicism in this work could have been suggested to Cicero by his study of Antiochus' view of man's supreme moral activity as the activity of one who does not loftily disdain things in the Stoic sense but who takes them into consideration, surveys all factors, and makes the right decision by a process of perfect reason derived from sense-perception.

We may sum up the main divisions of Cicero's sources as follows. In dialectic he probably confronted the contemporary arguments of Antiochus with those of the main men of the Academy after Carneades, i.e. Clitomachus and Philo. For the discussion of the ethical end and the structure of the virtues he drew the case of orthodox Stoicism from Diogenes Babylonius and the modification of it from Antiochus following suggestions of Panaetius. In cosmology and theology he set up the doctrines of Posidonius whose incorporation of Platonic doctrines was illumined by the translation of the *Timaeus,* and again drew the case of the New Academy from Clitomachus. The general contest in these divisions was between the Academy of the post-Carneadean era and the contemporary Stoics. But it was an earlier stage of Stoic theory that was in question in the *Tusculan Disputations* and so there Cicero drew on Chrysippus. Of course there are many incidental arguments drawn from a variety of sources. But this scheme does seem to describe the main sources for the Stoic, New Academic and Antiochean arguments. The treatment of the Epicureans I regard as subsidiary to the main argument. For them he seems to have relied on epitomes, on contemporary Epicureans such as his teacher Phaedrus and on Zeno the Epicurean, who also taught him.

However, I should like it to be clear that, in view of the complicated disputes about Cicero's sources during generations of scholarship, all decisions must remain conjectural. Consequently where I say 'the source was Posidonius' or 'the source was Clitomachus' it must be understood that I claim no more than probability but that the source does seem consistent with the broad issues of the argument as interpreted in the present work.

CHAPTER II

THE *ACADEMICA*

1. THE PRELIMINARY SURVEY

CICERO wrote two versions of the *Academica* and some knowledge of their arrangement is required for understanding the relations of the extant parts and especially the change of characters in the parts of the dialogue. The two versions were written in a period of three months (between mid-April and July 45 B.C.). The first was in two books, called 'Catulus' and 'Lucullus' after the main speaker of each. Of these we retain the 'Lucullus' only, i.e. *Academica Priora* II. The second version, the *Academica Posteriora,* was in four books, of which only Book I (corresponding to the first half of the original 'Catulus') is extant. Thus Book I of *Academica Posteriora* and Book II of *Academica Priora* give us substantially three-quarters of the original material. The part missing entirely is the second quarter (i.e. the second part of the 'Catulus' or Book II of the *Academica Posteriora*): about its contents we can make reasonable conjecture.

The rearrangement involved a complete change in the persons, but the arguments were substantially the same and this fact furnishes a hint of Cicero's method of composition. His method was to allot to his characters passages lifted from Greek works: thus the spokesman for the Antiochean case in *Academica Posteriora* I is Varro, but in the second half, *Academica Priora* II, it is Lucullus. It is clear that Cicero by no means intended his dialogues to be historical accounts of discussion actually held between his characters: his dialogues were quite fictitious, although, as his letters show, he did give care to the choice of appropriate characters.

In all Cicero's philosophical works that tendency to beat languidly about the bush which Montaigne censured manifests itself especially in the introductions. Where they attempt to give a natural setting to the dialogue they fail lamentably and instead of expressing clearly 'the strongest part of the doubt' they obscure the issue. Thus the first dozen sections of the *Academica,* which deal mainly with the value of using Latin in philosophic writing, form a clumsy introduction to the main question. This question is whether Antiochus or Philo is the true heir of the Academy. For Antiochus has 'returned to the

Old School from the New', which means that he considers the contemporary New Academy false to the true tradition. But Philo, who 'refused to allow that there are two Academies', claimed that his form of the Academy was correctly derived from the Old without any heresy or break in the tradition.

The first half of the work really forms a preliminary survey to the central examination which starts in *Academica Priora* II. To explain Antiochus' claim to be its heir Cicero offers under three heads—ethics, physics and logic—an account of the original system of the Old School, as Antiochus understood it, followed by an account, also drawn from Antiochus, of subsequent developments of which the Stoic are particularly important. Antiochus broadly identified the original Academy and the Peripatetics and so arrived at the conception of a common 'Academico-Peripatetic' tradition. This implies, of course, a rather peculiar view of the original schools and a disregard of distinctions between Plato and Aristotle. In the' phrases in italics in the following passage we may detect that tendency, which Zeller pointed out, to blend doctrines originally distinct:

> But because of the influence of Plato who was versatile and many-sided and fluent there was established a system of philosophy single and consistent but with two titles, Academic and Peripatetic: for these schools *agreed in substance* but differed in name. . . . Both groups enriched out of Plato's abundance drew up a certain definite code of doctrine full and rich in substance, abandoning the universal doubt of the Socratics and the practice of discussion without positive assertion. Thus was produced something which Socrates by no means sought—a certain artistic form of philosophy with a recognized order of topics and a *prescribed scheme of doctrine.* At first, as I said, it was a *single system* though it had two names: *there was no difference between the Peripatetics and the original old Academy.* In my opinion Aristotle was pre-eminent through a certain wealth of talent but both schools had the same source and made the *same distinction between the objects of desire and the objects of aversion.* (*Ac. Post.* i. 17f.)

The later philosophers could feel that the difference between Plato and Aristotle was incidental and not fundamental: probably the predominance of ethical enquiry diminished men's regard for differences in epistemology and the apparent agreement of the two schools in ethics ('they made the same distinction between the objects of desire and the objects of aversion') produced a blurring of distinctions and the identification of the two schools.

The distortion of the original position under the effect of later doctrines is particularly marked in the Antiochean account of the physics of the Old School. For here we find a conglomerate formed partly from the influence of Plato's *Timaeus,* partly from Aristotle and partly from Stoic influences. First is presented a twofold division of nature into active and passive parts which, while it is compatible with Plato's doctrine of forms and matter and with Aristotle's division of all material existences into a formal and a material part, yet shows a Stoic attitude in its rejection of the void, which no doubt implies the view that all existence is material. There follows an account of the four primary substances, air, fire, water and earth, which by treating them as ultimate factors, making no distinction between *initia* (ἀρχαί) and *elementa* (στοιχεῖα), shows a lack of discrimination since Plato, Aristotle and the Stoics do not regard them as ultimate: in Aristotle and the Stoics the real first principles are matter, and form or force. Next the Antiochean account accepts the Stoic division of these primary substances which regards air and fire as active and earth and water as passive. Aristotle's doctrine of a fifth element is mentioned but was probably regarded by Antiochus as a wrong development of the original system since Zeno's rejection of it is stated without further comment in the subsequent section on Stoic physics. Then having described the twofold division of nature and the primary substances the Antiochean account describes a general underlying material, formless and entirely destitute of quality. It underlies all forms of matter: it can receive changes and be transformed: it is not dissolved into nothingness but only into its own parts which can be subdivided without limit. Here is a close resemblance to the 'matrix' of the *Timaeus* (50), that 'third thing' distinguishable from the forms, of which sensible things are copies, and from the copies themselves—the receptacle in which the copies are located, which receives all kinds in itself yet is bare of all forms, just as a modeller's clay must be level and smooth. One must observe that the doctrine of infinite divisibility here included is an Aristotelian doctrine which the Stoics accepted. Finally the Stoic influence is manifest in the description of the governing force of the universe for the parts of the universe are held together by *natura sentiens* ('a constitution invested with sensibility') : it is the soul of the universe and is perfect wisdom: it may be called God or Providence: it may also be called Fate 'because nothing can happen otherwise than it has ordained, being linked in what we may term the destined and immutable chain of the everlasting order.'

Thus it is a composite system heavily affected by Stoic and other post-Platonic influences which is put forward as Antiochus' conception of the original position of the Academy in physics. The final survey of physics in *Academica Priora* ii. 114-28, will show that Antiochus accepted various Stoic doctrines which were consistent with this account so that, as well as being a statement of what Antiochus accepted as the Old School's physics, it probably states the system which Antiochus accepted for himself. But Cicero's intention in the *Academica* was to concentrate in the division of logic his whole examination of Antiochus' claim to be the true heir of the Old School. As regards physics his attitude was that, since scepticism was its true tradition, the Academy could not accept dogmatically any physical system. Consequently he did not intend by this account of the Old School's physics to raise any immediate issues in physical theory. That is, he did not propose to examine whether it was a valid account of the development of Academic physics or whether Antiochus rightly claimed descent. The main value of this account to students of Cicero is that, by its description of Antiochus' peculiar estimate of the original system of the Academy it gives an indication of the mentality of this man of whom Cicero said in *Academica Priora* ii. 113, that he 'strongly influences me, either because I loved the man as he did me or because my opinion is that he was the most cultivated and shrewdest of all the philosophers of our time' and who by virtue of his acceptance of Stoic influences had much in common with the contemporary Stoïc-Platonic system of physics which Cicero later examined in his group of cosmological works. In this way the account gives a pointer to Cicero's interest in problems which he will eventually raise in physics. But it would be suggesting an over-elaboration of his programme to say that he deliberately foreshadowed the problems here with the intention of reverting to them in detail later. For he did not commence his serious examination of physical questions until he had completed the *De Finibus* and *Tusculan Disputations*.

But in the discussion of ethics Cicero does raise an issue with the intention of examining it further. For in the account of the Old School he gives a definition of virtue which Antiochus accepted and this is contrasted with the Stoic definition which Antiochus rejected. The old view was that whereas virtue was supreme and could create happiness yet it did need the help of the 'natural advantages', for in addition to the supreme good there was a threefold division of other goods—'mental', 'bodily', and 'external'. The Stoics asserted that virtue alone is good, a doctrine which devised a peculiar category of 'things preferred' which were not actually good but were supposed in some way to account for the things commonly called good. Now this is the issue which Cicero intends to develop in the *De Finibus* and *Tusculan Disputations* for throughout those works he examines Antiochus' defence of his ethical conception against the Stoics.

It is in the division of logic that the real question of the *Academica* begins and the decision on Antiochus' claim to be heir to the Old School is treated as if it depended entirely on his development of dogmatism from what he supposes to be the original position in this division. The following outline of this supposed original position and of Aristotle's amendment reveals the origin of the problem which Antiochus felt the Stoics to have solved:

> They considered that the *criterion of truth* was *not contained in the senses* although it *had its origin in them.* They insisted that it was the *intellect that was the judge* of things: intellect alone they considered worthy of belief because it alone beheld the homogeneous, the simple and the unchanging. . . . Now they considered all *the senses dull and slow,* holding that they could in no way grasp those things which seemed to be in the realm of sense. . . . This was the original system they inherited from Plato. I shall now, if you desire, set forth those changes in their system of which I have heard. . . . [The speaker's companion's urge him to press on with this 'striking exposition of the doctrines of the Peripatetics and the Old Academy.'] Aristotle was the first who *shook the strength of the 'forms',* which I mentioned a little while ago and which Plato had embraced with such rare enthusiasm that he declared them to contain a divine element. (*Ac. Post.* i. 30-3.)

The significant point here is the view that, although it is only the intellect which can grasp true reality, it does require the aid of the senses in the first place: that is to say, although knowledge is itself an affair of the understanding it proceeds primarily from sense perception. Then if the senses are 'dull and slow' we

must have here the genesis of scepticism especially since the
forms are rejected. This was substantially the position which
the New Academy of Cicero's day accepted and accordingly they
accepted Plato as the progenitor of scepticism. As a result of the
facile rejection of the forms they assumed that his central theme
was the denial of certainty (*nil cognosci posse*), as may be seen
in this description of him probably taken from Philo:

> This Academy they call the New, but it appears to me to
> be the Old, if at least we count Plato as a member of the
> famous Old School: for in his books no positive assertion is
> made, though many arguments are advanced on both sides,
> with inquiry into all things but no definite conclusion. (Ibid.
> i. 46.)

The Stoics came to the rescue by attacking the view that the
senses were 'dull and slow' and developed their doctrine of
validity of perception, which Antiochus accepted. Having thus
strengthened that part of the old tradition which said that 'the
criterion of truth had its origin in the senses', the Stoics then
followed the other suggestion that it was 'the intellect that was
the judge of things' and so advanced the idea of conceptions
formed by the understanding (but still springing in the first
place from the senses) and leading to the discovery of reasoned
truth. This part of the Stoic doctrine Antiochus endeavoured
to develop consistently, trying to correct them when in their
ethical system they diverged from it. He thought that starting
from the facts derived from perception it should be possible to
develop a complete system of knowledge. This was to be a
perfect rationalism based on perception; for the rejection of the
forms and the insistence that knowledge must be derived from
the senses in the first place ruled out the possibility of knowledge
derived *entirely* from the operations of the reason. As the *De
Finibus* shows, the Stoics in their ethical theory went on to
base their pure morality mainly upon the development of the
virtues from the natural impulses and then supported it by
epistemological assumptions which had no connection with their
basis in logic. Here Antiochus sought to correct them and it is
clear that he thought that in the original tradition transformed
by the Stoic doctrine of validity of perception he could find the
grounds for a rationalist system of ethics.

Thus Antiochus advances a form of dogmatism as the correct
development of the Old School and the central argument of the

Academica turns upon the validity of its basic assumption, the Stoic doctrine of perception. But since the New Academy also claimed to be the heir it had to advance a positive case by explaining how its form of scepticism could provide a philosophy adequate for the conduct of life. This part of the argument will turn upon the doctrine of calculation of probability.

Book I of *Academica Posteriora* ends with a statement of the New Academy's view that the true development of the old tradition was scepticism. Cicero probably took this statement from Philo as an answer to the outline of the Old School which he took from Antiochus. It makes it clear that the reply to Antiochus' claim to be the heir is to be made in the division of 'dialectic'. There followed the second quarter of Cicero's work, *Academica Posteriora* II, which is now entirely missing. We can guess its theme from references and from an examination of the extant books. It appears to have contained an exposition of the positive teaching of Carneades about the New Academy's ability to establish a satisfactory criterion of truth and probably also included a foretaste of negative arguments against the Stoics, since part of the Stoic argument which follows next consists of replies to such attacks. The source was probably Clitomachus.

In the composition of this part Cicero probably followed a pattern which may be detected in other books: he led up to the Stoic case by asking the most important question which would arise from criticism of it ('If you reject Stoic validity of perception can you find any criterion at all?') and then advanced several well-known objections. In short, the missing part first stated the need that must result from a challenge to the Stoic position—the need to establish some working rule—and then foreshadowed the most obvious objections to the Stoic case. Thus it was not until the third quarter of his work that Cicero was ready to examine the crux of the whole dispute—the validity of the Stoic doctrine of perception which Antiochus adopted.

2. THE DIALECTICAL DISPUTE

(a) THE STOIC CASE

(i) *The Definition of a 'True Appearance'*. The dialectical argument begins in earnest with the statement of the case for the Stoics in *Academica Priora* II. Here, after an involved introduction concerning the relations of Philo and Antiochus and the true course of the old tradition, we have the first most important statement of the crux of the dispute—the Stoic definition of a valid 'appearance':

> An appearance fashioned and moulded from the object from which it comes in a form which it could not derive from an object from which it does not itself come—this definition of Zeno we declare to be thoroughly justified. . . . Wherefore our whole discourse is directed against the Academy in defence of that definition which Philo tried to overthrow. Unless we establish that definition we admit that perception is altogether impossible. (*Ac. Pr.* ii. 18.)

The Stoic definition implies the belief, ascribed to the Old Tradition as we have seen, that there does exist a true objective reality external to man on which all true perception is based. The term 'perception' has a special sense in the *Academica*: it means the valid grasping of existing reality. The basis of perception must always be a real object: a false appearance cannot be 'perceived' in the technical sense because either it does not have a real object behind it or, though it may have a real object behind it, it produces on the mind the impression that it comes from some other object.

The main positive arguments in support of the Stoic argument have a specious nature. They seem to have been tossed to and fro in the schools for years. They rest on various kinds of testimony to a general belief that there do exist external objects which can be apprehended as they are. For example it is asserted that art implies a basis of facts known, or that when men try to improve their use of the senses (e.g. by removing an obstacle which prevents one from seeing a thing clearly) they prove a fundamental trust in the ability of unhampered sensation to show us things as they exist, or again that the very nature of mind argues the existence of objects to be apprehended. The following assertion shows the type of argument used:

> I ask too why the typical good man who has determined to endure every form of torture and to be torn by insufferable pain rather than to be false to duty or obligation should have saddled himself with such oppressive conditions if, to justify this duty, he possessed no fact which was apprehended, perceived, known and determined. Therefore it is quite impossible for a man to place so high a value on his sense of fairness and good faith as to be willing to bear any penalty at all in order to preserve it unless he has given his assent to facts which cannot possibly be untrue. (Ibid. ii. 23.)

The Stoics relied on assertion rather than on proof. Nevertheless they made an almost emotional plea for the maintenance of their definition:

> Therefore those who deny that anything can be 'apprehended' are doing away with these very things that make life possible and make it attractive—nay they are absolutely overthrowing life from its foundations and actually depriving the creature of mind, so that it is difficult to describe their rashness in terms justified by the circumstances. (Ibid. ii. 31.)

(ii) *Replies to Sceptic Criticism.* The central part of the positive case of the Stoics was the assertion that true appearances have a conspicuousness sufficiently powerful to show us things which exist, exactly in their own nature, as they are. But the New Academy attacked this assertion with a variety of sceptical arguments. Sections 47-8 of *Academica Priora* II state how the Stoics viewed these arguments. The Sceptics, they said, argued that, since the gods made even such false appearance as dreams seem true, some possibility of error might also attach to those appearances which the Stoics accepted as conspicuously true: as examples of the indistinguishability of true from false the Sceptics pointed to the confusion of apparently identical things such as twins, eggs, bees and signet rings. In reply the Stoics said that most of this was argument of a sophistical kind relying largely on the logical device of the *sorites*:

> And first I must criticize them for this: they employ an exceedingly sophistical kind of argument—a kind which commonly finds very little approval in philosophy—the method of making a series of very small additions or subtractions. This device is called *sorites* because by the addition of one grain they make a heap. Truly a faulty and sophistical style! This is how you set up your case: If an appearance has been presented to a sleeper by a god of such a kind that it is probable then why not of such a kind as for it to be extremely like a true appearance? Then why not such as to be hard to distinguish from the true? Then why not such as not to be distinguished at all? Finally, such that there is no difference between the one and the other? If you reach this point because I yield to you each successive step, the error will be mine, but if you advance unaided, it will be yours. For who will ever allow you that a god either is omnipotent or would act in that way if he could? How is it that you assume that if one thing can be like another it follows that it is difficult to

distinguish them? then that they cannot even be distinguished? finally that they are the same? For instance, if wolves are like dogs you will end by saying that they are identical. And further some things not moral are like things moral, and things not good are like things good, and things quite inartistic are like things artistic: why do we hesitate then to declare that there is no difference between these classes of things? (Ibid. ii. 49f.)

The Stoics went on to prove that the appearances of real experience did have a conspicuousness that was lacking in the experiences of dreams:

There is one method of keeping off all the false appearances, whether they are formed by imagination, which, we admit, often happens, or in sleep, or through the influence of wine or madness. For we shall declare that all such appearances lack the conspicuousness which we must cling to tenaciously. For suppose a man who pictures something and sketches it in his imagination: yet surely as soon as he bestirs and recalls himself he realizes the difference between conspicuous and unsubstantial phenomena. The same argument applies to dreams. . . . So as soon as we have awakened we make light of those appearances and do not regard them in the same way as those acts which we have performed in the ordinary business of our life. (Ibid. ii. 51.)

What we say is that men who are sleeping do not have the same force and soundness in activity of mind or sensation as men who are awake. Nor do drunken men carry out their actions with the same decision as sober men; they hesitate, they waver, sometimes they check themselves, they are rather undecided in acknowledging the appearances that present themselves and when they have slept it off they realize how worthless those appearances were. The same thing happens to madmen—at the beginning of their madness they experience something which does not exist and declare that they can see it: then, when their frenzy passes, their thoughts and utterances are like those of Alcmaeon, who said, 'But my mind agrees not with the vision that my eyes behold.' (Ibid. ii. 52.)

As to the supposed indistinguishability of twins and such like, the Stoics insisted that things retain their identity—are distinctive pieces of objective reality—and are therefore distinguishable ultimately:

And why do you attach more importance to a proposition which the nature of things forbids? The nature of things

c

forbids that a thing should not maintain its identity in its own class and forbids that between two or more things there should be any confusion based on the absence of all differences. For example eggs may very closely resemble eggs and bees similarly resemble bees: then why do you continue to argue and what do you want with twins? For it is granted that they resemble each other and with this you could have been satisfied: but you insist that they are absolutely the same, not merely similar—and your contention is absolutely impossible. (Ibid. ii. 54.)

Now suppose that the famous Servilii of old, who were twins, were so closely alike as they say: then surely you don't think that they were identical? In public they were not recognized apart, but at home they were; they were not recognized by strangers but were recognized by their own folk. Surely it is our own experience that even though we would never have thought it possible to distinguish between certain persons yet after constant association with them we find it so easy to tell them apart that they don't seem in the least to resemble each other. (Ibid. ii. 56.)

That is to say, apparently indistinguishable things are found ultimately to be distinguishable, even such difficult things as eggs:

With regard to the proverbial resemblance of eggs one to another we have been told that at Delos when its prosperity was at its height, there were many persons who used to make money by rearing fowls in great numbers. They on examining an egg could tell which hen had laid it. (Ibid. ii. 57.)

Thus the Stoic sticks to his definition. He admits that some appearances are confused and likely to be mistaken: but things do preserve their classes and individual things their own identity: ultimately the man of wisdom can discern them and detect which appearances are true: on this power to detect true appearances depends his whole ability to understand the system of reality; but ultimately the man of wisdom can know that system for he 'has no fancied knowledge [i.e. does not move in the realm of opinion], I mean never yields "assent" to any matter which is either fallacious or unknown' (Ibid. ii. 59).

This part of the Stoic argument ends with a strong statement that the definition remains firm against the argument of indistinguishability of appearances:

Nor does this fact count against us, since we are content not to be able to tell eggs one from another; for it does not

result that we must admit that egg 'A' is the same as egg 'B',
implying that there is no absolute difference between the two.
For I have a guiding principle which is to consider as true
appearances which have such nature as they could not have
if they were false. From this principle I must not depart one
finger's breadth, as the saying goes, for fear of throwing all
into confusion. For not merely our theory of true and false
will be overthrown but also the natural order of them, if there
is to be no difference between them. (Ibid. ii. 58.)

(iii) *Attack on the Doctrine of Probability.* While defending his
own case the Stoic also attacks the New Academy's conception of
action based on probability. In the first place how can the New
Academy establish any canon at all?

> Now our opponents insist . . . that there is a 'probability',
> a sort of likeness to the truth, and they declare that they use
> it as their canon both in the conduct of their life and in
> inquiry and discussion. (Ibid. ii. 32.)
> But what sort of canon of true and false can that be if we
> have no conception of true or false because they cannot be
> known one from the other? For if we have such a conception
> then there must be a difference between true and false, as
> between right and wrong. But if there is no difference then
> there is no canon, nor can he to whom the true and false
> appear the same have any criterion or any sign of truth
> whatever. (Ibid. ii. 33.)

Moreover the New Academy, the Stoics argue, are untrue
to their whole doctrine when they try to establish a positive
criterion of action. The lost Book ii had contained some of the
argument for this. Apparently the Academy, despite its rejection
of the Stoic definition of true appearances, had assumed a degree
of conspicuousness adequate to sanction practical decisions:

> They make a similar mistake when, smarting under the
> reproaches cast upon them by the truth, they try to distinguish
> between 'conspicuous sensations' and 'perceptions' and try to
> show that there is something 'conspicuous' stamped indeed as
> true on the mind and intellect, and yet that it cannot be
> perceived and 'apprehended'. But how can you ever maintain
> that a thing is 'conspicuously' white, when it may happen that
> an object really black appears to be white? Or how shall we
> say that such things are either 'conspicuous' or accurately
> stamped upon our minds, when it is uncertain whether our
> senses are affected by a reality or by empty nothingness? In
> this way they leave us neither colour nor substance nor reality
> nor proof nor senses nor any 'conspicuous' thing. (Ibid. ii. 34.)

What then is that 'probability' accepted by your school?
For what could be more frivolous than that what presents
itself to any person and at first glance seems probable should be
accepted as certain? But if they intend to say that it is only
after a survey and careful reflection that they will act upon
an appearance presented to them, still they will find no way of
escape: first because all appearances which have no differences
between them are all equally deprived of credit: secondly
because since they declare it possible for a man of wisdom,
after taking every precaution and making a most careful
survey, to arrive at some result, which appears like the truth
and at the same time is very far from the truth, they will never
be able to trust themselves even if, as they want to say, they
advance a large part of the way to truth itself or get as close
to it as possible. For in order that they may have confidence
it will be necessary for the characteristic mark of truth to be
known to them; but if this is darkened and obscured what
kind of truth will they suppose themselves to reach? Again
what language can be so ridiculous as theirs when they talk
in this way: 'This is indeed a mark or proof of that matter
and for that reason I act upon it, but it is possible that the
matter indicated may be false or may not exist at all'? (Ibid.
ii. 35 f.)

And towards the end of the Stoic argument there is another
criticism of the doctrine of 'probability'.

But this is a ridiculous assertion that you make when you
declare that you act upon probabilities if nothing comes
to obstruct you. In the first place how can you fail to be
obstructed if false appearances are not different from true?
Secondly what criterion of truth is there if it is linked with
the false? Hence inevitably arose the doctrine of the ἐποχή,
that is 'suspension of assent'. In this Arcesilaus was the more
consistent if certain judgments about Carneades are true. For
if there can be no 'perception'—as they both held—then there
must be an end of 'assent'. For what is so futile as to give
approval to something which is not known? But we heard
just yesterday that Carneades sometimes used to drift away so
far as to say that the Wise Man would 'opine', that is, would
commit a sin. (Ibid. ii. 59.)

(b) THE CASE FOR THE NEW ACADEMY

(i) *True and False Appearances Indistinguishable.* The New
Academy denied that true appearances had that conspicuousness
ascribed to them by the Stoic definition. Arcesilaus had devoted

his whole strength to prove that 'there is no appearance derived
from a real object of such a kind that it is not possible that
there may be an appearance just like it but derived from a
falsity' (*Ac. Pr.* ii. 77). Now it was agreed between the schools
that, if false appearances were shown to be indistinguishable
from true, even though some appearances might represent the
objects from which they proceeded, man could not 'perceive'
them in the technical sense of recognizing them indubitably as
valid representations of the underlying reality. On this point the
New Academy even adopted from Epicurus, whom it rejected in
almost everything else, the view that 'if even one resemblance
imposes on us everything will be thrown into uncertainty' (Ibid.
ii. 84).

The general nature of the New Academy's arguments for
the indistinguishability of true and false appearances has been
shown in the description of the Stoic case and in this part of
the *Academica* there is a lot of running over the ground already
traversed. It is important to observe that the Sceptic of the New
Academy assumes that there does exist an underlying reality.
He is concerned not with its existence but with man's power to
interpret it. Allowing that mistakes may be due to taking one
object for another, he does not deny that there are differences
in the reality that underlies appearances: what he denies is
the ability of human faculties to grasp the difference and to
distinguish one object from another so as to arrive at perception
in its technical sense of 'correct understanding of objective
reality': 'We do not deny that something of the nature of truth
exists but we do deny that it can be perceived' (Ibid. ii. 73).
The Sceptic does not abolish truth altogether: 'We do not do
that for we discern truths as much as falsehoods. But there is an
aspect of things leading us to acceptance: we find no mark
leading to perception' (Ibid. ii. 111).

Hence the illustrations at this stage of the argument show, not
that there is no difference between real objects, but the inability
of the senses at the time when a mistake is made to distinguish
between them—as with indistinguishable statues or the impressions made by a seal on wax:

Tell me, could not Lysippus with the same bronze, the same
tempering, the same graving tool and the other equipment the
same, make a hundred Alexander statues of the same pattern?
By what mental conception then could you tell them apart?
Again, if I imprint a hundred seals with this ring, all on wax

of the same sort, will it be possible that there should be any
mode of distinction to help you to recognize them? Or will
you have to look out for some ring-maker since you found
your Delian poultry-keeper able to recognize the eggs? (Ibid.
ii. 85 f.)

The point is that the Sceptic admits that there may be really
a hundred statues and many separate impressions of the seal,
but man will not distinguish them and so will experience false
appearances: he will look at statue A and will feel: 'This is
statue B.' Nor does it save the Stoic's case for the conspicuousness of true appearances that he is able to show that there
is a difference in the reality underlying true appearances and
the visions of dreams, whence ultimately the true could be
distinguished from the false:

> Just as if one denied that a man on waking thinks that
> what he saw were the visions of a dream, or that a man whose
> frenzy has abated believes that the appearances which he had
> in his frenzy were not true. That is not the point: the point
> is what aspect the appearances had at the time when he
> experienced them. (Ibid. ii. 88.)

The Sceptic insists that at the time when the mistake was
made the false was indistinguishable from the true. He quotes
various delusions which prove that 'so far as the acquiescence
of the mind is concerned there is no difference between true
appearances and false' (Ibid. ii. 90). Granted that dreamers and
madmen may realize their error in a changed state, there are
still numerous errors in ordinary life which refute the Stoic
insistence on the conspicuousness of true appearances: even if
you correct delusions, even if you check some errors of identification by recourse to experts (be it admitted that experts can
distinguish things so alike as eggs), nevertheless mistakes occur,
the false is taken for the true: things may be found to baffle the
experts: and so the Sceptics insist on the indistinguishability of
false and true, whence, according to their assumptions, general
uncertainty.

(ii) *Criticism of the Stoic Logic*. It must be clear that one of
the Stoics' most urgent problems, if they were to make effective
use of their theory of perception, should be to show how the
valid perceptions could be made the basis of a complete system
of knowledge. That is to say they should link the significant

view that 'the criterion of truth had its origin in the senses' with
the other view ascribed by Antiochus, in his account of the old
tradition, to Plato and his successors who 'insisted that it was
the intellect that was the judge of things: intellect alone they
considered worthy of belief because it alone beheld the homo-
geneous, the simple and the unchanging.' The first step towards
knowledge must be the perception of some sense datum, on
which intellect must then work.

In the *Academica* there are several hints of the Stoic claims
for the power of their logic to 'establish an element of fact by
methodical procedure of reasoning'.[1] But it is a line of thought
not developed before the third book of the *De Finibus,* and in
the *Academica* the New Academy criticizes the vaunted Stoic
logic as if it expended its efforts, not on the broad problem of
epistemology, but on trivialities: and here, they said, it revealed
its incompetence to deal even with the *sorites*:

> The nature of the universe has granted us no knowledge
> of limits to enable us to determine how far we can go in any
> matter. Not only are we able to give no definite answer in
> the case of the heap of wheat (whence the name) but on
> no topic at all, when asked in gradual stages, are we able
> to reply what degree of addition or subtraction makes the
> answer definite—on questions such as whether a man is rich or
> poor, famous or unknown, whether things are many or few,
> large or small, long or short, broad or narrow. 'But,' say you,
> 'the soritae are defective.' Then refute them if you can so
> that they may not trouble you: but they will trouble you if
> you don't take care. 'But we have taken care;' says the Stoic,
> 'for Chrysippus when asked in gradual stages questions such
> as whether three are few or many, thinks it right to keep quiet
> a little before he comes to the many (that is the meaning of
> the term they use).' 'So far as I am concerned,' says Carneades,
> 'you may not only keep quiet, you may even snore.' But what
> good does it do you? For someone is coming to rouse you
> from sleep and pursue the interrogation: 'If I add one to the
> number at which you stopped short will that make many?'
> You will continue as far as you choose. Need I say more? You
> confess that you cannot reply where 'few' stops and 'many'
> begins. (Ibid. ii. 92 f.)

Similarly the New Academy asserts the inability of the Stoics
to expose the fallacy of the *mentiens*: 'If you say you are a

1. Cf. *Fin.* iii. 18.

liar and therein tell the truth, are you a liar or do you tell the truth?' (Ibid. ii. 95.)

(iii) *Action Based on Probability.* The part of the New Academy's argument which is put most forcefully is the account of how action may be based on probability. Having refuted the Stoic case for valid perception and having thus established the impossibility of distinguishing true from false, they yet had to make some concession to common sense. For men do base judgments on the information derived from sensation and in practice they make decisions that do seem to work. Now the Stoics had urged that the logical development of Arcesilaus' view must sweep away all activity from life. But Carneades had carried the Academic doctrine beyond Arcesilaus, making a strong practical and emotional appeal:

> Carneades allows that there are two methods of classifying appearances, first according to perceptibility, and secondly according to probability. Hence objections against the senses and conspicuousness concern the first class but there is no argument against the second: whence his decision: 'there is no appearance of such a kind as to lead to perception but many such as lead to acceptance.' Moreover it would be contrary to nature that there should be no such thing as probability and the result would be as you, Lucullus, used to urge, that the whole of life would be turned upside down. Therefore, there are many appearances for the senses to accept provided we hold fast just to this that there is not one among them of such a kind that there cannot also be a falsity of the same kind in no way different from it. Thus whenever anything happens with an appearance of probability, providing nothing presents itself to contradict its probability, the Wise Man will make use of it and thus will keep his life right on its course. For the Wise Man whom you bring on the stage will also be influenced by many probable appearances that are not apprehended or perceived or approved but are like the truth: and if he did not give assent to them the whole of his life would become impossible. Suppose he embarks on a ship: surely your Wise Man does not hold it in his mind as a fact apprehended or perceived that his voyage will be successful? How can he? But if today he should sail hence for the voyage of 30 stades to Puteoli with a sound craft, a good pilot and this calm weather it would seem probable to him that he would get there safely. Therefore it is on appearances of this kind that he will determine whether to act or not: he will be

more ready to accept the fact that snow is white than was
Anaxagoras: for Anaxagoras not only denied that it was white
but said that it did not even seem white to him because he
knew that the water of which it was made was black. And
whenever anything presents itself to him in such a way that
its appearance is probable with its probability unobstructed,
he will be influenced by it. He is not carved out of stone nor
fashioned out of wood: he has a body, he has a mind, he is
influenced through his mind and through his senses, so that
many appearances seem to him to be true though they may
not seem to have that distinctive and characteristic mark
which belongs to perception: and it is for this precise reason
that he believes that the Wise Man does not render assent,
namely that some deceptive appearance may spring up presenting the same form as any particular true appearance. Nor is
our argument against the senses in any way different from that
of the Stoics. For they declare that there are many false
appearances which are really very different from what they
appear to the senses to be. (Ibid. ii. 99-101.)

In the opening lines of this passage Cicero (quoting from
Clitomachus) means that the New Academy's arguments against
the evidence of the senses and conspicuousness reinforce the
denial that 'perception' in the Stoic sense is possible but do
not call in question the probability that there may be true
appearances mingled with and indistinguishable from the false.
Therefore the New Academy rejects the suggestion that its
doctrine must prevent all action. And in any case, they say, the
Stoic himself in his own practical life has to determine most of
his actions by calculation of probability:

Yet I still ask what will obstruct the activity of one who
acts on probabilities if there is no obstacle in his way. 'He
will be obstructed,' someone says, 'by the very fact that he
will decide the impossibility of perceiving even that impression
to which he gives assent.' You too will find the same obstacle
in making a voyage, in agriculture, in marriage, in rearing
children and in very many things in which there will be
nothing but probability to influence you. (Ibid. ii. 108 f.)

Now the Sceptic's refusal to admit absolute certainty by no
means, he thinks, binds him to declare all things indeterminate.
There are some questions about which he can make distinctions
sufficient for practical decisions. If you asked him whether the
number of stars were odd or even he would reply that that was

indeterminate and of no possible interest to man. But there is a great difference between that sort of question and questions that closely concern man. About these man wants to have as much certainty as is possible for him, and although he cannot be quite sure he may as a result of experience make reasonable calculations:

> And so he is not afraid of seeming to create general con-fusion and uncertainty. If he were asked whether the number of the stars is even or odd he would say that he did not know. But he would not in the same way profess ignorance on points of duty and many other subjects in which he has had experience and practice. For in matters indeterminate there is no question of probability but in subjects which admit of probability the wise man will not be at a loss what to do or what to answer. (Ibid. ii. 110.) [2]

The scepticism of the New Academy abandoned as insoluble the fundamental problem of distinguishing the *thing* from the *appearance,* the *noumenon* from the *phenomenon.* It was in this sense that it declared πάντα εἶναι ἀκατάληπτα, meaning that the thing behind the appearance is incomprehensible. This is to resign hope of speculative knowledge and to separate it from practical knowledge.[3] But it does not mean that in the field of practical knowledge all things are indeterminate (*incerta*). Here indeed there is room for calculation based on long and detailed observation.

(c) THE FINAL SURVEY

Cicero finishes the *Academica* with a broad survey of the advantages of scepticism. He introduces this by giving his verdict on the central dispute, rejecting the Stoic definition on which Antiochus' case rested. For he says that he can find nothing corresponding to the definition of apprehension as the grasping of 'a true appearance of such a form as a false appearance could not take.' By this he means that man cannot have per-ception indubitably true in the Stoic sense and he contends that Antiochus was quite wrong in ascribing this doctrine to the old Academy or the Peripatetics. He censures him also for asserting that the original tradition never allowed that the Wise Man could 'opine', i.e. 'decide on insufficient grounds': by this he

2. Cf. *Ac. Pr.* ii. 32.
3. Cf. T. W. Levin, *Six Lectures Introductory to the Philosophical Writ-ings of Cicero,* pp. 122 f.

means that the true tradition sanctioned the calculation of probability.

As regards physical inquiry Cicero first stresses the defects of dogmatism, then challenges certain Stoic doctrines held by Antiochus and then proclaims the advantage of the open mind. In the first place Antiochus' dogmatism demands that all knowledge be based on 'apprehension' as defined by the Stoic definition, but it is not possible for the principles of a universal system to be apprehended in this way. Thus the ideal Wise Man in the Stoic or Antiochean sense, when he accepts a doctrine, will hold it 'because he has "apprehended" it as thoroughly by mental effort as the "appearances" he "apprehends" by means of the senses': that is to say if he accepts the Stoic doctrine of the governing force of the universe it will be because he feels he has 'apprehended' it as forcibly as he might 'apprehend' a simple fact such as that the sun is shining. But, says Cicero, such a doctrine cannot be 'apprehended' and perceived. With this argument in section 119 should be compared the passage in section 128 which reinforces it. There Cicero criticizes the acceptance of theoretically based doctrines in the same sense as facts of sensual experience:

> When the crow croaks they will hold that it is issuing an order or a prohibition just as firmly as they will accept or grant assent to the fact that the sun is now shining, and they will have just as much confidence in declaring that the sun, which they cannot measure, is more than eighteen times greater than the earth as in declaring that that statue, if they measure it, is six feet high. Hence arises this argument: if it is impossible to perceive the size of the sun a man who accepts all other facts in the same way as he accepts the sun's size does not perceive those facts. Now the sun's size cannot be perceived. Therefore he who accepts it as if he perceived it perceives no fact whatever. Now suppose they answer 'You can perceive the size of the sun,' I shall not resist provided only they say that all other matters are perceived and 'apprehended' in the same way. Nor indeed can they say that one thing is 'apprehended' in greater or less degree than another since to all things the one definition of 'apprehension' applies. (Ibid. ii. 128.)

The obstacles to man's comprehension of the universal system are stressed by the fact that it is impossible to get at the exact truth even in matters of physiology:

All those matters, Lucullus, are hidden and enshrouded in the gloom of thick darkness: human genius has no penetrating ray so bright that it can pierce the heavens or plough into the earth. We do not know our own bodies: we don't even know the situation of the organs and their functions. Accordingly the doctors — who were interested in such knowledge — have opened up the body to bring the parts to view. But even then Empirics deny that this improves their knowledge since it is possible that the organs change when opened up and uncovered. (Ibid. ii. 122.)

Then how much more impossible is it to arrive at the secrets of nature which we cannot dissect, open up and cut into its parts! In any case there are quarrels among the Stoics themselves as to the correct physical system.

While the preliminary Antiochean account of the Old School ascribed to it various Stoic doctrines and implied Antiochus' own acceptance of them, this final survey makes a further identification of Antiochus and the Stoics in physics. Antiochus is shown to accept in general the Stoic account of the nature of the world, adopting such doctrines as the divinity of stars and other heavenly bodies, control of the universe by living intelligence permeating it and the design of the universe for human well-being. This confirms the impression derived from the preliminary survey that what we may call the 'Academico-Peripatetic' physical system upheld by Antiochus was a compound of Stoicism and Platonism with certain importations from Aristotle and this shows it to be fairly closely related to the physical system which Cicero set out to examine in his later works. In fact Cicero distinctly challenges here the doctrines of divination and fate: 'For I don't believe that there is any such thing as the divination which you accept and I reject the existence of that fate in whose chain you say all things are held' (Ibid. ii. 126). Now these doctrines Cicero examines in detail in his later works. Hence this part of the survey in the *Academica* reveals his awareness of problems to be taken up later. But while he raises various queries Cicero does not here expound any positive case in physics. Not that he rejects physical inquiry as such, for he ends with an appealing statement of the New Academy's conception of the scope of physical inquiry within the framework of scepticism:

Yet I do not think that those inquiries of the natural philosophers should be banished. For the study and con-

templation of nature is in some sense the natural food of
hearts and minds. We are aroused, we seem to be exalted,
we despise human things and in the contemplation of divine
and heavenly existences we despise this world of ours as puny
and insignificant. There is delight in the mere investigation
of matters at once so vast and so mysterious. If anything
presents itself to us that looks at all like the truth our soul
is filled with a most civilizing feeling of delight. Therefore
the Wise Man both of your school and of ours will pursue his
inquiries: but yours will do it with full acceptance, belief
and assurance: ours will act in fear of forming rash opinions,
and will think that he is doing very well if in matters of that
kind he finds anything at all like the truth. (Ibid. ii. 127 f.)

The main theme in the survey of ethical theories is the
Sceptic's difficulty of choosing amidst a multiplicity of systems.
But it includes a strong statement of the difference between the
Stoics and Antiochus. It thus develops a thought already put
forward in the preliminary survey and points to the need of
more detailed examination, which Cicero will make in the *De
Finibus* and *Tusculan Disputations*. There is an emphatic passage which states the irreconcilability of the two definitions of
the supreme good:

I now leave you to decide whom I am to follow. But don't
let anyone make such an ignorant and silly answer as 'anyone
you please, provided you follow someone.' There can be no
more ill-considered utterance. . . . Therefore the matter will
remain in dispute: the Wise Man must be understood to be
either a Stoic or a member of the Old Academy. He cannot
be both for the dispute between them concerns not merely
their boundaries but their whole territories. Indeed our whole
scheme of life is bound up in the definition of the supreme
good: those who differ about that differ about the whole
scheme of life. Therefore the Wise Man cannot belong to
both schools since they differ so widely. He must belong either
to the one or to the other. (Ibid. ii. 132.)

(Note that the phrase 'Old Academy' is here used to mean the
Old School as Antiochus understood it.)
The difference is shown to be that while Zeno supposed
happiness to flow solely from virtue, Antiochus said 'yes, but
not the greatest happiness,' by which he meant that virtue must
be accompanied by the 'natural advantages'. This doctrine
Antiochus ascribed to the Old School as was shown in the
preliminary survey:

They went back to nature to find that first portion which
relates to right living and said that they ought to obey her:
for nowhere else but in nature must be sought that supreme
good which was the standard by which all things were judged.
And they decided that the highest of the objects of desire
and the summit of things good was the acquisition of all
mental, bodily and external advantages which are in accord
with nature. (*Ac. Post.* i. 19.)

Thus Antiochus accepted the guidance of nature in morality
and, although the doctrine was actually first advanced by Polemo,
ascribed it to the original tradition, to whom, as he said, the starting point for action 'lay in the maintenance of those possessions
which were marked out by nature' (Ibid. i. 23). Now it will
be shown in the *De Finibus* that it was a basic view of the
Stoics that the primary ethical impulses came from nature and
Antiochus' quarrel with the Stoics will be that, starting likewise
from the 'commendation of nature', they then abandoned their
starting-point by asserting a transition to a transcendental realm
divorced from the things of nature.

Cicero states the Sceptic's objection to the Antiochean conception of 'virtue together with the natural advantages'. If material
factors must be allowed to have some effect on the virtuous man
some of them will be evils. But though Antiochus admits that
there are some evils which affect our persons and our fortunes
'he still pronounces that a man who is surrounded by all these
evils will be happy if only he is a Wise Man.' Surely, says the
Sceptic, the adverse factors will diminish the perfection of his
happiness in some way. Thus Cicero cannot at this stage decide
between the Stoic and the Antiochean definitions of the good.

Now as regards Antiochus' claim to be the heir of the Old
School, Cicero points out that despite the difference just now
discussed there are Stoic doctrines which Antiochus accepts and
his acceptance of two of them must invalidate his claim to be
the heir. The first is the doctrine that the Wise Man is free from
the influence of emotions, 'is never influenced by desire or elated
by pleasure.' Actually the *Tusculan Disputations* will show that
there was an important difference between Antiochus and the
Stoics concerning this. But they did unite in rejecting the doctrine of the mean, here ascribed to the Old School, according
to which 'in every excitement there were certain bounds marked
out by nature.' The second point of divergence from the original
tradition was the exaltation of the *sapiens*. Though again he

arrived at it in a different way from the Stoics, Antiochus maintained the perfection of wisdom as the necessary condition of
excellence, so that a man could not truly perform any function
unless he were perfectly wise. Thus only the perfectly Wise Man
could be called a king. This is the point of the anecdote in
section 137 where Lucullus said to Carneades, 'I do not appear
to you to be a praetor, nor do you think this capital a city nor
that it has a body of burgesses.' Carneades replied, 'It is the
Stoic who does not think you a praetor.' The meaning is that
Carneades as a Sceptic must regard everything as uncertain while
the intransigent Stoic thinks that lacking perfect wisdom an
ordinary mortal cannot truly fulfil any function.

In this part of the argument the identification of Antiochus
with the Stoics was made for the purpose of rebutting his claim
to be the heir of the Old School. That Cicero was aware of the
differences between Antiochus and the Stoics is shown by the
subsequent argument of the *De Finibus* and the *Tusculan
Disputations* in which the main contest in the field of ethics is
between the Stoics and Antiochus, with the New Academy as a
third party of observers. For the present in the *Academica*
Cicero is still mainly concerned with the general case for
scepticism. What he will not accept is the possibility of perfectly
valid perception by man and it is this that underlies the New
Academy's doctrine of 'qualified assent' which Cicero quotes
against Antiochus (here represented by Lucullus) :

> Do you think that I am not at all impressed when I hear
> these arguments and countless others? I am impressed, Lucul-
> lus, no less than you; don't think me less a man than you. The
> only difference is that you, when thoroughly impressed, agree,
> assent, approve while you insist that your 'truth' is definite,
> thoroughly apprehended, perceived, established, immovable
> and fixed and from that position you cannot be driven or
> dislodged by any reasoning: but I believe that there is nothing
> of such a kind that, if I assented to it, I should not often find
> myself assenting to what is false, since true is separated from
> false by no distinction, especially since your so-called criteria
> of dialectic are worthless. (*Ac. Pr.* ii. 141.)

Accordingly in ethics the Sceptic objects to decisions in particular cases, where the unreliability of perception must render
man liable to error. But this does not mean that he rejects the
possibility of a broad theory, and thus the willingness to investigate ethical theory in general remains. But what of practical

morality? Cicero is fully aware of the need to make decisions
in full seriousness and not at random choice. Already in several
places in the *Academica* he has quoted the dogmatists' criticism
of the difficulties that must impede the Sceptic in moral action
because of his denial of valid perception:

> Now the object which arouses desire should first be seen and
> command belief. But this is impossible if the object which
> appears to us cannot be distinguished from an unreality. Now
> how can the mind be influenced to feel desire if it is not
> clear whether the object which appears to it is consistent with
> nature or foreign to it? Again if the mind has never realized
> what course of action is consistent with its duty it will never
> do anything at all, never be impelled towards any undertaking,
> never be aroused. But if the mind is ever to act it must be
> that the impression which has struck upon it appears as a
> truth. (Ibid. ii. 25.)

> But these consequences again follow that without assent
> there can be no memory nor conceptions of things nor arts.
> Moreover the man who will refuse all assent will be deprived
> of the most important thing of all—the freedom of the will.
> Then what becomes of virtue if nothing rests with ourselves?
> (Ibid. ii. 38.)

Thus Cicero is aware of the issues: he knows the Stoic concern
that those who deny that anything can be 'apprehended' may
'do away with those very things that make life possible and make
it attractive' and may 'absolutely overthrow life from its foundations and actually deprive the creature of mind' (Ibid. ii. 31).
His task is to uphold a reasonable moral criterion while rejecting
the validity of perception and in his final statement on what has
been the chief topic of the *Academica,* dialectic, he gives the
New Academy's verdict. Here he finally censures the Stoics for
their rigidity amidst many diverse theories and for their inability
to make concessions to the requirements of practical life. How
much better is the Academy's readiness to act on due consideration but without insisting on perfect certainty—to give 'assent'
to something not perceived, that is to say, to 'opine' but in such
a manner as to be clearly conscious of 'opining'! — a decision
completely consistent with the Academic doctrine of calculation
of probability.

3. THE SIGNIFICANCE OF THE ARGUMENT OF THE *Academica*

Of all Cicero's philosophic works there is none whose interest
and method are closer to the spirit of modern philosophy than

the *Academica*. In the later works the analysis is imperfect and the standard of criticism is below the modern, but in the *Academica* the discussion of the nature and reality of the phenomena of perception is conducted with all the subtlety which the Greeks devoted for generations to questions which are still lively topics. Here we get in a very detailed form a manifestation of the negative side of Greek speculation with all that service to philosophy which is performed by expressing the grounds of negation and exposing falsehood and unsubstantiated affirmation.

In their search for some certain basis on which to establish the truths of science and morals the Stoics insisted on the realist theory of perception. Their theory of the relation of knowledge to existence, supported by the belief that every object had by nature a distinctive mark, implied that the object of thought was co-extensive with the real object. The image embraced and comprehended the object. In fact perception was intuitive and thus the gap between the object in thought and the object in nature was bridged. Their insistence on the distinguishability of appearances was directed to prove that, although objects might appear similar, no two objects were identical, so that for each true perception there existed a real object in nature. The external world then must be the object of immediate consciousness (καταληπτόν).

The New Academy's objection turned, as do modern criticisms of realist theories of perception, on the impossibility of escaping from subjective knowledge. How can man tell that the differences he detects when he compares objects are in the objects themselves and do not rise from differences in the points of view under which he considers them? In fact is he not comparing appearances rather than things and is not the theory of perception based on facts of consciousness which can only be interpreted by assuming the theory? Thus the New Academy was impressed by the subjective limitation. But in this it did not reach the extreme view which Hume expressed thus:

> By what argument can it be proved that the perceptions of the mind must be caused by external objects entirely different from them, though resembling them? . . . It is a question of fact whether the perceptions of the senses be produced by external objects resembling them. How shall this question be determined? By experience surely as all other questions of a like nature. But here experience is and must be entirely silent.

D

The mind has never anything present to it but the perceptions and cannot possibly reach any experience of their connexion with objects. The supposition of such a connexion is therefore without any foundation in reasoning. (*Essays*, ed. Green and Grose, vol. ii, p. 131.)

But the New Academy does not deny the existence of objective reality. They have not reached that point where scepticism overcomes its doubt that there may be truth behind the dogmatism. In fact their admission that true appearances may be intermingled with the false implies that they accept the existence of the world of things existing independently of human consciousness. Such scepticism cannot impose complete agnosticism. It questions not the existence of reality but man's ability to know it accurately. It thus leaves room for speculation and in fact there remains in the attitude of this phase of scepticism a positive impulse towards speculation which may be explained by its origin. This may be traced back to the quest for virtue in the post-Socratic schools. Dissatisfied with the Cyrenaic cult of hedonism and the proud Cynic disdain of wordly circumstances the scepticism of Pyrrho attempted to repress disturbing influences by cultivating doubt: doubt was to lead to suspension of judgment and tranquillity of mind in contrast to the Stoics who sought to achieve tranquillity by complete comprehension. The New Academy made some significant developments in the scepticism which it inherited from Pyrrhonism. These are summed up by Sextus Empiricus in the *Hypotyposes* (i. 33. 226) thus:[4] (a) The New Academy positively asserts that all things are incomprehensible, i.e. that there is no bridge from the subject to the object, while the Pyrrhonist does not despair of being able eventually to arrive at the comprehension of things. (b) The Academicians are more emphatic in judgment of good and evil, asserting with conviction that it is more probable that they are one rather than the other. (c) While the Pyrrhonists say that all mental representations are equally trustworthy or untrustworthy as materials for judgment, the New Academy says that some are probable, others improbable and that there are degrees of probability. Here the New Academy combines a denial of the possibility of ever bridging the gap with a positive case for calculating probability. It is emphatic in declaring that within the sphere of man's knowledge there is sufficient certitude on which to base principles of action. Thus while the

4. Cf. Levin, *op. cit.*

Pyrrhonists maintained that they could consistently behave like other men, provided it was understood that their behaviour did not imply a belief in the correctness of their impressions, the vitality of spirit of the New Academy, and its interest in human action, both carried it beyond Pyrrhonism and brought it into opposition with the principle of determinism which was linked with the Stoic theory of perception. Its desire to find some sanction for action is manifest even in the discussion of perception: this is the point of the doctrine of conspicuous sensations stamped on the mind. But of course it is especially manifest in the whole discussion of calculation of probability. For even when its investigation of the part played by man in perception convinced it of the limitations of man, it nevertheless pressed on with the quest for the criterion, refusing to be bound by the doctrine of suspense of judgment. Thus it believed that observation could show what was good or evil for man and that to maintain suspense when life called for action was absurd.

The New Academy realized the limitations imposed upon it by insistence on the sensual origin of all knowledge and by denial of supra-sensual communication of truths not derived from the world of nature, which followed from the rejection of the forms. They cannot claim more than that man by experience and observation may establish distinctions between what is probably false and what is probably true and thus make decisions for practical conduct satisfactory enough for ordinary life. They themselves realize that such judgments cannot be absolutely valid and when Antiochus, responding to that practical impulse to find a sure criterion, thinks that he can modify the doctrine of the Academy in its department of dialectic by allowing the validity of perception, they see that this is in fact a dogmatic acceptance of truth and quite unacceptable to the true tradition of the New Academy. Therefore they repudiate his heresy and in doing this they set a limit to their own claims for their criterion. This they realize and they admit it in the phrases quoted above: 'There is an aspect of things leading us to acceptance: we find no mark leading to perception' or 'there is no appearance of such a kind as to lead to perception but many such as to lead to acceptance.' Thus while Carneades had doubt and suspension of judgment as his main topics and the theory of probability only in second rank, his successors, Philo and Cicero, concentrated on this second doctrine and responding to the strong practical impulse of the age felt impelled to explore every possibility of establishing a criterion as certain as possible, knowing however that the nature of their case must prevent them from claiming complete certainty. There is indeed a passage (*Ac. Pr.* ii. 18) which seems to show that Philo went too far in claiming certainty for his criterion and in which Cicero gives Antiochus' view that such a claim is quite impossible unless the Stoic validity of perception is admitted. This proves that, whatever difficulties Philo may have got himself into in excess of enthusiasm, Cicero realized that the claims of the Academy for their criterion must, by the very nature of their fundamental assumptions, fall short of complete certainty. The following is an excellent statement of the Academy's attitude on free inquiry:

> But since we are accustomed to use our own arguments against all others we cannot show cause why others should not disagree with us. And yet the nature of our case is quite clear, for we want to find the truth apart from all party spirit and we seek it with every diligence and care. Now admittedly every branch of knowledge encounters many obstacles and in the nature of things there is such uncertainty and in our judgments such weakness that not without cause did very ancient and learned men despair of being able to find what they sought. Nevertheless they did not falter nor shall we through weariness abandon our earnest search, nor have our discussions any other purpose but this, to draw out by arguing on both sides, and, so to say, to give shape to some result which *is true or comes as near as possible to the truth*. Nor is there any difference between us and those who think that they possess knowledge except that they don't doubt that the propositions that they uphold are true while we consider many theories to be probable and can readily act upon them but *hardly declare them certain*. But in this respect we are freer and less restrained—we retain intact our power to judge for ourselves and are not forced by any compulsion to uphold all the doctrines which certain men may have tried to impose and force upon us. All others are held in close bondage before they can judge for themselves what is best; then when they are at the weakest age, either from deference for some friend or by the influence of a single speech of the first man they hear, they make up their minds about questions which they don't understand: to whatever school the storm sweeps them, there they stick as to a rock. (*Ac. Pr.* ii. 7 f.)

While this means that man must rely on what is given directly in his own consciousness and that the standard of decision must be personal, the New Academy was held back from intellectual anarchy, which might have resulted from complete scepticism, by the positive impulse which persisted from the era of the post-Socratic schools, the quest for virtue. In its attitude in the discussion of the theory of probability one can detect a disposition to accept by faith what can never be grasped by knowledge and this led towards positive acceptance in ethics. This can be seen in earlier works of Cicero. In the *De Legibus* i. 39, he had condemned the New Academy's vacillation in ethics and in the later philosophical works he tried to arrive at a system consistently argued. His reservation on perception which imposed the view that the truth attainable by man can only be provisional prevented him from becoming like Kant an absolutist in ethics while a sceptic in epistemology. But he did have great sympathy with the Antiochean system of ethics and was ready to admit that if only the doctrine of perception could be granted (though he himself could not grant it) then it would provide an acceptable theory of morality. Nevertheless, because doubt remained, he refused to be dogmatic or to assert clear distinctions. This attitude reflects itself in the end, in the *De Officiis*, in his inability to make a clear demarcation between individual rights and universal obligation and here his attitude is much like that of the modern philosophers who uphold a form of moderate relativism.

Finally in the *Academica* there are several points of general significance which are worth noting. To a certain extent the arguments of the Academy advance investigation into the scope of intellectual inquiry in those places where they inquire what are the questions in which man's calculation will avail. By contrast the Stoics make grandiose claims for the development of a system of conceptual knowledge by process of the intellect but they do not succeed in linking it consistently with the primary perception which was their starting point: their failure will be revealed in the *De Finibus* by the arguments drawn from Antiochus, who diverged from them after agreeing with their starting point.

From the *Academica* as a whole emerge two points significant for the ethical inquiry in Cicero's later works — the common acceptance both by Stoics and by Antiochus (in his so-called Old Tradition) of the existence of the material world (the 'order of nature', as we may call it) as the real basis of truth, and their further assumption of its essential goodness. For them both there is a direct connection between valid perception and fundamental valid impulse. Perception involves 'assent', i.e. acceptance as true, and at the same time because of the essential goodness of nature implies an impulse: 'For as no animated being can fail to desire an object which clearly seems agreeable to Nature so it cannot fail to "assent" to a "conspicuous" phenomenon which has been presented to it' (*Ac. Pr.* ii. 38).

These assumptions form an important link between the *Academica* and the *De Finibus*. For in the *De Finibus* the goodness of 'primary natural instinct' is the fundamental basis from which the ethical structure both of Stoics and of Antiochus is built up, but the examination of its validity does not yet go deeper than this assumption of the goodness of nature made in the *Academica*.

There is one further assumption in the *Academica* which has great significance in Cicero's social and political thought. It is the doctrine of the brotherhood of man: 'Man they considered to be in some sense a part of a community comprising the whole human race, and to be connected with his fellow-men by the link of a common humanity, as they called it' (*Ac. Post.* i. 21). In the *Academica* the doctrine is ascribed to the old tradition and is stated barely and without elaboration. In his later works we shall find that Cicero elaborates it and it will be our task, when we consider them, to discuss the origins and justification of the doctrine.

CHAPTER III

THE *DE FINIBUS*

1. CONNECTION WITH THE *Academica*

THE *Academica* and the *De Finibus* must be taken closely together. In point of time the composition of the two works overlapped: Cicero was already far advanced in the writing of the *De Finibus* when he was still busy with the revision of the *Academica*.

The full title of this work is *De Finibus Bonorum et Malorum,* which may be translated 'Various theories of the chief good and its opposite'. Already in his preliminary survey and again towards the end of the *Academica* Cicero had shown that the main issue in ethics was whether the supreme good is to be defined by the Stoic concept of 'moral worth' (*honestum*) or by Antiochus' 'Academico-Peripatetic' concept of 'virtue plus natural advantages'. Consequently his purpose in the *De Finibus* was to present the Antiochean criticism of the Stoics and then to state Antiochus' own conclusion. He himself stood outside the argument, intervening only at the end to indicate the need for further examination of the theory of Antiochus.

The Stoic view which was here being assailed upheld a pure morality, disregarding and unaffected by particulars. The positive case for it, given in Book III, is generally supposed to come from an author not earlier than Carneades: from similarities to Diogenes Laertius the source appears to have been Diogenes Babylonius. He accompanied Carneades on his famous mission to Rome in 156 B.C. Antiochus' purpose was to modify this contemporary version of the orthodox Stoic doctrine. Against the uncompromising definition of pure morality, detached and austere, he proclaimed a morality which must take account of particulars but could attain perfection nevertheless, an ethical system which had something in common with the theories of the modern naturalistic humanists. His criticism of the Stoics was that they were false to the starting-point on which, as we saw in the *Academica,* both schools agreed. For the origin of all knowledge they should be bound to perception: moreover the rejection of the doctrine of forms should cut them off from supra-sensual sources of knowledge. The question must be, how upon their basis they could reach a perfect system of ethics.

Now the orthodox Stoics, if they held consistently to their doctrine of materialism, might be able to make out a plausible case for the perfection of their system of knowledge. It would be knowledge of the sum total of the existing material plenum. As such it would be able to explain fully each particular detail. Surveying any given particular it would be able to make the right decision and it would be unaffected by particulars in the sense that none of them could sway it to a wrong decision. Thus it may be that the Stoic case, if correctly interpreted, was consistent. By the account in *De Finibus* III of the attainment of 'choice fully rationalized', it may be that the Stoics meant no more than that the vast complexity of the world could not be grasped by perception alone without the aid of the pure processes of reason. Thus their ideal of the complete system of knowledge may in fact have been knowledge of the whole sensible universe derived from perception but organized by reason. This process of organization may have been the function of the Stoic logic, treated so contemptuously in the *Academica* by the New Academy and not duly respected by Antiochus either. The Stoics may have felt that with its aid they were developing an account of the perfection of reason consistently from their first principles.

But this was not what Antiochus understood the Stoics to mean. The account of them given in the *De Finibus* and the Antiochean criticism of it which follows make it appear that they proclaimed the good as a thing entirely transcending the natural advantages: they seemed to Antiochus to imply, as the epistemological structure supporting their morality, a system of absolute knowledge above the world of the senses. If this was what they meant, it would imply the acceptance of an intelligible world, transcending the world of matter, and the recognition of intuitive reason, like that of the Platonists, capable of seizing on the essence of things. This would be inconsistent both with the physical doctrine of materialism and with the epistemological principles shown in the *Academica*. Therefore Antiochus accused them of abandoning their first principles and of making no use of perception on which they originally insisted. He treated them as if they did uphold an ideal of absolute knowledge divorced from the senses. The explanation may be either that Antiochus misinterpreted the Stoics or that the particular phase of Stoicism with which he was dealing did hold the doctrines he condemned. The latter alternative is not impossible because of the intrusion of Platonic elements into the Stoic theories of this era.

Rejecting what he understood to be the Stoics' transition to the transcendental realm, Antiochus himself set out to correct them and to build up an ethical system consistently from their principles laid down in the *Academica,* i.e., the validity of perception and the goodness of the order of nature. It was as if he said: 'the Stoics have gone about their task in the wrong way: I shall now show what is the right way, from their first principles, to attain their goal—pure morality.' Condemning the Stoics for their neglect of the things of the senses, he thought that by systematic compilation of information given in perception it was possible to build up a perfect system of knowledge. It is here that Antiochus differs from the modern naturalistic humanist. The latter recognizes 'that all explanation is offered in a specific context, that it departs from and ultimately returns to particular problems, and that therefore no explanation can be total or exhaust the nature of anything.'[1] But Antiochus, concentrating on establishing the perfection of his ethical end, reduces particular problems to negligibility and finishes not by explaining them but by explaining them away. This will be shown by his treatment of the relation of the good to the natural advantages.

The immediate connection of the *De Finibus* with the *Academica* can now be seen to be the discussion of whether the Stoic or the Antiochean system is the correct development from the common assumptions described in the *Academica.* But obviously it is the case of Antiochus that raises the most important issue, namely the possibility of constructing a satisfactory system of ethics upon the facts given in perception—an issue important in modern philosophy too. Accordingly his system now becomes the main centre of interest and the examination of the Stoic case is really a preparation for the study of him.

In pursuing his inquiry Cicero is quite consistent with the nature of his scepticism as revealed in the *Academica.* His attitude is that, though man may not know for certain in any particular case, yet the basis of truth is there, true appearances being mingled with the false. Therefore speculation is not idle.

1. S. Hook, 'Nature and the Human Spirit', *Report of the Amsterdam Conference,* 1948, p. 775.

Now instead of coming immediately to the difference between the two main rivals Cicero spends his first two books in discussing the Epicurean ethics and refuting them. He says:

> In the present work we believe that we have given a fairly complete account of the whole subject of theories about the chief good and its opposite: for we have aimed at giving, to the best of our ability, not only our own views but those of the various schools of philosophy. Then starting with the simplest account let us first pass in review the system of Epicurus which most men know best of all. (*Fin.* i. 12 f.)

This might imply an undiscerning purpose, merely to state the ethics of the various schools one after the other. But in fact Cicero's treatment of the Epicureans aids his general plan and leads up to the Stoic case by raising the vital questions 'What is the fundamental ethical impulse?' and 'What is the chief good that must be the final goal?' To these the answers of the Epicureans are respectively 'pleasure' and 'absence of pain'. These answers are rejected by the aid of Stoic arguments. This procedure is similar to that adopted in the lost part of the *Academica* where it appears that before giving the Stoic doctrine of perception Cicero gave the main alternative view which raised the most vital question and accompanied it by anticipatory objections to the Stoic case. Cicero's next step in the *De Finibus* was to expound and examine the Stoic answers to these questions, 'the instinct of self-preservation' and 'moral worth or absolute virtue'. Up to this point the argument assists the subsequent development of the case of Antiochus in that it necessitates first the discussion of the theory of the primary impulse, in which he has a common starting point with the Stoics, and then the statement of a final goal whose lack of connection with that starting point he considers to be the fatal weakness in the Stoic case. Then beginning from the same principles and retaining in particular the instinct of self-preservation as the primary impulse, the Antiochean account tries to trace the progress up from the things of nature to the highest good. The improvement that it endeavours to make as compared with the Stoics is that, as each higher grade is reached in the progress up to virtue, it supposes the retention of the things already admitted to be good. Thus it advances the conception of a complete structure of virtue in which the things of nature retain some force, whereas the Stoic, after using them in the early stages of the upward progress, abandoned them entirely when the highest stage was reached and thus presented a conception of virtue entirely divorced from the first grounds which gave it meaning.

In this continuous endeavour to arrive at a more complete account at each successive stage, rejecting the faults but retaining the sound principles of each school examined, we observe a sustained development of the case for Antiochus from the starting point laid down in the preliminary survey of the *Academica*. Then at the end of the *De Finibus* Cicero, who has stood outside the argument, states the attitude of the New Academy. He is not yet satisfied about the Antiochean account of the relationship of the things of this world to the supreme good. Thus he points the way to a further examination of this problem in the *Tusculan Disputations*.

2. DISCUSSION OF EPICUREAN ETHICS: BOOKS I AND II

(a) SOURCES

The purpose of the discussion of Epicureanism being to throw into relief the main Stoic doctrines, it is natural that Cicero should use the traditional Stoic arguments against Epicurus. He probably found these in some work of Antiochus. The description of moral worth, which we shall quote, may derive ultimately from Chrysippus.

For his Epicurean arguments Cicero drew on a compendium lent to him by a friend. It probably contained an epitome of a work by Epicurus *Concerning the End* ($\pi\epsilon\rho\grave{\iota}$ $\tau\acute{\epsilon}\lambda ovs$) and an appendix which condensed the points of difference between Epicureans and Cyrenaics.[2]

(b) THE PRIMARY IMPULSE

(i) *The Epicurean Case for Pleasure*. The starting point for the Epicurean morality is the doctrine that pleasure is the primary impulse. But the arguments for this are weak. Their general lines are these: the world of nature is the basis of all true knowledge and man through his senses can have direct and valid perception of it (observe the similarity to the Stoic account of perception): that is to say, man can have true knowledge of what is in accordance with nature and therefore his pure and uncontaminated choice is for what is in accordance with nature: now his pure and uncontaminated choice, when he is an infant

2. Hutchinson ed. *Fin.*, pp. xxxi f.

and free from wrong influences, is for pleasure: hence pleasure is the primary natural impulse: but of course it is exactly that assumption, that the first choice is pleasure, that the Stoics will attack. Moreover the Epicureans make the unjustified assumption that knowledge of what is in accordance with nature implies its choice. These two passages bring out the general nature of their case:

> Every animal as soon as it is born seeks for pleasure and delights in it as the chief good: but it recoils from pain as the chief evil and makes every effort to avoid it. This it does while as yet it remains unperverted under the pure and unbiased guidance of nature. Therefore Epicurus refuses to admit any need for theoretical argument to prove why pleasure is desirable and pain to be avoided. The facts of sense perception are, he thinks, such things as that fire is hot, snow white, honey sweet; there is no need to establish any of these facts by elaborate argument: it is enough merely to draw attention to them. . . . Now since, if mankind is stripped of sensation, nothing remains, it follows that nature herself must be the judge of what is in accordance with nature and what is contrary to it. Now to control nature's desire or avoidance what object of perception or judgment has she other than pleasure and pain?
>
> But there are some of our school who would refine upon this doctrine: not satisfied for the decision of questions of good and evil to rest with the senses, they declare that it is a matter of intellectual comprehension that pleasure is in itself and for its own sake desirable, and pain to be avoided in and for itself. Hence they declare that our perception that the one is desirable and the other to be avoided is, as one might say, a natural idea implanted in our minds. (*Fin.* i. 30 f.)

He attached most importance to physical inquiry. By the knowledge that it produces can be grasped the meaning of terms, the nature of predication and the law of consistency and contradiction. By the knowledge of the facts of nature we are relieved from the burden of superstition and from the fear of death and we cease to be bewildered by sheer ignorance which often produces terrifying apprehensions. Finally, we shall also be better in our own characters when we learn the requirements of nature.

Besides it is only if we hold fast to a well established scientific system—by preserving the canon which we have as a gift from heaven to afford us understanding of the universe and by making it the test in all our judgments—that we shall resist the persuasions of eloquence to betray our belief.

Now if we have no clear knowledge of nature we cannot possibly hope to uphold the truth of sense perception. Every mental presentation derives from the senses; only if they are all true—as the theory of Epicurus holds—are knowledge and perception possible. Those who deny the validity of sensation and say that nothing can be perceived cannot—by virtue of the exclusion of the senses—expound even their own argument. Moreover, the rejection of knowledge and science renders impossible every theory of life and conduct. Thus from physical inquiry are derived courage against the fear of death, resolution to face the terrors of religion and peace of mind, for it abolishes ignorance of the mysteries of nature: and again it promotes self-control by explaining the nature of the desires and distinguishing their different kinds: and, as I just now showed, the canon or criterion of knowledge, established by that same philosopher, provides a means of distinguishing the true from the false. (Ibid. i. 63 f.)

This thorough-going attempt to base morality on direct perception of the order of nature might be expected to produce a doctrine that would march closely with the Stoics. But the Stoics hotly reject the theory that the primary impulse is to seek pleasure and this difference on the primary impulse causes a complete divergence of the ethical theories of the two schools.

(ii) *The Stoic Case for Self-preservation.* The Epicurean having asserted his primary impulse without penetrating examination, the Stoic retorts in kind with an even barer declaration that the primary impulse is not pleasure but self-preservation. With this doctrine Antiochus will agree and a fuller justification of it is deferred until the case for Antiochus is developed in Book v. For the present this is what the Stoic spokesman says:

Again the natural instinct of the infant is not to seek pleasure, its instinct is for self-regard, for self-preservation and protection. For every creature directly after birth has a feeling of regard for itself and its members, embracing primarily its two main parts—body and soul—and then the divisions of each of them. For there are certain distinctive excellences of soul and body, the first slight recognition of which impels the creature to make distinctions, seeking the primary endowments of nature and spurning their opposites. As to whether these primary endowments of nature include pleasure that is a stormy question, but to think that they really include nothing except pleasure, neither limbs, nor senses nor intellectual activity nor bodily vigour and health, that seems to me the depths of ignorance. And from one's decision on this topic [i.e. one's view as to the objects of instinctive desire] must derive one's whole theory of goods and evils. (Ibid. ii. 33 f.)

One can see that this is not so much disproof of the Epicurean view as flat denial and substitution of another primary impulse. The Stoic assertion of self-preservation as the primary impulse is assumed to be axiomatically true. But though at this stage it does not support its case by detailed argument the Stoic account does go on to make a specific attack; the Epicurean, says the Stoic, has claimed too much for the evidence of the senses:

> In his assertion that the verdict of the senses is that pleasure is good and pain evil, he ascribes more power to the senses than the laws allow us as judges of private suits. For we cannot give a verdict on any matter which is not within our jurisdiction. . . . Then what does come under the verdict of the senses? Sweetness, bitterness, smoothness, roughness, proximity, distance, stability, squareness, roundness. There-fore it is reason that will give a fair decision with the aid of the knowledge of the universe, which may rightly be called wisdom, and then with the additional aid of the virtues: the virtues reason pronounces to be the mistresses of all things but you insisted that they are the handmaids and servants of the pleasures: in consultation with all these reason will pronounce first concerning pleasure that she has no claim either to be enthroned in that seat of the chief good which is the object of our search or even to be associated with moral worth. (Ibid. ii. 36 f.)

In this statement that the verdict of wisdom 'in consultation with the virtues' is superior to that of the senses the rational side of the Stoic ethics emerges. In criticizing the Epicurean reliance on the evidence of the senses the Stoic is moving towards the view—inadequately expounded in the *Academica* because of the deficient treatment of the Stoic logic—that a complete system of human knowledge, although it has its origin in the facts of perception, must mainly develop by processes of the reason. This desire to conduct the ethical inquiry at a level higher than that of the evidence of the senses manifests itself with increasing urgency as the positive argument for Stoic ethics unfolds and we shall find that in Book iii they pass quickly from the instinct of self-preservation to 'facts established by methodical reasoning'. But from the outset, because of their insistence on the derivation of truth from perception by which Antiochus has declared them to be bound, the Stoics appear to be handicapped in their effort to attain to perfect knowledge and absolute morality. One must always ask whether the transition is made correctly and with due regard for the starting point of the perception and the primary impulse on which they insist so strongly.

(c) THE THEORY OF THE CHIEF GOOD

(i) *The Epicurean Theory of Absence of Pain.* In the Epicurean passages quoted above we observed the attitude of those who sought to 'refine upon the doctrine' and to raise the calculation of pleasure from the level of the senses to the level of intellectual cognition. No doubt it was their influence which produced the conception of absence of pain as the highest form of pleasure. From this they went on to advance the doctrine that the chief good was absence of pain, despite its apparent incompatibility with their starting point where the primary impulse was stated to be pleasure in an active form:

> We do not seek solely for that sort of pleasure which affects our physical being with a definite feeling of delight, a sense experience of positive enjoyment. But we consider that the highest form of pleasure is that which is experienced as a result of complete freedom from pain.
> In relief from pain the actual release and freedom from all discomfort affords us joy: and since everything that gives us joy is pleasure and everything that gives annoyance pain, complete release from pain is rightfully called pleasure. For example, when hunger and thirst are quelled by eating and drinking the actual removal of discomfort brings pleasure in its train; so generally, the removal of pain causes pleasure to take its place.
> Therefore Epicurus would not admit that there was any intermediate state between pain and pleasure. That state which some thought intermediate—the complete absence of pain—he regarded as not only pleasure but actually the highest form of pleasure. However, a man who realizes the nature of his feelings must be experiencing either pleasure or pain. But Epicurus thinks that complete absence of pain is the limit and highest point of pleasure; beyond this, however the pleasure may vary in kind, it cannot vary in intensity or degree. (Ibid. i. 37 f.)

This tendency to theorize about the nature of pleasure is carried further by argument about its relation to the virtues. The Epicureans present the virtues not as ends in themselves but as means to pleasure, and even wisdom is portrayed as its handmaiden:

> Now if those transcendent virtues which your school rates so highly did not produce pleasure who would think them praiseworthy or desirable? We value the art of medicine not for its interest as a science but because we want good health: the art of the pilot wins esteem not for its scientific but for its practical value, since it involves the rules for sailing a ship successfully: similarly wisdom, which must be considered the art of living, would not be desired if it achieved no results, but actually it is desired because like an artist it points the way to the attainment and acquisition of pleasure.
>
> Now you see my definition of pleasure. You must not let my explanation fail because of the discreditable associations of the term. What most of all upsets human life is ignorance of good and evil; it is because of mistaken ideas about them that we are frequently deprived of the greatest pleasures and racked by the cruellest mental pain. So we must call in the aid of wisdom to banish fear and greed, to root out all the rash decisions of prejudice and to show itself as our surest guide to pleasure. Wisdom is the one thing that can drive sorrow from our hearts and prevent us from being a prey to fear; with her to instruct us we can live in peace and extinguish all the blazing flames of desire.   (Ibid. i. 42 f.)

The Epicureans felt satisfied with what seemed to them to be a systematic explanation of the nature of pleasure. They thought it a thing much more substantial and soundly based than the Stoics' vague concept:

> for they say that there is no good thing except that vague phantom which they entitle moral worth, a title more splendid than substantial; and they say that virtue resting on this moral worth has no need of pleasure; but is sufficient in herself for happiness.   (Ibid. i. 61.)

(ii) *The Stoic Refutation.* It is not difficult for the Stoics to demonstrate a fundamental confusion in the Epicurean case. The Epicureans had urged that the univeral instinct was to seek active pleasure. This 'kinetic' pleasure was quite a different thing from the 'static' pleasure, i.e. absence of pain, at which the Epicurean finally arrived:

> For the origin of the chief good he goes back, I think, to the state of living creatures immediately after birth. As soon as the creature is born it rejoices in pleasure and seeks it as a

good, shunning pain as an evil. The best verdict of good and evil is, he says, that of creatures which have not had time to become contaminated (that is what you asserted and the phraseology is that of your school).

But what a mass of fallacies! Will a wailing child distinguish between the chief good and the chief evil? And by which kind of pleasure is he to decide, static or kinetic? For we learn our language, heaven help us, from Epicurus. If the criterion is 'static' pleasure then natural instinct is obviously for self-preservation, which we grant. But if it is 'kinetic' pleasure as you say, then no pleasure will be so base that we should do without it and at the same time that new-born creature does not find its first motive in the highest pleasure you assert to be absence of pain.

Yet Epicurus cannot have sought this argument from children or again from beasts which he considers the true reflection of nature: he could not say that natural instinct guides them to seek that pleasure which consists in absence of pain. For this pleasure cannot excite appetition nor has this condition of freedom from pain any driving-power to give an impulse to the mind. . . . It is the positive feeling of pleasure that supplies an impulse. Consequently Epicurus, to prove that pleasure is naturally desired, makes use of this argument that it is the 'kinetic' pleasure that attracts children and animals, not the 'static' which consists merely of absence of pain. Then how can it be right to say that natural instinct starts from one kind of pleasure but that the chief good is found in another? (Ibid. ii. 31 f.)

Again, the Epicurean account of the virtues as 'means of pleasure' is refuted by detailed argument which takes up most of the second half of Book II, its length being rather disproportionate. Briefly the Stoic case is that the Epicurean principles reduce the virtues to a calculation of self-interest, which is inconsistent with the natural order of things; as the Epicureans tacitly admit by their own conduct:

But I ask you . . . don't you realize that the force of natural instinct is the more firmly established because you yourselves, who make your own interests and, as you admit, pleasure the standard in all things, nevertheless show by your own conduct that your standard is not pleasure but duty and that natural impulse towards the right is stronger than corrupt reason? Suppose, says Carneades, that you know that there is a viper lurking somewhere and that someone by whose death you will profit is going to sit on it unwittingly, you will be wrong if

E

you don't warn him not to sit down. Yet your wickedness will
go unpunished: for who could prove that you knew? But I
need not labour the point; it is obvious that if fairness, honour
and justice are not to have their origin in nature and if all
these things are to be valuable only for their utility, then no
good man can anywhere be found. (Ibid. ii. 58 f.)

(iii) *Stoic Conception of Moral Worth.* In the course of his
refutation of the Epicurean highest good the Stoic has had
to state his own conception of moral worth, which he calls
'*honestum*'. The preliminary description of it, revealing it as
something desirable for itself, serves as a preparation for the
criticism by Antiochus of the Stoic failure to link it with the
doctrine of the primary impulse:

> My own view is that if I can establish the existence of
> moral worth as a thing essentially and for itself desirable,
> your whole case falls. Therefore I shall define it briefly as
> time demands . . . .
> Moral worth then we define as essentially such that, with-
> out any consideration of utility and without thought of profit
> or reward we can commend it in and for itself. Its precise
> nature is to be realized not so much by my definition (although
> that is not entirely useless) as by the general verdict of man-
> kind and the aims and actions of all men of high character;
> for in many of their actions they are guided purely by con-
> siderations of propriety, right and morality, even though they
> see no likelihood of profit. (Ibid. ii. 44 f.)

In this passage the *honestum,* described as 'desirable for itself',
is presented as an affair of the reason. This is a further stage in
the development of the rational side of Stoic ethics. But as yet
it gives us no actual description of the nature of the *honestum.*
However, it is supported by an account of the virtues as rational
activities, assisting the recognition of 'that which is itself desirable without any consideration of utility'.

The Antiochean account will eventually develop the conception of complete morality as an outcome of the development of
the virtues. But, in keeping with its proclaimed role of correcting
the Stoics and resisting their exaltation of the reason, it will
insist that the perfection of the structure of the virtues and the
consequent achievement of the ethical end by man's full self-
realization require the continuous development of the whole
man from his first impulses. Thus this Stoic statement of moral

worth and its support by the virtues serves to present a point of view which the Antiochean argument will finally correct.

In this part of the *De Finibus* should also be observed a reinforcement of the attitude already foreshadowed in the *Academica* and destined to expand to a conception of social obligation:

> This same reason has endowed man with a fondness for his own kind with conformity of nature, speech and habit; she has prompted him, starting from affection for the members of his own household, to extend his interests and form social ties first with his fellow-citizens and then with all mankind. Reason reminds man that, as Plato wrote to Archytas, he was not born for himself alone, but for his country and his fellow-men so that only a small part of him is left for himself. (Ibid. ii. 45.)

(d) THE FUNCTION OF *De Finibus* I AND II

In the preliminary survey in the *Academica* Cicero forecast the limitation of the ethical inquiry to two schools and he confirmed his intention in the final survey. The *De Finibus* again makes it very clear that one must accept none but the Stoics or the 'Old Tradition'. There is a short list of ethical theories classed according to views on the primary object of desire and the highest good. It shows that there are three classes (Ibid. ii. 34 f.) :

(i) Theories which do not include moral worth in the highest good (Aristippus the Cyrenaic, Epicurus, Hieronymus and Carneades). The first three aimed at pleasure in either the kinetic or the static sense.

(ii) Theories which combined moral worth with some further element, e.g. Polemo of the 'Academico-Peripatetic' tradition, who thought that the highest good was enjoyment of the primary natural goods in accordance with virtue; or Callipho, who was midway between Stoics and Epicureans and aimed at a combination of virtue and pleasure; or Diodorus, who aimed at virtue together with freedom from pain.

(iii) The theory by which the highest good was moral worth alone, i.e. Stoicism.

Of these, all theories which include in the chief good pleasure or absence of pain and all those which do not include moral worth are rejected, i.e. all in the first section and all but the

'Academico-Peripatetics' in the second. Two views only are worth considering:

> Thus two views will be left which Reason must ponder again and again. *Either* she will decide that there is no good but moral worth and no evil but moral baseness and that all other things either have no importance whatever or so little importance that they are not objects of desire or aversion but only 'things to be selected' or 'things to be rejected' *or* she will prefer that theory which she sees not only to possess the full beauty of moral worth but also to be enriched with the primary natural objects and a full perfection of life. (Ibid. ii. 38.)

Then if Cicero would not in any case accept the Epicurean ethics, what has been the function of his survey of them? Actually it has substantially advanced his argument. The *Academica* was concerned with perception as the first problem of epistemology and only touched incidentally on questions of morality, as when in its general introductory account it described the acceptance by the Old School of the guidance of nature: 'they went back to nature to find that first portion which relates to right living . . . for nowhere else but in nature must be sought that supreme good . . .' and the starting point for action 'lay in the main-tenance of those possessions which were marked out by nature.' The Stoic doctrine of perception imposed on this basis implied that man's perception gives him accurate knowledge of some part of complete reality which is good in itself and which can be known completely and that knowledge of this reality through perception furnishes impulse to action. But to develop the Stoic case it was necessary to define the two conceptions of the 'primary impulse' and the 'moral end'.

Now the merit of the treatment of the Epicureans in the first two books of the *De Finibus* is that it has enabled Cicero to dispose of the main rival popular theory while stressing the chief points on which ethical argument must turn and at the same time foreshadowing the positive exposition of the Stoic morality. Of course it was not his purpose at this stage to give a positive exposition but he has not been able to refute the Epicureans without some explanation of the Stoic concepts of the funda-mental instinct of self-preservation and moral worth viewed as the chief good. His next task is to give a positive account of the Stoic morality. But although this task becomes quite clear about the middle of Book II he fills the second part of the book

with lengthy argument on the Epicurean views concerning the
virtues, friendship and hedonism in general. This does not really
advance Cicero's quest. It must be regarded as one of those
annoying digressions which were caused by Cicero's method of
using his sources. Here he went on copying from the epitome
of Epicurus with no real attempt to adapt his material to his
particular purpose.

3. POSITIVE EXPOSITION OF STOIC ETHICS: BOOK III

(a) THE STOIC ETHICS AND THEIR RELATION TO CICERO'S ARGUMENT

From the discussion of Epicureanism have emerged two aspects
of the Stoic case. One is the doctrine of the brotherhood of man.
As yet it has received little prominence but it will be expanded
in some detail in Book III with increasing significance in the
development of Cicero's social theory. The other is a contro-
versial matter. It concerns the relationship of the primary ethical
impulse to the supreme good. It arises from the view that from
man's essential nature, as determined by the definition of the
primary impulse, can be developed the whole structure of the
virtues by the perfection of which, according to Stoic doctrine,
man should achieve his ethical end. For the Stoics proclaimed
a system of natural morality in which the supreme good was the
full development of man's nature. But we have already seen
that, despite their insistence on the impulse as the starting point
for the ethical structure, they went on to speak of moral worth
as an affair of the reason, desirable for itself alone and separated
entirely from the world of the senses. Therefore the question
must arise whether in the end the primary impulse has any real
connection with the supreme good.

This is the question which Antiochus raised about the Stoic
case, as we shall see. His objection was that, as the Stoic case
developed, the good was removed to a transcendental realm apart
from the world of the senses and the continuity of the structure
based on the primary impulse was broken. Therefore Antiochus
set out to correct the Stoic desertion of their principles. He
believed that their starting point was correct: that is to say, he
accepted the goodness of the system of nature and believed that
man's essential nature could be defined by the determination
of the primary ethical impulse. From this starting point he
believed it possible to explain the attainment of the ethical good
by the full development of man as a moral creature and he
insisted that the development should be continuous, retaining

what was granted at each stage and avoiding that transition to the transcendental realm which he condemned in the Stoics. In short Antiochus claimed to be able to construct the complete system of morality from the starting point of the primary impulse. Although he condemned their methods he recognized the importance of two of the Stoics' assumptions. The first was the attainment of a perfect system of understanding on which the moral decisions must be based. The second was that the perfect morality remains pure and unimpaired by concern with the problems of practical morality. The first of these assumptions Antiochus did not examine thoroughly and the epistemological weakness in the end remained his chief defect. But it does seem that, impressed by the doctrine of validity of perception, he was confident that from it could be constructed a complete system of knowledge. This was why he incorporated that doctrine into his own interpretation of the Academic tradition. By avoiding on the one hand the sceptical attitude to perception and on the other hand the Stoic transition to a transcendental realm, he thought it possible to construct a complete system of knowledge from the facts of experience.

The other question Antiochus did face and it provoked the argument concerning the relation of the 'natural advantages' to the good which starts in the *De Finibus,* which underlies most of the *Tusculan Disputations* and which is resumed again in the *De Officiis.* The Stoics, when they said that virtue was quite unaffected and unimpaired by concern with mundane things, supposed that pure morality preserved towards practical activity that relationship which might be supposed to exist between the Platonic form and the particular. But Antiochus' doctrine of continuous development upward from the impulses implied that perfect morality could be attained only through experience of the practical. Therefore it must be difficult for him—if not impossible—to establish such a pure relationship that in the end the practical could be denied any effect at all.

Now I believe that Cicero's main purpose in the *De Finibus* was to expound the Antiochean case as a basis for further criticism. What then was the function of his account of the Stoic ethics? Since Antiochus professed himself to be the corrector of the Stoics, it would be valuable to have a statement of their position, and particularly so since Stoicism upheld those two assumptions of a system of pure morality, the purity of reason and its transcendence over particulars. Therefore a statement of the Stoic case would serve as a challenge to Antiochus, showing the standards which he must establish in his attempt to uphold a perfect morality developed from the impulses and the ability of this morality to cope with the practical without having its own perfection impaired. In short I think that Cicero put forward the Stoic case not with any intention to examine it metaphysically but in order to use it as a preparation for the exposition of the Antiochean ethics.

Accordingly our two main points of interest in the Stoic account are the description of the perfect Wise Man's progress up from impulses to perfect wisdom and the relation of the good to particulars. On the first of these Book III offers a more elaborate description of the rational side of Stoic ethics whose emergence we have noted already during the argument with the Epicureans. From the primary ethical impulse the perfect man is supposed to rise to 'choice fully rationalized', which implies perfect goodness of will based on perfect understanding.

One can detect three stages in this argument. First is the expansion of the description of self-preservation as the primary impulse. As when he was refuting the Epicureans, the Stoic relies on statement rather than on proof:

> It is the view of those whose system I adopt that immediately after birth (for that is where we must start) a creature feels an attachment for itself and feels an impulse to preserve itself and to feel affection for its own constitution and for whatever tends to preserve it: and they think it feels antipathy to destruction and all that seems to threaten destruction. They feel that this theory is supported by the fact that even before there is any experience of pleasure or pain children seek things conducive to health and reject their opposites: and they would not do this if they did not feel affection for their constitution and fear destruction.
>
> Now it would not be possible that they should feel any desire unless they had self-consciousness and consequently felt an affection for themselves. From this we can realize that the primary impulse to action springs from love of self. (*Fin.* iii. 16 f.)

From this basis the Stoic moves towards the conception of impulse also as an affair of the understanding. For his assumption of the essential goodness of the natural order induces the decision that anything that is in accordance with nature is in some degree 'deserving of choice': this category he extends to include facts discovered by reason and finally the sciences:

Again acts of cognition (which we may call acts of comprehension or perception or, if these terms are not satisfactory
or are not understood, καταλήψεις) according to our view
should be adopted for their own sake since they contain an
element which, as it were, embraces and enfolds the truth.
We can observe this in children when they experience pleasure
in discovering something through their own powers of reason,
even though they gain nothing by it. We also think that the
sciences should be adopted for their own sake: for not only
do they contain an element worthy of adoption but also they
are composed of acts of cognition and contain an element of
fact established by a methodical procedure of reasoning. Again
the Stoics think that men feel stronger repugnance towards
assent to what is false than towards all the other things that
are contrary to nature. (Ibid. iii. 17 f.)

Here we have an expansion of the hint in the *Academica* that,
whereas perception is the first step to acquaintance with nature,
it should lead afterwards to 'conceptions' imprinted on the mind,
'which conceptions enable us to find out not merely the first steps
but certain broader avenues leading to the discovery of reasoned
truth' (*Ac. Post.* i. 42) .

Finally in the third stage the Stoics pass from the impulses
derived from the sciences to the conception of the pure impulse
of absolute morality. From the rather facile picture of progress
up from attraction to things in accordance with nature, through
the stage of 'duty incompletely rationalized', they arrive at the
'good properly so called' which is 'choice fully rationalized'.
This on the highest level turns out to be moral worth: this alone
they declare good, so that the primary objects of nature which
were first admitted to be deserving of choice are now found not
to be desirable for their own sake. An account of the progress
upward is given in Book iii. 20 ff. Thus the crowning point
of the whole Stoic system—moral worth, which implies perfect
knowledge—is now declared to be completely divorced from
utility. Being itself the only good, it denies all other things a
share in goodness.

But this *honestum* remains a vague concept itself unanalysed,
whose goodness is asserted but not established on metaphysical
grounds. It is precisely here, where we look for the full explanation of their morality, that this account of the Stoics is incomplete. What we have observed is a description of the progress
up to the supreme good rather than a description of the concept
itself, and we shall find likewise that the Antiochean criticism

of the Stoics is rather a criticism of the deficiencies in the account
of the development from the impulses than an attempt to analyse
the meaning of the Stoic *honestum*.

Antiochus seems to have spoken as if he understood that
the Stoics supposed a transcendental realm of pure being to
correspond to the level of perfect understanding: but if this was
what they meant it would have been quite inconsistent with
the physical theory of orthodox Stoicism which, as Reid said,
considered even abstract notions such as virtue to be corporeal,[3]
and concerning which we have in the *Academica* the view
ascribed to Zeno 'that it was impossible for anything which
exerted force, or for anything which was acted upon, to be
non-corporeal.'[4]

Now it may be that there was some confusion between the
physical doctrine and the conception of the moral end. Reid
has said that Stoicism was 'in its details a tangled web of inconsistencies even as expounded by its highest authorities.'[5] Or on
the other hand it may be that, with the extreme complexity
of their physical doctrines,—which conceived even spirit as corporeal—the orthodox Stoics could have offered an explanation
of their concept which would have done it better justice than is
done in Cicero's account and the criticism which he drew from
Antiochus. For example, Antiochus declared that in arriving
at the idea of the good the Stoics repudiated their principles
because they made no proper use of the starting point of the
impulses and attended to the mind alone instead of to the
development of the whole creature which they had first proclaimed. Against this the Stoics might have argued that their
assumption that the good is to be attained by the full development of man rested on the view that the nature of each thing,
as the normal law of its being, is a manifestation of the reason
which governs the universe, whence harmony with its own
nature is harmony with the divine law. Therefore for man life
according to nature requires that he should realize his true
being. But for man's 'true being' the Stoics could advance a
peculiar definition, saying that a thing was in harmony with its
own nature when it was determined by its ruling principle: and
the ruling principle in man was reason. That is to say, the
Stoics might have found defence against Antiochus' criticism and

3. J. S. Reid, trans. *Academica*, p. 96.
4. *Ac. Post.* i. 39.
5. J. S. Reid, ed. *Academica*, p. 27.

somehow, with their extreme ingenuity, they might have related it to their doctrine of materialism. But of such arguments we find no trace in the Ciceronian account.

It is more likely that in the *De Finibus* we are dealing not with the orthodox Stoics but with those later ones who incorporated Platonic elements in their doctrines and that they did in fact endeavour to rise above the limits of materialism and proclaim a morality based on independent intelligence. But if this is what they attempted they are condemned out of their own mouths, for their acceptance of the kingdom of nature is revealed in the description in *De Finibus* III of a science not as a pure process of intellect but as an interpretation of some part of nature, so that knowledge of good and evil is said to require an understanding of the 'whole plan of nature':

> The same honour is paid to natural philosophy and with good cause, because he who desires to live in accordance with nature must make his start from the system and government of the whole world. Nor can anyone give a true verdict about things good and evil unless he has a complete understanding of the whole plan of nature and of the life of the gods and knows whether or not the nature of man is in harmony with the nature of the universe. Think of those old maxims of the wise man such as 'Yield to circumstances', 'Follow God', 'Know thyself', 'Moderation in all things'! Without natural philosophy no man can tell what is their value; and it is very great. Again this is the one science that can tell us the power of nature in the fostering of justice and the preservation of friendship and other valued relationships. Nor again without unfolding the secrets of nature can we understand the devotion to the gods or our debts of gratitude to them. (Ibid. iii. 73.)

By virtue of this admission of the kingdom of nature these later Stoics must come under the objection which Kant directed against the orthodox Stoics—an objection which in the end must apply in some degree to the system of Antiochus also. When the Stoics declared that *honestas* was the only good and *turpitudo* was the only evil they meant that to the Wise Man nothing is good but the good will and only the bad will is evil. This is what Kant meant when he said that the Stoics in proclaiming the good will had hit upon the correct ethical principle but could not justify it on metaphysical grounds.[6] He said that to proclaim the good will was an attempt to free morality from

6. K. Reich, 'Kant and Greek Ethics', *Mind*, xlviii (1939).

concern with the things of nature and that this was fundamentally unsound according to the whole Stoic conception of
the universe. They were bound to the kingdom of nature and,
Kant insisted, freedom is incompatible with the kingdom of
nature. The Stoics had not reached that point of theory where
they could justify the goodness of a thing without reference to
some end. They revealed this when they proclaimed that virtue
was sufficient for happiness, for happiness denoted mastery of
external factors and they thus equated

> common well-being in the sense of human happiness—some-
> thing which . . . is not conceivable as the supreme determining
> ground of an absolutely good will—with that which *ought* to
> be the common interest of mankind i.e., with what follows as
> a common interest from 'obligation out of respect for a mere
> idea'.[7]

Within their system moral worth, as the principle of morality,
is void and meaningless unless it is related to some end, and
yet Kant taught that 'no principle into which there enters as
condition of its possibility an object of the will, or in other
words an end, is fitted to be the original principle of morality.'[8]
Thus the conception of the autonomy of the will lay beyond the
Stoics' horizon: yet that, in Kant's view, is the only thing that is
good without limitation.

Whatever the strict Stoics themselves may have intended, the
Ciceronian account of those whom Antiochus criticized suggests
that they did try to free morality from the kingdom of nature
and it was on this point that Antiochus mainly attacked them.
But in Cicero's version of his argument he does not raise the
metaphysical issues raised by Kant. Instead he makes a more
simple approach by raising the question of the continuous
development from the impulses to the good. That is why on
the question which Antiochus did face the statement of the Stoic
view was such an excellent preparation for the examination of
Antiochus' main problem. It was for Antiochus to show that by
continuous development upward from the impulses one could
arrive at a morality which, though not freed from the kingdom of nature, could yet be unimpaired and pure. What was
important was the relationship between the good and practical
morality. Therefore the Stoic case, by stating an entirely pure

7. Ibid., p. 463.
8. Ibid., p. 458.

relationship of the good, completely transcending particulars, set up a standard which Antiochus sought to establish for the relationship of his own supreme good to the natural advantages. He wanted it to be perfect and, though concerned with particulars, remain unaffected by them.

In contrast to Antiochus the Stoics, after admitting the importance of things in the first place, went on to assert that pure morality was completely independent of them. Thus on the one hand the importance of the natural order of things was acknowledged in the assertion that 'the highest good is life aided by knowledge of natural causes and by the ability to select what is in accordance with nature and reject what is contrary to it, that is, life in agreement and harmony with nature' (*Fin.* iii. 31). And again the Stoic said: 'For the good and the evil, as we have often said already, develop subsequently, but the primary things of nature, whether favourable or not, fall under the judgment and choice of the Wise Man and provide as it were the material for wisdom to work upon.' (Ibid. iii. 61.)

But on the other hand the Stoic asserted that, although the Wise Man must consider the things of nature and take account of differences between them, they could not have any effect upon him. Thus, while upholding the complete supremacy of virtue, he allowed that some other things such as health 'deserve a certain value', but would not call them 'good'. Accordingly a large part of the Stoic case is taken up by plausible and intricate attempts to explain this category of things 'deserving of value' but not good and its relation to the good. First is the illustration of the sun's eclipse of all inferior lights: just similarly was the supreme brilliance of virtue supposed to eclipse every other claim to goodness:

> The light of a lamp is dimmed and overwhelmed by the light of the sun. A drop of honey disappears in the vastness of the Aegean. The addition of one coin is insignificant in the wealth of Croesus and one step in the road from here to India. Similarly if the supreme good of the Stoics stands it must follow that all the value which you set on bodily advantages perishes in the majestic splendour of virtue. (Ibid. iii. 45.)

Next in explanation of the status of the primary natural objects, as factors which are devoid of goodness and yet have to be considered by the Wise Man, the Stoic invented peculiar categories of 'things preferred' and 'things rejected':

Next comes an account of the differences between things: if we denied differences we should confuse the whole of life as does Aristo nor could we find any function or task for wisdom: for there would be no difference between the things that have a bearing on the conduct of life nor would any choice among them be possible: then since it was sufficiently established that moral worth was the only good and baseness the only evil, the Stoics went on to affirm that among those things that have no power to effect happiness or misery there was nevertheless some difference; so that some of them had positive and others negative value while others were neutral. Among those things that were valuable some had sufficient justification for being raised above others—I mean health, unimpaired senses, freedom from pain, or fame, wealth and the like: others were not of this nature; likewise of those which were not worthy of any value some had sufficient grounds for being rejected, grounds such as pain, disease, paralysis, poverty and disgrace and the like, but others again had not. Hence the distinction in Zeno's terminology between the προηγμένον and its opposite the ἀποπροηγμένον. (Ibid. iii. 50 f.)

These peculiarities of terminology were explained by the following illustration:

In a royal court, says Zeno, no one says that the King is promoted to his high estate (that is the meaning of προηγμένον) but they apply this term to those who enjoy some office, whose rank most nearly approaches but is second to the royal preeminence. Similarly in life we call προηγμένον, i.e. 'promoted', not the things in the first rank but those in second place: let us call them by this name (that will be a literal translation) or 'advanced' or 'degraded' or the expression we have been using, 'preferred' or 'superior', and let us call the opposite 'rejected'. If we understand the meaning we should become lenient about the exact use of words.

But since everything that is a good holds the first place, according to our view, it follows that what we are calling 'preferred' or 'superior' is not a good nor an evil; and we define it to show that it is indifferent but possessed of moderate value; for it has struck me that I may use the term 'indifferent' for their word ἀδιάφορον. (Ibid. iii. 52 f.)

Finally the Stoic supported his contention that practical activity is devoid of ethical significance, when performed by the Wise Man who has attained perfect morality, by advancing the conception of *officia* (καθήκοντα) as neutral things to be classed neither among things good nor among their opposites:

But although we assert that moral worth is the only good, nevertheless it is consistent to perform an 'appropriate' action although we count appropriate action neither as a good nor an evil. For in these neutral things there is an element of reasonableness; it is such that we can give an account of it and consequently it is possible to give an account of an act reasonably performed. Now an 'appropriate action' is one done in such a way that a reasonable account can be given of its performance; whence we realize that an 'appropriate action' is a sort of intermediate thing to be classed neither among things good nor among their opposites. And since in those things which are neither among the virtues nor among the vices there is nevertheless an element which may be useful, we must be careful not to lose it. Now in this (neutral) class there is also an action of a certain kind such that reason demands that we should do or produce one of those neutral things; but what is done with reason we call 'appropriate action'. Therefore 'appropriate action' belongs to the kind which is classed neither among the goods nor among their opposites. And it is also clear that the Wise Man performs some acts which are in the sphere of these neutral things. Therefore when he acts he decides that it is an 'appropriate action'. And since the Wise Man is never wrong in his verdict an 'appropriate act' will be one of the neutral things. (Ibid. iii. 58 f.)

It will help us to understand the Stoic attitude if we examine the original motives for the Stoic system. As Bevan says, Stoicism was a system put together hastily, to meet a desperate emergency. It was put together at a time when the standards which man had long accepted were overthrown and when there was great need of security for 'minds shivering naked'. It aimed above all at securing absolute tranquillity and independence for the Wise Man. It was this desire to ensure his freedom from fear and to prevent any breach in his security—rather than any metaphysical examination of the nature of pure being—which caused the repudiation of 'things' and the assumption that intelligence and will could function in complete independence of them. The result was the insistence on the imperturbability of the perfect understanding. Although the Wise Man must be allowed to engage in selective activity his attitude towards external things must be one of 'intention' but not of 'desire', so that it would not matter to him if events turned out in this way or in that: what mattered was the goodness of the act of will. Hence the

Stoics denied that the natural advantages or disadvantages could have any effect upon their Wise Man. In particular they took the question of pain as the test case and asserted that the Wise Man would be completely unaffected by it.

A natural consequence of their attitude was that the Stoics spurned all degrees of understanding that had failed to achieve perfection: a man of imperfect understanding must be quite unable to assess the particulars with which he must deal. Thus they denied any merit at all to those who were advancing on the upward path, the προκόπτοντες — in fact they would go so far as to deny that they *were* making progress: this is the point of the famous 'drowning man' argument for which the critics condemn the Stoic intransigence.

This had two effects. In the first place their contempt of the imperfect caused the Stoics to disregard the need to demonstrate the continuity of development upwards from the primary impulse. Antiochus upbraided them severely for breaking the continuity and making a complete transition to the transcendental realm. But on their side the denial of progress in the προκόπτοντες would make them less perturbed at such a transition. In the second place the repudiation of the 'natural advantages' rendered them obdurate against the claims, on which Antiochus was to insist, that their pure morality was meaningless unless it were linked with the practical.

But Antiochus detected the paradox of admitting actions appropriate 'according to the order of nature, to every living being after its own kind' while denying that such actions had ethical significance and set out to establish a system of morality based on Stoic principles but in which practical activity should be reconciled with perfect morality. His objections to the Stoics were that their transition to the transcendental realm was inconsistent with their original project of demonstrating a continuous development from the primary impulse and that likewise, instead of demonstrating the development of the whole man, they attended to the mind alone. He felt that the right remedy was to go back to the old ideal of the good somehow embracing 'all mental and bodily advantages which are in accordance with nature' (*Ac. Post.* i. 19). He felt that in their transition to the transcendental realm the Stoics were disregarding the significance of the basis of perception on which they had insisted so strongly and which he supported, as was shown in the *Academica*. By using the principles of the original 'Academico-Peripatetic' tradition and incorporating the Stoic doctrine of perception, he thought it possible to establish the ethical structure on the epistemological basis. True knowledge would be comprehension of the material system in its entirety by perfect intelligence. There could be no case for the repudiation of things, for they would be the material on which intelligence would act. Then since the primary ethical impulses were derived from perception of the facts of nature, it should be possible to demonstrate a consistent development of morality from the primary impulses. Thus should be justified the old ideal of the chief good, set out in the preliminary survey in the *Academica*. It was not to be a 'vague phantom' nor an absolute something divorced from the things of nature. It was to be the crown of the natural order of things.

Thus Antiochus thought it possible to admit the ethical significance of practical activity without imposing any limitation on the perfection or freedom of the understanding. In short he thought that man, attaining complete understanding, can grapple with practical factors and yet make the decisions proper to perfect reason—undeterred, for example, by pain. But against his case there are certain objections. The first is the difficulty of supposing that man can in fact attain perfect understanding by that consistent development from the impulses on which Antiochus insisted. For, as we have seen in the preliminary survey in the *Academica*, he started from the Old Tradition as he understood it; and this must impose a bar against any suggestion of conceptual processes independent of the senses. For it was laid down that, though true knowledge is an affair of the intellect, it must be based on perception of objective facts. Thus the conceptual processes require for their first material the truths of perception and these truths derive from the world of nature. This, together with the denial of forms, seems to deny complete independence for reason.

Antiochus should then have faced the question whether from direct and valid knowledge of nature man can compile a complete system of reasoned truths. Here he did not pursue the epistemological inquiry. Had he done so he might have become less confident of attaining a perfect morality through a system of knowledge developed from the compilation of the facts of perception. One might say that from the outset the mere limitation of possible experience must impose an incompleteness on the sum of knowledge that any man can hope to build up for himself: for there is the objection, which Taylor makes, that perception cannot be of the universe in its entirety but must be only of some part of it.[9] And again he might have become aware of the argument which Scholastic philosophers use that increase in understanding of the physical world does not necessarily imply increase in man's capability for moral action. Thus 'there is no *a priori* reason why every addition to our knowledge of human nature should give us a more perfect knowledge of our rights and duties.'[10]

But the main defect of Antiochus was his uncritical acceptance of the doctrine of the attainment of the good through man's full self-realization. In him it was less defensible than in the Stoics. They might have found some plausible justification of it in terms of their physical doctrine, according to which man was an organic part of nature and in fact a miniature representation of the cosmos, so that the full and perfect realization of man should accord fully with the perfection of the cosmos.[11] But Antiochus relaxed the extreme materialism of the Stoics and may have here followed a trend in some of the later Stoics, e.g. Panaetius. He asserted some degree of freedom and thus debarred himself from the argument of identification of individual with the cosmos. Yet at the same time he did not free himself from the kingdom of nature. In fact his insistence on the continuity of development from the first natural impulse seems to confirm his acceptance of it. Consequently he too must fall under Kant's criticism, as one whose acceptance of the goodness of the order of nature makes it illegitimate to proclaim the autonomy of the good will without reference to some end.

In fact Antiochus concentrates on inquiry into what Scholastic philosophers would call the 'subjective final end' without realizing that, by virtue of his acceptance of the goodness of the whole order of nature, such inquiry cannot by itself arrive at a complete definition of the ethical end. Since Scholastic philosophy also developed a form of natural morality from similar grounds (possibly derived in part from the Stoics) a comparison with it may serve to reveal the weakness of Antiochus. The main advantage that the Scholastics have—I mean an advantage as regards the development of their case to their own satisfaction—

9. A. E. Taylor, *A Commentary on Plato's Timaeus*, p. 70.
10. Cronin, *The Science of Ethics*, 1910, p. 168.
11. See Arnold, *Roman Stoicism*, pp. 238 ff.; Hicks, *Stoic and Epicurean*, pp. 74 ff.

F

is that they distinguish both the subjective and the objective final ends.[12]

Both Antiochus and Scholastics start with the assumption that the primary natural objects of man's understanding are external, that the whole system of reality is good, and that the primary criterion of moral goodness is to be found in the natural objects of the appetites. (Note Antiochus' adoption of the Stoic doctrine of perception of real objects, the Stoic assertion of the goodness of nature, and the Stoic insistence on inquiry into the primary impulses.)

The implications of these common grounds are that, since nature is good, knowledge of the natural objects of the appetites reveals man's essential nature as a creature of will and that this is the key to knowledge of man's highest capacity: whence it should be possible to determine his moral end, as that which fills up the measure of his highest capacity.

But the Scholastics stress more firmly the implications of the first assumption, the externality of the primary objects of understanding; and this leads them to distinguish between man's objective final end and his subjective final end. Thus they deliberately define the nature of the objective final end. On the ground that it must be that which fills up the capacity of the will for desiring—for, as Aquinas says, 'Nothing can be our final end which still leaves something to be desired'—and since the natural object of the will is the good-in-general, the Scholastics assert that man's final objective end is *the infinite uncreated good*: 'for nothing short of an "infinite" can fully exhaust the possibilities of that object and of the capacity of the will of which it is the end.'[13] They strongly insist on the need to define the objective final end as an end beyond man himself.

As for the subjective final end, Aquinas goes back to the assumption that the desire for happiness is natural and to the principle that nature does not act in vain, whence he asserts that it is possible for man to attain perfect happiness. He goes on to establish the final happiness of man as a condition of the intellectual faculty consisting in knowledge of the infinite accompanied by delight of the will in the attainment of its final end: and although he is not certain that attainment of this intellectual happiness excludes all the delights of the senses which in the natural order, before the attainment of perfect wisdom, seemed

12. For the interpretation of Scholasticism see Cronin, op. cit., ch. iii.
13. Cronin, op. cit., p. 70.

to have a worth of their own, yet on the whole he considers it likely that the lower order of delights will lose their attraction altogether in the higher order of the supernatural.[14]

But he insists that man's own development is not his final end. 'As St. Thomas puts it, the attainment and enjoyment of the end belong to the soul, but the end itself which is sought is quite distinct from the soul or self.'[15] In fact it is a fundamental part of Scholastic doctrine that man is not self-sufficient.

By contrast it was precisely on the subjective final end that Antiochus insisted in his development of the Stoic theory that the good is man's full self-realization. Accordingly it will help us to appreciate the Antiochean argument if we remember that its purpose was to uphold this ethical end with regard to the two requisites on which Stoicism insisted—the perfection of the end in itself and its absolute freedom from limitation by concern with particulars. Antiochus devoted great care, as the *De Finibus* shows, to the demonstration of the continuity of development, within man, of the virtues from the impulses—an argument which Cicero illumines in the *De Officiis* by the Panaetian account of the structure of the virtues. But this was to assert the perfection of the structure, not to prove it. There is no serious theoretical examination of the claim for its completeness and no discussion of the principles of epistemology, although surely they should be involved in such inquiry.

As for the relation of pure morality to the practical the Antiochean treatment is more detailed. But here again, where a Platonist might have discussed the relation of forms to particulars according to principles of epistemology, Antiochus' approach is made at no high level of theory: the argument is based almost entirely on the power of virtue, as conceived according to his theory of natural morality,' to triumph over the particulars of experience. This is the main theme of the Antiochean case in the *Tusculan Disputations*. But to demonstrate the power of virtue to triumph is an argument which in itself admits conflict with inferior factors: and this is a very different thing from establishing the pure transcendence of virtue in the sense in which the Stoics claimed it.

To remember that the main purpose of Antiochus was to uphold the perfection of this ethical end will also help us to avoid misinterpretation of him at a later stage of his argument.

14. Ibid., p. 83.
15. Ibid., p. 63.

We have seen that the Stoics refused to admit that the natural advantages could be called 'good' and called them 'things preferred' instead: Antiochus however, rebelling against the Stoic repudiation of practical morality, started by affirming the ethical significance of the natural advantages. In short, he called them 'good'. But later he went on to assert that his difference from the Stoics was purely a matter of terminology. He said that, whereas the Stoics called them 'things preferred' and he called them 'good', they both meant the same thing, namely that these things could have no effect upon the decisions of pure morality.[16] Now this might be taken as a repudiation of the admission of ethical significance in the natural advantages—as the negation of his original plan to develop morality from the impulses. But I do not think that that was what Antiochus meant. We must remember, as I said, that his main object was to uphold the perfection of his ethical end: accordingly what he intended to say was that its perfection was so complete that to allow ethical significance to things could not diminish it. He did not mean 'Whereas I formerly allowed that these things were good, I now deny it' but 'Even though I admit things to be good, the perfection of pure virtue remains unimpaired.' This of course would be a very difficult thing to prove and in the end Antiochus' proof of it remained deficient. But he does not seem to have realized his own limitations and in effect claimed to have established a system of perfect morality.

As for the Stoics, their attitude may have been more correct than Antiochus suggested. What he condemned as their transition to a vague realm may have been no more than a proper insistence on the systematization of the facts of experience by the principles of logic, and when they hotly repudiated Antiochus' claim to attain to a morality as pure as theirs it may have been because they were conscious of differences which escaped Antiochus and of the hopelessness of his attempt to build up to perfect knowledge from the facts of experience. But the Ciceronian account is by no means a critical and theoretical examination of the Stoic system and this may be because he did not understand it or, on the other hand, because he had it as his main purpose to examine Antiochus and did not feel the need of exhaustive criticism of the Stoics.

16. On the whole question of the difference of terminology see *Fin.* iii. 41; iv. 56 f.; *T.D.* ii. 30; iv. 6; v. 32 f.

(b) THE DOCTRINE OF SOCIAL OBLIGATION: BROTHERHOOD AND RIGHTS OF MAN

Book III of the *De Finibus* is important for its account of the doctrines of the brotherhood of man and of private rights. Cicero's transmission of Greek thought on these topics constitutes in itself a most important contribution to the development of European political philosophy.

It was the Stoic school which first properly developed the idea of universal brotherhood. Socrates seems to have had no more than the germ of the idea: it is found in the statement ascribed to him by several authorities that he was 'a citizen of the world'.[17] Since the same sentiment was ascribed to Aristippus and to Diogenes the Cynic, we may infer that the Cyrenaics and the Cynics took up the idea to some extent.[18] It is not found in Plato and Aristotle. Where Aristotle in the *Nichomachean Ethics* deals with the mutual obligations of men we can see that the society which he envisages is a form of partnership for the interchange of services. The bond of his society, the principle of justice which regulates it, is the principle of 'reciprocity' ($\tau\grave{o}$ $\mathring{a}\nu\tau\iota\pi\epsilon\pi\sigma\nu\theta\acute{o}s$) and though the members of such a community have common interests it is found that, when an individual subordinates his immediate interest, what determines him is his desire to share in the greater good of the whole community: that is to say, the individual really considers his own ultimate interest. In this society of Aristotle there is no real suggestion of the common bond of men as such. Where he does qualify his rather brutal description of a slave as a 'living tool' — a creature with which a master could have nothing in common — by the admission that, although the master could have no friendship for the slave 'as a slave', yet he could have some for him 'as a man', nevertheless we find that the reason for this admission is not the warm sense of a common humanity but the rather grudging concession that after all the slave could in some sense participate in the justice of the community: 'For there seems to be room for some element of justice in the relations of any man with any person who can share in law and contract. Consequently there can be friendship so far as he deserves the title 'man'.[19] Our denial of Aristotle's interest in this doctrine might seem to be contradicted by our previous statement that the account

17. Arrian, *Epict.* i. 9. 1; Plutarch, *De Exilio*, v; Cicero, *T.D.* ed. Dougan, v. 108. On this whole question see Reid's edition of the *Academica*, p. 120.
18. Diog. Laert. ii. 99; vi. 63.
19. Aristotle, *Eth. Nich.* viii. 11, 7.

of the Old Tradition in the *Academica* included acceptance of the brotherhood of man. But this was really a mistake by Antiochus, who was ascribing to the early stages of the school beliefs currently accepted by the Peripatetics who were his own contemporaries. In fact the Peripatetics of the early first century B.C. had a doctrine of humanitarianism that closely resembled the Stoic doctrine of universal brotherhood. We shall find their attitude in *De Finibus* v and it will be clear that on this whole topic, in regard both to the general conception of social obligation and to the arguments by which it is justified, they agree closely with the Stoics.

In keeping with his whole system of morality the Stoic founds his theory of society upon the order of nature. To determine what is good for man he inquires into the nature of his primary impulses. Already we have seen his use of the instinct of self-preservation as the basis of man's personal morality, for he declared that it sanctioned man's preservation of the highest part of himself, the soul, and this was regarded as the highest good of man considered as an intelligent creature. But for his theory of social obligation he does not use this which he has already declared the fundamental ethical impulse: instead he finds another impulse or perhaps more than one, as we may see in this passage:

> They consider it important that man should understand that *nature causes parents to have affection for their children.* This is the starting point from which derives *the social community of mankind* to which we attain. This must be clear first from the conformation of the body and its parts which themselves make it obvious that nature's scheme contemplated the procreation of offspring. Now it would be inconsistent that nature should desire the creation of offspring without providing that the offspring should receive affection. Even in beasts we can observe nature's operation: in their efforts in the bearing and rearing of their young we seem to detect the very voice of nature. Wherefore, just as it is clear that it is natural for us to shun pain, so it is clear that *it is from nature herself that we receive the impulse to love those whom we have begotten. This impulse produces that mutual attraction* for each other which men feel, a gift implanted by nature: and it makes them feel that the mere fact of their common humanity should bind men together in kinship. (*Fin.* iii. 62 f.)

Here we can distinguish two impulses, parental affection and men's mutual attraction for each other. They really are separate and the Stoic makes no case for the derivation of one from the other. Nor do they appear to be derived from the instinct of self-preservation. The justification of all three is similar. First they are assumed from observation to be natural impulses and then, because the order of nature is supposed to be good, their goodness is assumed. The weakness of the Stoic case against the Epicureans remains: the Stoics said that the aim of the primary instinct was self-preservation, the Epicureans with as much reason said that it was pleasure: both sides relied on observation and their assumptions were matters of opinion.

By the same process of analysis one might arrive at a number of so-called primary impulses. They might even conflict, as we shall find in the case of the instinct of self-preservation and the impulse of mutual attraction; and then, as they all appear to be equally valid and it is purely a matter of opinion which is more fundamental than the rest, there would be no criterion for the solution of the conflict. The defects of the Stoic argument are that, whereas it sets out to found its morality upon natural primary impulses, it does not push its analysis far enough, it is not free of confusion (e.g. it makes no clear distinction between parental affection and mutual attraction) and it does not critically examine the complexity of man's nature as composed of possibly conflicting impulses.

From the plausible assumption of men's feeling of mutual attraction the Stoic develops his conception of a common bond of humanity which provides him with his justification of the duties of individual to society. He supports this with evidence of acts which certain creatures do to aid each other—creatures such as the ant, the bee and the stork—from which he infers that man is fitted by nature to form unions, societies and states since in him 'this bond of mutual aid' is stronger still.

Human society is declared to be in accordance with the natural order of things, as we may see in the passage which follows: it is in keeping with the divine plan which rules the universe: it develops from men's nature, the key to the understanding of which is the recognition of that common affection which should bind men as such and which provides the sanction for devotion to society and to mankind in general:

> Now they think that the universe is ruled by divine will and that it is, so to speak, a society and civic community of gods and men, each single one of us forming a part of that universe with the natural result that we should prefer the interests of

the community to our own private interests. The laws rate the
safety of the whole citizen body more highly than the safety
of the individual: similarly a man who is good and wise, who
obeys the laws and realizes his duty as a citizen, considers the
general interest before that of any single person, including
himself. A traitor to his country deserves no greater blame
than the man who for the sake of his own interests or safety
jeopardizes the interests or safety of the community. This is
why he who faces death for his country deserves praise, because
we should hold our country dearer than ourselves. And again
it is regarded as an impious and wicked utterance when men
say that they don't mind if the universal conflagration should
come after they have died (a thought commonly uttered in a
familiar Greek line). Consequently it is undoubtedly true
that we should give some thought for their own sakes to those
who are destined to be. (Ibid. iii. 64.)

With his discussion of social obligation the Stoic intermingles
the declaration of man's personal rights to possess private
property and to marry. And here his procedure is uncritical.
In the passage that follows he allows the possession of private
property because it seems compatible with his conception of
society, but he attempts no analytical justification of it. He
rests content with the bare statement that 'there is no principle
of justice working against the possession of private property':

They think that men are united together by the bond of
right; but they think that there is no bond of right between
men and beasts. Chrysippus well said that all other things
were made for the sake of men and gods, but that they exist
for their own community and society so that without injustice
men may use beasts for their own advantage. A man's nature,
he said, is such that there is a code of law between him and
the rest; therefore the man who observes that code will be
just, but he who breaks it will be unjust.

Although the theatre is public yet it is reasonable to say
that the seat which a man has taken is his own: similarly in
the state or in the universe though these are common to all,
there is no principle of justice working against the possession
of private property.

Now since we see man designed by nature to protect and
preserve his fellow-men, it is in accordance with this natural
disposition that the Wise Man should desire a share *of
government* and *administration* and to *marry a wife* and have
children by her *so that his life may be in accordance with*

nature. They don't think that even love when pure is out of keeping with the character of the Wise Man. (Ibid. iii. 67 f.)

If he had followed his process of analysis consistently the Stoic would have sought justification for private property in one of man's primary impulses: presumably in accordance with his own theory he could have based it on the instinct of self-preservation which sanctions man's full development of himself in accordance with his nature. Had he done this he might have become aware, through conflict of private and social interests, of a fundamental opposition between his primary impulses. And this might have caused him to consider the high complexity of human nature and the resulting temerity of his suggestion that he could quite simply pick out the primary impulses to provide the basis of his ethical system. For as things stand with his argument the Stoic is naïve. He thinks that social obligations, based on mutual attraction, and private rights, which according to his theory ought to be based on the instinct of self-preservation, must be good and compatible on the ground that they derive from man's nature: and on this ground he accepts them uncritically as good and sees no need to investigate the possibility of conflict between them.

Our objection to the Stoic case apart from whether it is wrong is that it is incomplete. Its deficiency in the discussion of private property is obvious. The same incompleteness impairs the whole treatment of social obligations. Whereas the Stoic set out to base his system on an analysis of man's nature, he rests satisfied with the arbitrary and uncritical adoption of the several impulses. But the effects of the doctrine, as handed on by Cicero, were enormous. Although the analysis of human nature did not go far enough it did give a hint of emotional influences on conduct: the resulting conception of a bond of union with some basis of emotional warmth was more readily acceptable than the cold Aristotelian 'principle of reciprocity'. It was not the proof of the Stoic doctrines but their results—the conception of brotherhood of man and of individual rights, incompletely argued as they might be—that profoundly influenced European thought. As a matter of fact we cannot say that at this point Cicero has said very much at all about the rights of man. But he has pointed to the need to fit them in to the general ethical system. In the *De Officiis* he will have more to say about these doctrines inadequately treated in the *De Finibus.*

4. The Criticism of Stoic Ethics: Book iv

In Book iv Cicero gives the criticism of the Stoic ethics by Antiochus. Antiochus regards the Stoics as wanderers from the true 'Academico-Peripatetic' tradition rather than upholders of a completely independent system, and he adopts the role of their corrector; he endeavours to bring them back to a position consistent with what he assumes to be their first principles and to remedy their weaknesses. Therefore the criticism gives a fore-taste of Antiochus' own positive system in which he tries to be more systematic than the Stoics themselves.

The introduction stresses the common starting point in the acceptance of the goodness of nature as the primary fact of significance in the ethical theory and the acceptance of the instinct of self-preservation as the fundamental impulse.

The main attack of Antiochus is against the unsatisfactory nature of the Stoic's intermediate processes: he criticizes the break in the continuity of the progress up from the natural impulses to the highest good and the final establishment of moral worth as a vague phantom, a crowning point divorced from the very structure on which it was supposed to have been erected. In particular Antiochus objects to the Stoic's discarding of the lower faculties and attention to mind alone: this, he says, is false to the ideal of the self-realization of the whole man. He protests against the intricate terminology devised to account for the importance of external things without allowing them any value. And he makes a strong plea for practical morality, protest-ing against the Stoic denial of 'things conducive to life' and the intransigence which repudiates any progress that falls short of perfection.

The main part of the book consists of detailed refutation of the Stoic inconsistencies, but at the same time gives a strong indication of Antiochus' positive case for the continuous develop-ment of the structure based on the primary impulses. It will be most convenient to set it out under headings.

(a) neglect of the basis assumed

Antiochus points out that, although they start from the prin-ciple of self-preservation and might be expected to build up an edifice of virtue by the retention of things that are found to have some positive force by being 'in accordance with nature', the Stoics discard the body and all the things that are 'in accordance with nature' and so arrive at a conception of the chief good which would not satisfy even a 'disembodied mind':

But let it be granted first that we feel affection for ourselves and that our first natural impulse is for self-preservation. On this we agree; the result follows that we should realize our own nature in order to preserve ourselves in the proper condition. Well then, we are men; we are composed of soul and body and these are of a certain kind, and it is our duty—as the first natural impulse demands—to esteem these parts and from them build up our end, the chief and ultimate good: and this task, if our premises are true, we must pronounce to be the attainment of the greatest number of the most important things in accordance with nature.

This then is the end on which they insisted and this conception—which I have explained in detail and they briefly, in the phrase 'life according to nature'—they believed to be the supreme good. Well then let your leaders show us—or rather you should do it (for who could deal with these questions better than you?)—how in the world you manage, starting from the same first principles, to make out that morality of life (for that is what we mean by 'life in accordance with virtue' or 'in conformity with nature') is the chief good? Tell us how on earth or at what point you suddenly abandoned the body and all those things which, though in accordance with nature, are outside our control and finally 'appropriate action' itself. My question is, how comes it that these things so strongly recommended by nature and derived from her have been suddenly abandoned by Wisdom? Now if the chief good of our search were that not of man but of some living creature consisting of nothing but mind (to aid our search let us suppose that we can imagine some such thing) yet this end of your definition would not be appropriate for that mind. It would desire health and freedom from pain, it would aim at self-preservation and at security for the goods just mentioned, and it would conclude that its end was life in accordance with nature. And that, as I said, is the possession of the things which are in accordance with nature—either all of them or the most and the most important.

Whatever the kind of the creature which you construct, it must happen—even if it is without body as we are supposing—that in its mind there are some attributes analogous to those in the body: accordingly it cannot be set up as the end of goods except in the way which I have described. But Chrysippus in his account of the different species of living creatures says that in some of them body is the chief part and in others the mind, while some are strong in both: then he discusses the ultimate good appropriate for each species. His classification of man required him to assign to him mind as the chief part. But his definition of man's chief good made it appear not that mind was his principal part, but that he consisted of nothing else.

There is only one way in which it would be right to place the chief good in virtue alone. We should have to imagine a creature consisting solely of intellect and imagine moreover that that intellect had in it no single element that was in accordance with nature, such as health. But a conception of the nature of this creature could not be formed without inherent contradiction. (*Fin.* iv. 25-9.)

The consequent denial of the goodness of all things other than moral worth involved the Stoic in many inconsistencies. It was based on his assertion that 'nothing but moral worth is good and . . . virtue cannot be established if among the rest of things any one thing is better than any other' (Ibid. iv. 54).

But observing the importance of external things in the upward path to virtue, and remembering the positive impulse of the primary natural objects, which the Stoic admitted at one stage of his argument, Antiochus held that though virtue was pre-eminent some value, even if small, must be given to external things. This the Stoic tried to deny, but he could only preserve the austere detachment of virtue by an unconvincing subtlety of terms and by such absurdities as that the Wise Man 'if to the life of virtue be added an oil flask . . . will choose the life so augmented but yet will not on that account be any happier.' That is, he will choose the thing but will not admit that it is good (Ibid. iv. 30). But for all his subtlety of terms the Stoic 'in fact set no lower value on the things he himself denied to be good than did those who said they were good' (Ibid. iv. 57).

With the desperate intricacy of the Stoic attempts to find an adequate description for the things of nature which influence conduct but yet to refrain from admitting them to be good Cicero is able to contrast Antiochus' attempt to place them in proper relationship to the supreme good. Antiochus said that while the 'ancients' called these things 'good' they did not really rate them higher than Zeno who resorted to subterfuges of terminology:

Now of all those advantages to which they who declare them good ascribe no more value than Zeno (who denies that they are good) they declare that by far the most outstanding is the one that is morally worthy and praiseworthy. But if a choice is offered between moral worth accompanied by health and moral worth accompanied by disease there is no doubt to which of them nature will lead us. But such is the force of moral worth and such is its complete pre-eminence above all other things that it cannot be deterred by any punishments or rewards from what it has decided to be right. . . . In short what Zeno called 'valuable' and 'to be adopted' and 'suited to nature' they call 'good'. And they say that the happy life is that which comprises those things which I have mentioned, or most and the most important of them. But Zeno calls that alone good which has its own peculiar charm and attractiveness and that life alone happy which is spent with virtue. (Ibid. iv. 59 f.)

But the Stoic resorts to distorted terminology, trying at all costs to find for these things some term other than 'good':

Now hear what follows and restrain your laughter if you can. These intermediate things, he says, which have no difference between them are nevertheless of such a kind that some of them are to be chosen and others to be rejected and others to be entirely disregarded. That is to say some you must desire, others reject, and to others be indifferent.
— But you just now said that there is no element of difference in them.
— And I say so now, he will say, but I mean no difference in respect of virtue and vice.
— That is obvious. But let us have your account.
— Those things you have mentioned, says he, health, wealth, freedom from pain, I don't call goods. I shall use the Greek term προηγμένα or our term 'promoted' (although I prefer the terms 'preferred' or 'pre-eminent': that sounds smoother and more acceptable). And again I don't call their opposites—disease, want, pain—'evils' but, if you like the term, 'things to be rejected'. Therefore I say not that I 'desire' one class but that I 'select it' not that I 'wish for it' but that I 'adopt' it and the opposites I don't 'avoid' but—shall I say?—'discard'.
— What say Aristotle and the other pupils of Plato?
— They say that they call 'good' all the things which are in accordance with nature and their opposites 'bad'.
— Then do you realize that your friend Zeno agrees in terminology with Aristo but differs from him in substance, whereas with Aristotle and the followers of Plato he agrees in substance but differs in terminology? (Ibid. iv. 71 f.)

The point of the last sentence is that Aristo (a heterodox Stoic of Chios, who flourished about 260 B.C.) taught that there was no value at all in external goods. For example he said that there was absolutely nothing to choose between the most perfect health and the most serious sickness. This view he shared with Pyrrho.[20] Now Zeno agrees with Aristo verbally in denying that the externals can be called 'good', but in fact he allows them some value despite his verbal contortions. Thus in substance he agrees with the philosophers who frankly call them 'good'.

(b) INCONSISTENCY OF ATTENTION TO MIND ALONE

The Stoics had agreed that every creature's fundamental instinct was for the preservation of itself, that is the whole of itself. But the Stoic elevation of mind and denial of body implied that the primary instinct is to cherish only the best part of oneself. If that is what they meant, they should alter, says Antiochus, their definition of the fundamental instinct:

> Then why do you hesitate to alter your conception of the primary instincts? Why do you say that every creature immediately after birth is entirely devoted to the love and preservation of itself? Why don't you say instead that every creature is devoted to the best element in itself and spends itself entirely in guarding that alone? (Ibid. iv. 34.)

But wisdom's task is to perfect the whole man:

> What then is man as first formed by nature? What is the function and task of wisdom? What is the perfect product that must be the task of wisdom? If in the organism to be perfected this product is solely a certain operation of the intellect, that is, reason, then it must follow that for such an organism the highest goal must be activity motivated by virtue, for virtue is the consummation of reason. But if that product is nothing but the body then the chief things will be things such as health, freedom from pain, beauty and the rest. But the organism whose chief good we are seeking is man. Then surely it is the ground-plan of man in his whole nature that we ought to discuss. All agree that the whole duty and function of wisdom is devoted to the perfection of man. Nevertheless some schools (you must not think that I am arguing against the Stoics alone) advance opinions to support them in placing the chief good in that class of things that lies beyond our control, as if they were to talk about some creature

20. Cf. *Fin.* ii. 43.

devoid of mind. But others on the other hand attend to nothing but the mind, as if man had no body. (Ibid. iv. 35 f.)

(c) INCONSISTENCY OF DISCARDING THE LOWER FACULTIES

Whereas the Stoic by his assumption of the fundamental instinct allows that there are natural motives of action, he goes on to dissociate the chief good entirely from these. But the whole plan of nature reveals that when higher faculties are added the lower are not taken away. The following passages, though their purpose is polemical against the Stoics, are most important for their positive argument for the progress up from the primary impulse to the highest good and for their description of the Antiochean view of the relation of virtue to external goods:

> Consequently I feel that you don't give sufficient thought to nature's method of procedure. In crops nature controls the development from blade to ear but then discards the blade as worthless. But she does not act similarly with man when she raises him to possession of the faculty of reason. Her procedure is continually to make additions without discarding her previous gifts. Thus she added reason to sensation. (Ibid. iv. 37 f.)

> Similarly sensation when added to a natural species protects that species, it is true, but also protects itself; but when reason has been super-added it holds such complete sway that all these primary endowments of nature are brought under its protection. Thus it does not abandon its task of safe-guarding those elements: its duty is to govern the whole of life by controlling them. And so I cannot adequately express my wonder at the inconsistency of those friends of yours. For they insist that there is a natural tendency (which they call ὁρμή) to seek the things according to nature and that duty and virtue herself are concerned with them. But when they want to reach the chief good they make a complete leap and leave us two tasks instead of one. They impose on us the necessity of 'adopting' some things and 'desiring' others. whereas they should include both in the same end. (Ibid. iv. 38 f.)

> Man's constitution itself, if it could speak, would say that its first movements, so to speak, of desire were directed to preserving itself in the natural character with which it was born. But at that stage it had not yet been sufficiently revealed what was the principal intention of nature. Then suppose it revealed: then surely the whole intention will be understood to be that no part of nature is to be ignored. If man's nature

contains nothing but reason we may suppose that the end of
goods is contained in virtue alone: but if it also contains body
then the result of the revelation of nature as you describe it
will surely be our desertion of the elements to which we held
before that revelation took place. (Ibid. iv. 41.)

But you say that it is impossible to establish virtue if the
elements which lie outside virtue have any bearing on happiness of life. But the opposite is the case: it is impossible to
find a place for virtue unless the things that she chooses and
rejects are counted towards the one sum-total of good. (Ibid.
iv. 40.)

Thus the truth is the contrary of what you say; it is quite
impossible to establish virtue unless it retains, as elements
essential for the sum total of good, the first endowments of
nature. The search for virtue has contemplated not the abandonment but the preservation of nature: but according to your
view she protects a part of our nature and discards the rest.
(Ibid. iv. 41.)

This means that life in accordance with nature is the
desertion of nature. Now some philosophers, starting from
sensation, have discarded sensation after beholding faculties
greater and closer to divine nature. Similarly your school,
rising from material desire to the recognition of Virtue in all
her beauty, casts aside everything that they previously saw
other than Virtue herself. For they forget that the whole
instinct of appetition is so wide in its range that it exercises
influence from the primary objects of desire right up to the
ultimate ends. Nor do they realize that they are taking away
the foundations of the very things that they found beautiful
and admirable. (Ibid. iv. 41 f.)

(d) INTRANSIGENCE

The Stoic's denial of goodness to anything that falls short
of absolute virtue not only forces him to these absurdities of
terminology but produces extremely false analogies, as in the
famous illustration of the 'drowning man':

And at this point you used to bring forward those extremely
false analogies on which they base their arguments. It must
be clear that, if a number of men are striving to rise from the
depths, those who are getting close to the surface of the water
though nearer to breathing will not actually be better able
to breathe than those at the bottom. Hence you argue that
advance and progress in virtue avails not to rescue a man from
complete wretchedness before he actually obtains virtue, since
to rise in the water does not avail: similarly puppies who are

just getting ready to use their eyes are just as blind as those just born: and in the same way Plato who had not yet beheld wisdom was just as blind in spirit as Phalaris. (Ibid. iv. 64.)

This intransigence distorts their verdict on questions of practical morality, as when they deny that there is any gradation in transgressions, so that the skipper who loses a ship with a worthless cargo is as guilty as one who loses it with a cargo of gold and a man who beats a slave is as bad as one who beats his father, while in the case of a number of lyres if not one of them were strung so as to be in tune, they would all, in the Stoic view, be equally out of tune. (Ibid. iv. 75 f.)

The book ends with a vigorous condemnation of the Stoics' failure to connect the concept of moral worth with the basis of the primary impulse:

> What is so inconsistent as to say that moral worth is the only good and to say in the same breath that we have a natural instinct to seek things conducive to life? Thus when they insist on retaining those ideas that are consistent with their former doctrine they fall into the same position as Aristo, but when they try to avoid that they actually uphold the same view as the Peripatetics while clinging tooth and nail to their own terms. (Ibid. iv. 78.)

In other words, if the Stoics reject Aristo's complete denial of the value of external things they must admit the theory of Antiochus and the 'Academico-Peripatetics' which will be stated in Book v.

5. The Ethical System of Antiochus: Book v

(a) its relation to cicero's general argument

In Book v Cicero's plan is to present the positive ethical teaching of Antiochus and then, in the last few sections, to reveal the part in which the New Academy requires further proof: thus he will point the way to the lines of inquiry which he must follow in his later work. For we shall find that the system of Antiochus presented in the *De Finibus* is by no means complete but opens up questions for further examination in the *Tusculan Disputations*.

Cicero as usual obstructs the reader's sense of the continuity of the argument. In Book v he changes the persons and scene of the dialogue and sets it at a fictitious date about thirty years earlier than that of the setting of Books iii and iv. Moreover the introduction includes much irrelevant matter. However, a

G

glance at the headings under which the argument is arranged in the next section makes it clear that Antiochus' purpose was by no means to repudiate entirely the Stoics' theory of ethics. Rather did he seek to remedy their defects — the gaps in the theory of the development from impulses to virtues, the neglect of the essential parts of the creature and the discarding of the humbler faculties in the progress towards the higher ones. In short he adopts and amplifies the Stoic doctrine that the good of man is his full self-realization. He endeavours to develop the argument in a manner more consistent with the common basis from which the Stoics and he both set out.

But after advancing this conception of the good it was necessary to ask if the theory offered a solution of that most pressing problem, the relation of the good to the natural advantages. It could not be correct to say, with the Stoics, that goodness of character was all that counted and that beside it nothing else had any value at all. The school of Antiochus saw that other things did count and that implicitly the Stoics admitted that they did but, with their obstinate determination to reserve the terms 'good' and 'bad' exclusively for moral perfection and its opposite, relied on the invented terminology of 'things preferred' and 'things rejected' to conceal their admission. Against this intransigence Antiochus rebelled and sought a definition of morality that gave to external things the recognition due to them in a system whose goal in epistemology was complete understanding of the order of nature. Therefore the discussion of the several aspects of the achievement of the ethical goal through man's self-realization is followed by discussion of the relation of the chief good and external goods. Here, however, Antiochus wavers and it is on this topic that Cicero, for the New Academy, requests further argument.

(b) THE DEVELOPMENT OF ANTIOCHUS' NATURAL MORALITY

(i) *Self-preservation as the Primary Instinct.* The Stoics advanced their doctrine that self-preservation is the primary instinct when they rejected the Epicurean theory of pleasure. The treatment of this doctrine in the present book offers a fuller statement of it, some attempt to justify what had been pronounced as axiomatic, and a fairly full examination of its implications. The main parts of the statement are these:

Every creature loves itself and as soon as it is born directs all its efforts to preserving itself because the first impulse granted to it by nature for the protection of its whole life is the instinct to preserve itself and maintain itself in the best possible state in accordance with nature. At first it has this tendency in a vague and uncertain form—the mere blind instinct to protect itself, whatever its character: at this stage it has no understanding of what it is nor of its powers nor its own nature. But when it advances a little and begins to realize the effect and bearing on itself of various things then it gradually begins to make progress and to be conscious of itself and to realize why it has that instinctive appetition which I mentioned and then it starts to try to win the things which it feels to be in accordance with its nature and to repel their opposites. Therefore for every creature the object of appetition is found in what is suited to its nature. Thus the end of goods stands revealed, namely to live in accordance with nature, maintaining oneself in the best possible condition which is most in accordance with nature. (*Fin.* v. 24.)

Hence finally we may embrace them all in one broad generalization and declare without hesitation that all nature is devoted to its own self-preservation and has set before it as its end and goal the duty to protect itself in the best possible form appropriate to its kind; hence it follows that all those things endowed by nature with life have a goal that is similar but not the same. Thus we should realize that for man it is the highest good to live in accordance with nature and *this we understand to be life in accordance with the nature of man developed to its full perfection and lacking nothing.* (Ibid. v. 26.)

The attempted justification of this doctrine that the primary impulse is the instinct for self-preservation is unconvincing. It is based on the argument that self-love is universal. This is said to be axiomatic—a fundamental fact of nature which men may grasp by the evidence of the senses and which no sane man could deny. This supposed axiomatic truth is supported by a series of proofs. There is a syllogistic proof that to desire one's own harm is a contradiction in terms: fear of death is also used as evidence that men desire their own preservation. Now we may admit that men do have affection for themselves and do desire their own preservation: but this does not suffice to establish self-preservation as *the* fundamental impulse.

The validity of this whole argument is no more deeply based than that of the Epicureans had been. The whole thing turns on *what in fact is the fundamental impulse.* Antiochus accepts the Stoic arguments but they are inadequate. Nevertheless he feels no doubt about it and emphatically asserts his ability to use the instinct of self-preservation to detect what is fundamentally good for man:

> For it will be easier for a man to abandon himself than to lose the impulse to seek those things which are good for him. Rightly then have the most serious philosophers gone to nature to seek the starting point of the chief good and rightly did they consider that in all men is implanted by nature an impulse to seek those things which are suited to our own nature because it is based on that natural attraction which makes them love themselves. (Ibid. v. 33.)

The argument proceeds to show how a complete morality can be developed upon this basis by remedying the defects observed in the Stoic system. We shall find, however, that as well as the instinct of self-preservation Antiochus later without examination counts as fundamental impulses other things such as parental affection and the mutual attraction of men.

(ii) *A Morality Embracing every Aspect of Man's Nature.* The great defect of the Stoics had been that, after starting their inquiry by an investigation of the primary impulse and declaring that the later stages of man's development must be in harmony with the primary impulse, they had then, on arriving at their conception of moral worth, declared that this alone was good so that now it appeared that none of the primary objects of nature was desirable for its own sake; hence in man, whereas the primary instinct sanctioned the preservation of the whole creature, it turned out, in the Stoic view, that all that mattered was the preservation of man's highest part. The Stoic morality in fact proceeded just as if man consisted of mind alone. But the Antiochean account will consider every aspect of man's nature. The line of argument is this: since the system of nature is good the fundamental instinct, being in accordance with it, shows what is good for man; now the fundamental instinct enjoins the preservation of the whole creature; therefore an examination of man's whole nature will reveal what must be preserved; hence knowledge of man's nature and obedience to the impulse to preserve it provide the key to human morality.

But the proclaimed conviction that, since man consists of both mind and body, a theory of good must consider both parts is assailed by a sneaking regard for the absoluteness of the Stoic good. A tendency to assert that the virtues of the mind alone are good may be detected in this passage:

> With this explanation it is easy to guess that the most desirable of our possessions are those which have greatest intrinsic worth so that the excellences which are the most desirable are the excellences of the best parts which are desirable for their own sake. Thus it will come about that excellence of mind will be placed before excellence of body and that the volitional virtues of the mind will surpass the non-volitional. For it is the volitional virtues that rightly are called virtues and they are quite outstanding because they are derived from reason, the most divine element in man. For the supreme good of the things which nature produces and protects and which either are without mind or practically so is in the body; hence the aptness of the saying about the pig that it was endowed with mind as with salt to stop it from going bad. But there are some animals with an element like virtue, for example, lions, dogs, and horses, in which we see not only physical movements, as with pigs, but even to some extent mental activity also. Now in man the supreme end pertains entirely to the mind and to the rational part of the mind and from this springs virtue which is described as the perfection of reason. (Ibid. v. 38.)

But Antiochus realizes the need to save his principles. He therefore tries to check this tendency to exalt the reason and tries to avoid the Stoic fault of jettisoning the lower parts. To this end he advances an illustration of the behaviour of a vine which receives an endowment of various superior faculties. As it receives each higher endowment its new nature becomes more important but nevertheless its old faculties have not altogether lost their value:

> Now suppose a vine receives a gift of sensation so as to have some degree of appetition and power of movement; what do you think it will do? Will it not seek to win by its own efforts the benefits which it normally receives through the vine dresser? Do you see that it will become anxious to safe-guard its senses and all their appetitive instincts and any additional members? So to the properties which it had before it will join its subsequent acquisitions: it will not have the same end as its cultivator had but will desire to live in accordance with the nature which it has subsequently acquired. Thus its end of good will be similar to what it was before

but not the same; for it will seek the good not of a plant but of an animal.

But suppose furthermore that it gains not only sensation but human mind. Must not the result be that, while it retains and protects those early endowments, the subsequent additions will be much dearer and that the best parts of the mind must be the dearest? Must not its goal of the chief good consist in this crowning development of its nature, since the superiority of intellect and reason is great and marked? Thus emerges the highest of things desirable—derived from the first attraction of nature it rises by many steps to reach the summit, the consummation of perfect bodily integrity and the perfect development of the mental power of reason. (Ibid. v. 40.) [21]

We can see that this is an attempt to close the gap which the Stoic had left in his abrupt abandonment of his starting point by linking the argument about the primary impulse and the discussion of man's chief good and by making man's chief good dependent not only upon the main part of him but upon the whole of him.

(iii) *The Development of the Virtues.* The next step is to establish the virtues upon the declared ethical basis. There is a broad survey of man with particular attention to his fondness for activity and since this appears to be part of the design of nature it is decided that activity must be desirable for its own sake: whence the virtues—as the characteristic activities of man's highest nature—are desirable and part of nature's scheme of things. There is a sustained attempt to demonstrate a continuous connection between the first impulses and the developed perfection of the virtues: thus it is for man himself by process of reason to develop the embryonic ideas of the virtues implanted with the instincts:

But of virtue herself she gave the first beginnings and nothing more. Therefore it is within our power—I mean within the sphere of our science—to seek the proper development of the elements which we have received until our purpose is achieved: and this is much more important and more intrinsically desirable than either the senses or the physical endowments aforesaid, which the matchless perfection of the intellect surpasses by an almost incredible degree of superiority. Therefore all honour, all admiration, all enthusiasm are directed towards

21. Cf. Aristotle's argument from the scale of existence; and Mayor's edition of *N.D.,* ii 33-5.

virtue and to the activities which are in accordance with virtue and all such properties or processes of the mind are included in the one term 'moral worth'. (Ibid. v. 59 f.)

Thus in the Antiochean account moral worth is not in an absolute realm to which the human mind can attain only by abrupt transition and abandonment of all the things of the world of the senses; man is to reach it by development of his own powers. And at first this seems plausible: justice, for example, is described as a development from the original impulses of parental affection and mutual attraction between men. Then, since justice is the leading virtue and 'diffuses its agency' through the rest, these primary impulses are in a sense the basis of all the virtues:

> But in the whole moral sphere of which we are speaking there is nothing so glorious or of wider influence than the solidarity of men and their virtual alliance and partnership of interest and the actual affection between members of the human race: this develops from the first implanting because children are loved by those who beget them and the whole household is united by the ties of marriage and lineage; then it gradually extends its influence outward first by blood relationships and then by marriage relationships, then by friendships and later by ties of neighbourhood; then it expands to fellow-citizens and those whose friendship depends on public relationships and finally expands by embracing the whole human race.
>
> Now this attitude of mind which ascribes to each his own rights and with generosity and fairness upholds the aforesaid human solidarity and alliance, is called justice: to it are joined devotion and friendliness, generosity, kindness and gentleness and everything of that same kind. While these are peculiarly associated with justice they are also elements shared by the rest of the virtues. For man's nature is so formed at birth that it has inborn in it an element of civic and national feeling which the Greeks call πολιτικόν. Therefore whatever each virtue does will not be out of keeping with the community of interests and the affection and solidarity of mankind which I have explained; and in turn justice, just as it will spread its agency over the other virtues, will likewise aim at the promotion of them. (Ibid. v. 65 f.)

In this passage should be observed the general agreement with the Stoic view of the nature of the primary impulses of parental affection and mutual attraction and the agreement also with the Stoic view of universal brotherhood founded on these impulses.

(iv) *The Relation of the Chief Good to External Goods.* Up to this point in Book v the aim has been to support the ideal of 'life in accordance with the nature of man developed to its full perfection' as the supreme end in morality. But now it is found that this concentration on the subjective final end has caused neglect of the problem of the apparent antithesis of external things and the good. The Stoics thought they could avoid the dilemma by their transition to the realm of absolute morality. Antiochus challenged this transition: but in so doing he admitted the dependence of the good on externals which did seem to impair its perfection. Yet at the same time he tried to cling to the Stoic ideal of absolute perfection. His difficulty was that he formed a conception of the absoluteness of the good, like the Stoics, but could not reconcile it with the elements from which he had led up to it and would not jettison those elements, as the Stoics had done. Consequently the last part of the *De Finibus* is taken up with desperate efforts to account for the positive force of external things without impairing the perfection of the supreme good.

First Antiochus attempts a subterfuge. He says that only those things which are intimately part of man—goods of mind and body—can constitute the chief good: goods which belong neither to mind nor body are 'external goods': they may be desirable for their own sakes, but they are not part of the chief good:

> Therefore since there is in every virtue a sort of aim (*cura*) which directs itself outwards and embraces other men and makes them its end, this result arises that friends, brothers, kinsmen of blood and marriage, fellow-citizens, in short all men (for we insist that there is one society of mankind) are things desirable for their own sake. Yet none of them is of such a kind as to be contained in the end and chief good.
>
> So it comes about that we find two classes of things desirable for their own sake; one class consists of the things which constitute the chief good, namely in *mental and bodily* goods. But the other group consists of external goods, that is, those which are neither in mind nor body such as friends, parents, children, relations, even one's country; these things are indeed intrinsically dear but are not in the same class as those others. *Nor could anyone ever achieve the chief good if all these things, which, although desirable, are external to us, were included in the chief good.* (Ibid. v. 67 f.)

This virtual repudiation of the connection of the external goods with the good is supported by an attempt to minimize the amount of weight allowed to them:

> For those things which we count as bodily goods, certainly go to make up the full happiness of life: *nevertheless a happy life is possible without them.* For so slight and trifling are those supplementary goods that, like stars in the rays of the sun, they are not even seen in the bright light of the virtues.
>
> But although the saying is true that those elements of bodily advantage are of small importance to happiness of life, still *it is too sweeping to say that they are of no importance.* Those who argue thus seem to me to forget the first principles of nature that they have themselves established. Therefore we *must ascribe some value to these provided you realize the proper amount of value.* For a philosopher who seeks truth rather than ostentation must not consider as valueless the things which even those boastful persons admit to be in accordance with nature; but he must also realize that the power of virtue is so great and so great too—if I may say so— the authority of moral worth that *the other goods, though not indeed of no value, are so small that they seem to be of no value.* (Ibid. v. 71 f.)

Thus, though he has insisted all along on the importance of external things as steps up to the good, Antiochus now says that they are eclipsed by virtue, a thing takes its name from its predominant part and in the supremacy of virtue all else is as nought. But in the phrases in italics we may detect equivocation and inconsistency.

Here we see the inevitable result of Antiochus' attempt to base a system of pure morality on information derived entirely from the facts of perception. He believed that he could construct a perfect understanding of the whole order of nature. In that order all things must be real parts and must be granted some weight. This he was willing to grant them. But as he pressed on towards his main goal, which was to establish the perfection of the ethical end, he realized that he must not, by allowing ethical significance to things, detract from its perfection. This was the point of his claim to differ from the Stoics only in terminology: he called the external things 'good', the Stoics called them 'preferred': both schools, said Antiochus, admitted that external goods counted—the Stoics merely concealed their admission by their terminology. But, said he, the external goods counted only in a limited sense and not in such a way as to detract from the completeness of the supreme good.

It was easy for the New Academy to detect the weakness of this position. Immediately the question was raised whether 'virtue could be so great as she is if anything outside virtue be classed as a good': that is to say, is Antiochus justified in saying that the allowance of other goods does not impair the perfection of virtue? Speaking for the New Academy, Cicero reduced the problem to the practical question whether the Wise Man is always and invariably happy.

Now to judge virtue by its power to ensure happiness is to abandon the metaphysical quest for its perfection. For it implies the power, and the necessity, to dominate external factors. It is an admission of other goods and their opposites, evils, and an admission of their power to affect the Wise Man. Fighting desperately, Piso, the spokesman for the Antiochean tradition, is forced to admit that there are degrees of happiness, thus implying that virtue is in fact affected by external factors. Nevertheless, says Piso, the Wise Man is always happy. 'Well, Piso,' says Cicero, 'that is a position which you will find to need a great deal of defending.' And in my opinion the first four books of the *Tusculan Disputations* give Cicero's statement of the defence which the school of Antiochus had to offer.

6. The Transition from the *De Finibus* to the *Tusculan Disputations*

By adopting the Stoics' doctrine of perception, by checking their abandonment of their first grounds in their transition to the transcendental realm, and by filling the gaps in their account of the development from impulses to virtues, Antiochus thought that he had found a satisfactory epistemological basis for morality in the foundation accepted in common by the Old Tradition and the Stoics. He claimed to correct the Stoics and give a right account of their theory. Thus, early in Book v, Cicero makes the spokesman for Antiochus say that 'the Stoics took over their whole system from the Peripatetics and the Academics, adopting the same ideas under other names.' And at the end, despite the Stoics' repudiation of the alleged compatibility of the two systems,[22] Antiochus persists in declaring that the difference—which should be vital—over the relation of external advantages to the good is merely a matter of terminology.

22. *Fin.* iii. 41.

The glaring fault of Antiochus' argument was the poverty of his criticism of the ethical end. Admittedly he did brand the Stoics' *honestum* as a 'vague phantom' and the transition to the transcendental realm as a betrayal of principles. But the criticism all dealt with details in the account of the development from impulses and with gaps created by the sudden transition: in short it was criticism not of the conception itself but of the methods by which it was established. As for his own case, again he left his concept of virtue without metaphysical justification and, whereas it should have been his main concern to prove the completeness of his system of knowledge, he did not attempt the task. In short it is characteristic of Antiochus to be undiscerning in all matters requiring a discussion of epistemology and to be over-elaborate in matters of detail.

Neglecting epistemology, Antiochus spent the main part of his efforts in an attempt to establish what the Scholastics would call the subjective final end. Here he was defective both in his conception of the broad requirements of moral theory and in the details of his proof. On the first point we have observed the Scholastics' views of the inadequacy of the establishment of the subjective final end as proof of a theory of morality; as regards the details, we find an arbitrary and uncritical assertion of the nature of the primary impulses, and a plausible and incomplete account of man's essential nature, as witness the use of the figure of the vine successively endowed with fresh faculties as an illustration of man's continuous development.

This interest in the subjective final end determines the lines which the school of Antiochus will follow in defending their system. For them the main problem becomes not the theoretical justification, according to principles of epistemology, of the supreme good embracing natural advantages but the ability of man to act rationally, overcoming factors which may assail him, fears, pains and emotions. This is the theme of the *Tusculan Disputations*. In them we shall find that what is important is not the contrast of perfect knowledge of the transcendental, according to the Stoic ideal, with the conception of a complete system of knowledge built up from perception, according to Antiochus. What is important is the conception of man consistent with the Antiochean account of the *De Finibus* — man not serenely disregarding the things of the world, like the Stoic *sapiens,* but affected by them and taking them into his calculations, man with his feet on the ground and his knowledge developed from perception of the things of nature.

Thus the problem for Antiochus becomes very much the same as that of modern theories which endeavour to found a practical morality on the explanation of the empirical traits which human beings manifest in their everyday life, for example naturalistic humanism.[23] The difference between Antiochus and modern naturalistic humanism is that he does suppose the possibility of attaining complete understanding. But he does not prove it: it is in fact unjustifiable within his general system: and in the last resort he does not argue consistently from the assumption. The distinctive part of his theory is the development of morality from the conception of man's essential nature expounded in the *De Finibus* and here it resembles those modern theories which likewise derive their ethics from analysis of man's nature, such as that of McDougall with his basis of instincts, or even those more recent attempts to establish a connection between ethics and psycho-analysis: for these follow Waddington's view that 'the psycho-analytical discoveries, which are concerned with the development of the ethical system of individuals, are the most profitable basis from which to begin our examination of the scientific basis of ethics.'[24]

In the *Tusculan Disputations* we shall detect the effect of this conception of the *De Finibus* of man gradually developing from his first impulses and retaining the humbler faculties in the progress towards the higher so that his emotions have an active effect within him. In such a nature it is the task of reason to cope with the emotions and reduce them to order: this contrasts with the Stoic ideal that the perfect Wise Man is not in any way affected by such forces. Consequently we must expect to find a conflict of the Stoic belief in the eradication of the emotions and the Antiochean doctrine that they must always remain factors to be considered even by a man who has attained the highest virtue. And here it must be noted that the Antiochean theory differs again from the Peripatetic theory of emotions as desirable 'mean' states.

As regards Cicero's own position there are obvious reasons why he should wish to continue the examination of Antiochus' system after the *De Finibus*. A thorough-going Sceptic, after

23. Cf. S. Hook, 'Nature and the Human Spirit', *Report of the Amsterdam Conference,* 1948, p. 775.

24. J. Wisdom, review of *Science and Ethics,* ed. C. H. Waddington, *Mind,* lii (1943) , p. 278.

rejecting the claims about validity of perception in the *Academica*, might have been expected to throw out the whole of Antiochus' system without further examination. But we have seen that Cicero's scepticism was not complete: he did not challenge the existence of the world of nature, or the view that it should give rise to the primary impulses, or the ethical significance of these impulses based on the assumed goodness of the order of nature. But he was troubled about the problem of establishing valid connection between man and the world of physical reality. He was somewhat in the position of Kant who, while not denying the existence of the world of things, was yet unable to admit that human faculties could grasp things as they are in themselves. There was this difference that whereas Kant found an essential limitation in the nature of man's knowledge which must always keep him separated from 'the thing in itself', Cicero admitted that some of man's perceptions might be correct without his knowing it. That is to say, Cicero felt that Antiochus was right in his account of how a true perception (i.e. a direct and valid grasping of the thing, as it exists, without any 'bifurcation of nature', to use A. E. Taylor's phrase) could be formed *if only* it could be distinguished. His objection was the impossibility of disentangling true from false. In short Cicero was worried over the *confusion* of true and false perceptions, Kant over the *essential limitation* of perception. Cicero realized the limitation of subjective knowledge but was not so clear about the issue as was Kant.

Now because of his admission of the existence of the world of things and because he did not altogether reject Antiochus' account of the nature of the relation that can be formed between the person perceiving and the object perceived (with the reservation that there will also be false perceptions which will render certainty impossible) Cicero could not stop short at the end of the *Academica*. He must examine the next part of Antiochus' system in the *De Finibus*. But almost the whole of this was taken up by the exposition of the case for Antiochus which had to include first the refutation of the rival schools and then the positive statement of its own system. Then obviously Cicero could not stop short at the end of the *De Finibus* either. For the Sceptics had no space to state their criticism: they had merely asked one pertinent question. And in any case the exposition of Antiochus, so far as it was intended to state an ethical system, was far from complete. There was not even any need for Cicero to make an independent choice of his next theme, for he had only to follow the order of topics commonly discussed in the school of Antiochus. He would know that the next stage of the Antiochean case after asserting the Wise Man's ability to act rationally despite the influence of mundane factors was to prove his assertion by demonstrating his ability to overcome fear, pain and emotions. In short, in the *Tusculan Disputations* Cicero maintained a sincere and continuous examination of the case of Antiochus against the Stoic ethics commenced in the *De Finibus*.

CHAPTER IV

THE *TUSCULAN DISPUTATIONS*

1. THE STRUCTURE OF THE ARGUMENT

THE first four books of the *Tusculan Disputations* are a statement of the Antiochean view that man can act rationally despite the influence of fears, pains and emotions in general. The fifth book is Cicero's review of the issue between the Stoics, with their ideal of moral worth as the only good, and Antiochus with his view that the moral end is virtue together with the natural advantages. Thus Cicero shows that, although the case for Antiochus which he expounds in the first four books may prove that virtue has the *power* to override inferior influences, it is not yet certain whether the allowance of some force to these inferior influences may not *impair the perfection* of virtue. In other words, can the Antiochean system establish a perfect morality? This is what is implied in the question raised in Book v and already asked at the end of the *De Finibus,* whether virtue is sufficient for happiness of life; for the implication of this question is that, if man is in any way influenced by mundane factors, even granted that he may subdue them by reason, yet the happiness that he may attain may not be the complete happiness of perfect virtue.

The divisions of the Antiochean case in Books i-iv are:

Book i. The proof that man can overcome the fear of death: *either* the soul is immortal so that the death of the body confers a blessing by releasing the soul to its true life of purity, *or* death, as complete annihilation of soul and body, renders impossible any experience of evil after death.

Book ii. A general affirmation of man's ability to overcome pain, resting mainly on the dominance of the rational part of the soul.

Book iii. The explanation of the dominance by reason over emotions, based on the argument that emotion (e.g. distress, *aegritudo*), being due to an act of will and wrong opinion, can therefore be overcome by the will and by right reason.

Book iv. Further support for the theory that emotion is due to wrong opinion based on an examination of the nature of emotions; this involves the rejection of the Peripatetic doctrine of emotion as a 'mean' state in favour of the view (compatible with Antiochus' theory of man's moral nature in the *De Finibus*) that emotions are conditions which affect the Wise Man but which he can control: this view differs from the Stoic view that emotions must be eradicated and can have no effect upon the Wise Man.

The continuity of the argument may be explained by the fact that Cicero, from his association with Antiochus and his sustained interest in contemporary philosophy, knew the order of topics requisite for the exposition of the Antiochean case. These books do, however, elaborate particular topics in a manner disproportionate to the main plan; for example, the great detail of the theories on immortality in Book I or the minute Stoic subdivisions of emotion in Book IV. This happened because, since the topics had been thrashed out in the school for generations, Cicero drew his arguments from a variety of sources and, while reproducing them in the right order, translated whole slabs of his Greek originals without due care in adapting them to his argument.

The fact that various of these sources were Stoic is quite consistent with our view that these first four books present the Antiochean modification of Stoicism. For although the Stoics strongly denied the influence of emotions on the ideal Wise Man they frequently discussed the practical problems in overcoming emotion of the ordinary man who has not attained pure wisdom; and by such Stoic discussions of practical morality the case of Antiochus could be supported seeing that he asserted that his ideal Wise Man, supposing he could anywhere be found, must be subject to the influence of the emotions.

In arguments drawn from various sources some inconsistency was inevitable. We shall detect in the *Tusculan Disputations* two theories of the nature of the soul, the Platonic-Pythagorean and the Stoic. Cicero makes no attempt to reconcile them. Each gives some support to the thesis of the ability of man to control emotions. Therefore Cicero will use both theories from his various authorities feeling that the distinction between them is not relevant to the main argument.

A word of warning must be given against the danger of accepting passages in Books I-IV as statements of Cicero's own views. Some confusion may be caused by his abandonment of his system of characterization and by his distinction of the speakers simply by the letters M and A. What these letters mean is not certain. For A have been suggested *Adulescens* or *Auditor* and for M either *Marcus,* Cicero's own name, or *Magister.* It is even possible that they are later additions which formed no part of the original text. Reid in his addition to Dougan's note[1] is reluctant to jettison 'M for Marcus' on the grounds that there must have been some mode of distinguishing the interlocutors and that M as the principal is 'thoroughly identified with Cicero'. But I do not think that Cicero intended to do more at this stage than to explain the case of Antiochus without indicating his own verdict upon it.

2. IMMORTALITY: BOOK I

The task of Book I is to state the reasons why man can overcome the fear of death. The broad lines of the case are simple: either the soul is immortal, which is the belief of the 'Academico-Peripatetic' tradition in general and of some contemporary Stoics, or the soul perishes with the death of the body, which is the view of other Stoics. In either case death can be no evil, for it is accepted as a corollary of the doctrine of immortality that in its own pure life the soul enjoys complete happiness. Certain other possibilities are considered and rejected, such as the theory of yet another section of Stoics that the soul lives for some time only after separation from the body, and the view of death as evil because it means loss of the blessings of this life.[2]

Now Cicero might have shown the case for the possibility of overcoming the fear of death quite simply by stating that both the main theories deny that death is evil. But he has given both theories, concerning immortality and the denial of it, in great detail just as in the early part of the *De Finibus* he expanded the account of the Epicureans more than was necessary. His own affiliation with the New Academy gives him a general sympathy with the Platonic case for immortality, which he reveals especially at the end of the book.[3] But he is not required to make a decision for or against immortality, his purpose being to state the case for overcoming fear as part of the general Antiochean case for man's control of fears and emotions which he himself will weigh in Book v.

1. *T.D.,* ed. Dougan, vol. i, p. 13.
2. See sections 83 ff.; cf. Dougan's important examination of Cicero's discussion of the meaning of *carere* (in *T.D.,* ed. Dougan and Henry, vol. i, p. lix, and *Class. Rev.,* xvi, 1902).
3. *T.D.,* i. 118.

H

It is probable that Antiochus as an adherent of the 'Academico-Peripatetic' tradition supported the doctrine of immortality, and a distinction made in Book i. 77 between the Stoics and the case argued up to that point points to him because of the distinction between him and the Stoics in the *De Finibus*. But it is not suggested that Cicero's source was Antiochus himself; it could be a source acceptable to him. This could quite well be Posidonius. Into his Middle Stoicism he fitted the Academic doctrine of immortality. This was typical of the eclecticism of the Middle Stoa and explains why he could be used to support Antiochus on one topic but not on another. For example, in Book ii. 61 he seems to be the source of the Stoic denial that pain is evil, which is there used against Antiochus. Thus of the many sources that have been suggested I favour Posidonius as the main source for the arguments for immortality. The alternative view, that the soul is destroyed with the death of the body, would naturally come from more orthodox Stoic sources. Panaetius is not impossible as a source but it does seem that, while denying immortality, he did suppose that the soul lived on for a time.

In short, this book consists in the main of the case for immortality, drawn from a source favourable to Antiochus and the case against it, probably from orthodox Stoic sources. Their combined effect is to support the thesis of Antiochus that man can overcome fear of death. In addition there are various parts of the argument such as the preliminary statement of the problem and the short survey of various theories of the soul where Cicero could choose from a variety of sources and may have done some original composition himself. We need not investigate them here since they have little bearing on our main thesis that Cicero's purpose in this book as a whole is to give one part of the general case for Antiochus.

In the details of the argument there are two points that deserve special attention. The first reveals the deficiency of Cicero's critical sense. In sections 57-61 his main purpose is to support the immortality of the soul by arguing from the pre-eminence of its powers. Now one of these powers is memory ($\mu\nu\acute{\eta}\mu\eta$) but he brings in Plato's argument on $\mathring{\alpha}\nu\acute{\alpha}\mu\nu\eta\sigma\iota\varsigma$ as if it were a subdivision of $\mu\nu\acute{\eta}\mu\eta$, thus treating it as an instance of the marvellous powers of the mind of man and missing Plato's point. Next it should be observed that sections 36-52 supporting immortality state certain doctrines which agree with the cosmology of the *Timaeus*, e.g. the description of the earth as the centre of the universe,[4] the escape of the soul to its own pure realm,[5] the soul's survey of the earth by its own pure power whereas in the body there are limitations on the senses,[6] the discussion of the composition of the soul,[7] the conception of the control of the world by intelligent purpose,[8] the divine power of mind whose seat is in the head.[9] Now if these sections are based on Posidonius this implies some agreement between him and the *Timaeus,* a point of significance in our examination of Cicero's purpose in translating the *Timaeus.* But there are points of difference also inevitable because of the nature of Cicero's sources. Thus the argument that the soul, being self-moving, never had a beginning and will therefore never have an end, which agrees with *Phaedrus* 245, is not compatible with the doctrine in the *Timaeus* of the creation of the soul.

3. ENDURABILITY OF PAIN: BOOK II

Book II is the first stage of the proof of the endurability of pain and the emotions. It has two main divisions, the demonstration that pain is an evil affecting the Wise Man, which the Stoics deny,[10] and the proof that man can overcome pain:[11] for this division Stoic arguments are available despite the previous denial, for, as we have said, the Stoics did grapple with the practical problem.

In the first division it can be seen that the issue is precisely the same as at the end of the *De Finibus.* Just as there the Stoics used their peculiar terminology to avoid conceding value to anything other than moral worth—calling 'preferable' what Antiochus called 'external goods'—so now they pour forth a flood of terms, 'unpleasing', 'against nature', 'hard to endure', 'melancholy', 'cruel' for what Antiochus would call in a single word 'evil'.[12] By this means they seek to avoid conceding that there is any evil other than moral baseness (*turpitudo*). But in section 30 the argument rejects as 'mere aspiration, not proof'

4. *T.D.* i. 40 f.; *Timaeus* 34b.
5. *T.D.* i. 42-4; *N.D.* ii. 118.
6. *T.D.* i. 45 f.; *Timaeus,* 64 ff.
7. *T.D.* i. 60 f.; *Timaeus,* 35a, 41d.
8. *T.D.* i. 70; *Timaeus* 47e.
9. *T.D.* i. 70; *Timaeus* 44d.
10. *T.D.* ii. 28-34. The introductory sections, with their general statement of the topic and their criticism of unsatisfactory accounts of pain as an evil by poets and philosophers, need not concern us here.
11. Ibid. ii. 35 ff.
12. Ibid. ii. 29 f.

the Stoic assertion '*nihil bonum nisi quod honestum, nihil malum nisi quod turpe*' and states a preference for the obviously Antiochean view '*omnia quae natura aspernetur, in malis esse: quae adsciscat, in bonis.*' Renounce the difference of terminology, says the argument, and it may readily be admitted that moral worth is pre-eminent and all else by comparison slight and microscopic while moral baseness is so bad that no other evil, not even all evils combined, can compare with it. Here the Antiochean attitude is unmistakable: it insists, as in the *De Finibus*, that to external things must be allowed some weight, however negligible.

The argument that pain may be despised falls into two parts. There is a practical account with historical examples of the endurance of pain by practice, preparation and habituation.[13] But this is much less important than the following part which tries to establish the endurability of pain on philosophic grounds. This takes up the last third of the book from section 42.

In the philosophic justification Cicero calls in the aid of the Stoics on behalf of the case of Antiochus. He has already in sections 31 and 32 shown the latter's sympathy with the Stoic conception of the cardinal virtues which demands that 'courage must go by the board or else a grave be found for pain.' By this Antiochus would imply the complete dominance of the virtues while allowing to pain a small but negligible force. A phrase in section 46 relevant to the attitude of Antiochus demands explanation. Cicero here, expounding the case for Antiochus, says that 'far the best for man is that which is desirable in and for itself, is derived from virtue or rather based on virtue, is of itself praiseworthy "*quod quidem citius dixerim solum quam non summum bonum.*"' This reading would be consistent with the attitude of Antiochus, the last clause meaning 'and indeed I should prefer to describe it as the only good rather than as not the highest good.' That is to say, rather than admit virtue is not supreme he would even go over to the Stoics and declare it the only good. King omits the *non* of the MSS. and translates 'and in fact I should prefer to describe it as the only good rather than the highest good.' This would express a preference for the Stoic definition of virtue and would be inconsistent with the general argument which Cicero is here expounding on behalf of Antiochus.[14]

13. Ibid. ii. 35-41.
14. J. E. King, ed. *T.D.* ii. 46 (Loeb).

The philosophic justification of man's ability to endure pain, so far as it is based on theory, rests on the doctrine of the control of the lower nature by reason (sections 47-53). This supposes the division of the soul into two parts, τὸ λογιστικόν and τὸ ἄλογον, of which the latter may be subdivided into τὸ ἐπιθυμητικόν and τὸ θυμοειδές.[15] This was a doctrine of some later Stoics and is probably drawn from Posidonius. Now this conception of the soul implies that reason is in the upper part alone: 'the soul is divided into two parts of which one is gifted with reason and the other is devoid of it.'[16]

This is quite different from the argument in Book III that emotions are all functions of some grade of intellect. This difference might be urged in refutation of the claim of the continuity of the two books. But we must observe that Cicero makes only very general use of the argument of the divisions of the soul and does not investigate its details. His purpose is to open up the general case for the endurability of pains and emotions and he is content to use the theory of the mastery of the lower part by the higher without investigating its compatibility with the view of emotions as due to acts of reasoning, which will be the basis of his later arguments. Finger, who accepts Posidonius as the source for the Stoic sections of Book III, also argues that the dualistic psychology of Posidonius does not, either in Cicero or Seneca, influence the teaching on the moral character of the πάθη.[17] Hence the incompatibility of the dualistic psychology in Book II with the later description of the emotions does not invalidate the theory of the continuity of Cicero's argument.

We can now see that the professed philosophic justification of the endurability of pain is not penetrating. Apart from this unexamined theory of the dominant power of the higher part of the soul the argument consists mainly of examples, exhortations and generalizations.

Dougan[18] ascribes Cicero's poverty of material and use of padding in Book II to the fact that the endurability of pain has been partially established by the argument in Book I show-

---

15. See Dougan's notes on *T.D.*, vol. i, pp. 28, 216; cf. our discussion and the references to Dougan and Henry in section 5 of this chapter.

16. *T.D.* ii. 47. This dualistic psychology, involving the subdivision of the irrational into two parts, corresponds with the Platonic tripartite division.

17. Philipp Finger, 'Die beiden Quellen des III. Buches der *Tusculanen* Ciceros', *Philologus*, lxxxiv (1928-9), 51 ff., 320; cf. *T.D.*, ed. Dougan and Henry, vol. ii, pp. xxxiii, xxxvi.

18. Op cit., vol. i, p. xxvi.

ing that death is to be despised. I prefer to think that in Book I Cicero had his mind entirely on the question of fear of death and that in Book II he commenced a fresh problem, man's ability to master pains and emotions, which was to be continued through the next two books. Thus the structure of Book II is explained by the fact that he intended it as an introduction to a general thesis whose details were to be studied more closely in the later books.

For the sources for the two main divisions of the argument I have the following suggestions.[19] The refutation of the Stoic denial that pain is an evil in sections 28-34 is so consistent with the attitude of Antiochus in the *De Finibus* and with my theory that Cicero in Books I-IV was elaborating the case of Antiochus that the source for this part was probably Antiochus or possibly a Sceptic, such as Philo, who might have contrasted the Stoic and Antiochean views. Either of these suggestions seems preferable to the choice of a pure Stoic source for these sections. The general proof of the mastery of pain probably came from Posidonius. The dualistic psychology was consistent with his Academized Stoicism. There is much pure Stoicism in this part of the book but Posidonius, who was probably the source for the opposition to the Stoics in Book I concerning immortality, could quite well represent the Stoic tradition on endurance of pain. Here Cicero has interpolated various Roman illustrations and, if the main source was Posidonius, then the description of his denial in section 61 that pain is evil must be an addition by Cicero. In the book as a whole Cicero must have done considerable independent composition, using various books for reference.

4. REMEDIABILITY OF EMOTION BY REASON: BOOK III

The general purpose of Book III is to explain the theory that emotion is due to error of judgment and can therefore be remedied by reason. Cicero's method of introduction is confusing since it states that the thesis for discussion is to be 'that the Wise Man is subject to distress' (*aegritudo*).[20] This might be taken as a reversion to the first problem of Book II, but the preliminary argument, up to section 22, reveals a general intention to discuss the nature of *aegritudo* and its remediability. Moreover, these sections reveal a preference for a conception of

19. Cf. Dougan, op. cit., vol. i, p. xxv; M. van Straaten, *Panétius*, pp. 266, 285 ff.; M. Pohlenz, 'Das Zweite Buch der *Tusculanen*', *Hermes*, xliv (1909), 23-40.
20. *T.D.* iii. 7.

the emotions intermediate between the extreme Stoic view, that the Wise Man excises all emotion from himself, and the Peripatetic doctrine (which allows too much sensitivity) that emotion is desirable 'as a mean state'.[21] Here then we see again the characteristic difference of Antiochus from pure Stoicism: his difference from the Peripatetics will be examined in detail in Book IV.

Hirzel has rejected Antiochus as a possible source for Book III on the ground that he 'could not have subscribed to Cicero's polemic against the Peripatetics.'[22] But that reveals a misunderstanding of Antiochus' position. The essence of his case is that man, even the ideal Wise Man if he existed, is subject to influences which he must control. This view is well represented in section 22: 'For every evil, even a moderate one, is an evil; but our object is that there should be no evil at all in the Wise Man.' By this he meant that emotions are influences to be considered. They cannot be dismissed in the airy fashion of the Stoics. But they must be mastered without allowing the retention of a certain amount of emotion as natural, necessary, and desirable according to the Peripatetic view.

This interpretation might seem to conflict with an argument in section 13 where it is proclaimed that though we must endeavour to tear out weakness by the roots, 'yet even then there may be some left; the roots of folly go so deep; yet only that much will be left which must be left.' But this is quite consistent with the whole Antiochean case that the evil is an evil and must be mastered. It does not support the Peripatetic view of the positive desirability of the retention of a certain amount of emotion. The position of Antiochus was that of the Academico-Peripatetic tradition in general, but on the emotions the Peripatetics had their particular theory, much as various Stoics diverged in details from the main Stoic tradition. The manner of reference in section 22, '*Peripatetici familiares nostri*', suggests a recognition of some distinction between the speaker, who here is expounding the Antiochean case, and the Peripatetics.

The original question whether the *sapiens* is affected by *aegritudo* is tacitly dropped and the main part of Book III advances a theory of the nature of distress and so of emotion in

21. For criticism of the attempts of Stoics by syllogisms to vindicate the excision of emotions see sections 14-21 and for the rejection of the doctrines of the mean see sections 22, 74.

22. R. Hirzel, *Untersuchungen zu Ciceros philosophischen Schriften*, vol. iii, pp. 414 ff.; cf. *T.D.*, ed. Dougan and Henry, vol. ii, p. xxxii.

general as a thing which reason can control. Here again, as in the discussion of pain, Stoic arguments are available. Although in strict theory the Stoics denied that distress could affect the Wise Man, yet they did discuss its nature and the means of remedying it in the practical life.[23]

Just as in Book I the case for immortality was argued in much greater detail than was necessary for Cicero's main purpose, so here we have an elaborate analysis of the relation of *aegritudo* to the other emotions and of its nature. It involves the examination of theories of various schools and it is typical of Cicero that he goes off for ten pages into a tirade against Epicurus. But the essence of the argument is that grief is a voluntary matter: people grieve because they form the opinion that they are affected by great present evils and that it is their duty to be distressed at what has happened: people mourn because they think it is a duty to mourn. Then if distress is a voluntary matter it can be remedied by reason. One must show the sufferer that the evil is negligible. Better still is it to convince him that his grief is due to his own volition.

One can now see that this theory of distress as an act of will and erroneous opinion could be extended to the other emotions. In fact in Book IV we encounter the Stoic view that all emotions are due to a mental decision and to the forming of a mere opinion. From this it is reasonable to say that Book III leads up to the next book and our sense of the continuity of Cicero's exposition is strengthened.

The advice of Books III and IV on the remedial treatment of annoyance is obviously a fruitful source for all future philosophers concerned with mastery of grief and we can see great similarity between these parts of the *Tusculan Disputations* and Seneca, Epictetus, Marcus Aurelius and the French philosophers of the sixteenth and seventeenth centuries who sought comfort in times of trouble. But in our examination of the structure of Cicero's programme we are more concerned with the theoretical development of the case for man's ability to control fears, pains and emotions. In Book III we have found the theory to rest on the conception of emotion as a wrong opinion, or due to a wrong opinion. There is some confusion in the description,[24] but the implication is clear, that the remedy is an act of reasoning. This differs, as we have said already, from the dualistic

    23. Cf. Dougan and Henry, op. cit., vol. ii, p. xlvii.
    24. Dougan and Henry, op. cit., vol. ii, p. xxxiv; cf. our later discussion in section 5.

psychology of Book II according to which emotion would be a disturbance of the inferior part which is devoid of reason. In the last section I have given reasons why this difference does not suffice to upset the theory of the continuity of Cicero's exposition. Of the two the account of the emotions in Book III is the more consistent with Antiochus' conception in the *De Finibus* of the continuous development of man's understanding with the retention of the humbler faculties as the higher ones are attained.

As for the sources of Book III, the parts which concern us most are: (a) The statement of the Stoic syllogisms in sections 14-21. These were clearly from a pure Stoic source in the style of Zeno and Chrysippus. (b) The statement of the need to find an account intermediate between Stoics and Peripatetics, in section 22. This has a distinctly Antiochean tone but could be Cicero's own. (c) The analysis of the nature of *aegritudo*. In this part the Stoic doctrines probably came in the main from Chrysippus. But here Cicero has made digressions on the Cyrenaics and the Epicureans and quotes either directly or at second hand from a great number of Greek authors, some of whom, such as Crantor and Clitomachus, he had used for his *Consolatio*.[25]

5. Remediability of Emotion and Refutation of the Peripatetic Doctrine of the Mean: Book IV

In Book IV the case for man's ability to control the emotions culminates. There are three main parts which support our thesis of the continuity of Cicero's exposition by amplifying doctrines already raised in Book III. They are:

(a) The elaborate classification of the emotions and explanation of them as due to a mental decision and to forming a mere opinion (sections 14-33). This builds upon the particular study of *aegritudo* in Book III.

(b) The full refutation, in sections 38-57, of the Peripatetic doctrine of emotions as 'mean' states which urges the desirability of the retention of a certain amount of emotion.

(c) Discussion of the treatment of the emotions in sections 58-81 which expands the advice of Book III on the treatment of *aegritudo* that, since the emotion is due to wrong judgment, it may be controlled by reason.

In short, Book III has stated the case for the remediability of one form of emotion, arguing that, since it arises from wrong

---

25. On the whole problem of the sources see Dougan and Henry, op. cit., vol. ii, pp. xxx-xlii.

opinion, it may be remedied by reason and rejecting the Peripatetic claim for its retention as a 'mean' state; and Book IV expands the same argument for the remediability of emotions in general and attacks the Peripatetic claim in detail.

The analysis of emotions as due to mental decisions and to forming of mere opinions, which is a pure Stoic conception, is preceded by a brief statement in sections 10-11 of a dualistic psychology specifically ascribed to Pythagoras and Plato. Thus we have in juxtaposition the two theories of the structure of the soul which were advanced separately in Books II and III without any recognition by Cicero of their incompatibility. Here again either he is not conscious of the distinction or considers it irrelevant.[26] He bases no specific arguments on the Platonic psychology. He is content to state it as support for the thesis that reason can control emotions. But he does not examine how the control would be effected according to that psychology, namely by strife and the victory of the rational part. For explanation of the control he relies entirely on the Stoic conception of emotions according to which, since reason pervades all parts of the soul, all correction is an act of reasoning.[27]

Although all the argument on the nature of emotions is Stoic, the final result of rational control in man, which it supports, admirably suits the Antiochean ideal, as in the description in section 34 of virtue as an 'equable and harmonious disposition of the soul' and the delineation of the Wise Man which ends this part of the book. This is most probably from a Stoic source, yet the ideal of human understanding, especially in its reference to the contemplation of the vastness of the universe, is precisely true to the Antiochean ideal of the system of understanding of the order of nature; and the whole picture is that of a man who grapples with mundane influences and controls them:

> Therefore the man, whoever he is to whose soul restraint and consistency have brought peace and who is at peace with himself,—so that troubles do not sap his power, fear does not break him, nor longing pursuit of some ambition burn and torture him, nor does the quest of vain baubles waste his strength in frantic efforts—he is the Wise Man whom we seek, he is the happy man who can think nothing in the life of man so intolerable as to break his spirit or unduly delightful

26. Dougan and Henry, op. cit., vol. ii, p. xliv.
27. For details of the Stoic psychology see ibid. note to *T.D.* iv. 78 and p. xlvii.

so as to rouse him to ecstasy. For in the life of man what can
seem important to one who knows all eternity and the vastness
of the universe? (*T.D.* iv. 37.)

The classification of the emotions and explanation of their
nature is so consistent with Stoic doctrine that it is reasonable
to think that these sections derive mainly from Chrysippus'
περὶ παθῶν or from a related source. Chrysippus is known to
have delighted in minute subdivisions. The persisting confusion
as to whether the *opinio constituted* the emotion or *caused* it
may transmit traces of arguments which Chrysippus is said to
have directed against Zeno on this topic.

The refutation of the Peripatetic doctrine of emotions as
'mean' states is obviously Stoic. It is so vigorous and so insistent
on the need to eradicate emotions that it might be taken for
an attack upon the Antiochean theory that some weight must
be allowed to things other than pure virtue. In fact the Stoics
would use such arguments against Antiochus: for example in
section 42 the thought 'he who sets a limit to vices admits a
part of them' could quite well be directed by them against the
Peripatetic 'mean' and Antiochus' retention of 'some weight'
for other things. But it was also possible to use those Stoic
arguments against the Peripatetics without considering their
applicability to Antiochus. What he urged was the need to
master the emotions as real forces: he would not consent with
the Stoics that they could be eradicated in the sense that they
could have no influence at all on the Wise Man. But he could
unite with the Stoics in condemning the Peripatetic desire to
retain them as necessary states. Thus in section 4 above we
considered the consistency of Antiochus' condemnation of the
Peripatetics on the doctrine of 'means' with his general acceptance of the 'Academico-Peripatetic' tradition. Now it was just
as consistent for him to correct the Peripatetics in one doctrine
as to correct the Stoics in some parts while upholding them in
others. On the relation of the emotions to pure reason he sought
a position intermediate between Stoics and Peripatetics. The
Stoics he called back from the empty absoluteness of reason: the
Peripatetics he called back from too much concession to emotion.

While the general origin of the criticism of the doctrine of
the 'means' is clearly Stoic, either Chrysippus or someone who
followed him, the copious historical examples and quotations
point to independent composition by Cicero.

The difference between the Stoic conception of the perfect Wise Man and the Antiochean conception is well made in the phrase with which the third main part of this book opens: 'I think that your inquiry is concerned not so much with the Wise Man as with yourself—for you think that he is free from all disorder while you *wish* to be free.' Antiochus, bound by his concession of some weight to mundane factors, cannot assert perfect freedom from emotion. In the various Antiochean descriptions of the supremacy of virtue, especially in Book v, we must realize that there is always this qualification that the Wise Man, as this tradition conceived him, must grapple with inferior influences: on the other hand the Stoic definition supposed complete freedom from them.

This third part reinforces the discussion in Book iii of the remedies of *aegritudo* by similar discussion of the means of remedying *perturbationes* in general. Here again the correct treatment is described as an appeal to reason: one must show that the object of fear and annoyance is not evil or that the object of desire and delight is not good or one must persuade the sufferer that mental disturbance in general is vicious. The arguments in section 79-81 on the voluntary nature of anger are consistent with the view of Book iii that *aegritudo* is voluntary. In the appeal to reason, with its assumption that *perturbatio* is a matter of opinion, we still see the Stoic standpoint nor in the cure is any use made of the dualistic psychology: the cure is to be effected by reasoning and not by strife of the rational part against the inferior part, supposed to be devoid of reason. Thus the argument here is Stoic and is probably derived from Chrysippus or one of his viewpoint. Strict Stoic doctrine, of course, ought not to recognize any need in the Wise Man to overcome evils but in practice the need for cures was recognized, especially by Chrysippus. Thus although at the beginning of this book Cicero specially observed the interest of the Peripatetics '*ad placandos animos*', there is no need to think that he drew from other than a Stoic source.

6. THE STOIC AND ANTIOCHEAN DEFINITIONS OF THE GOOD: BOOK V

Having thus in Books i-iv presented the Antiochean case for the power of virtue to override mundane factors, Cicero now reverts to the issue between Antiochus and the Stoics. That is to say, the question remains whether Antiochus can establish a perfect morality supposing his first grounds are granted. And so again the question is asked as it was at the end of the *De Finibus,* 'Is the Wise Man always happy?' or 'Is virtue sufficient for leading a happy life?' Since the Antiochean case by presenting the Wise Man's concern with the things of the world implies that virtue is not isolated but requires the addition of 'other goods', the argument comes back to the crux of the dispute with the Stoics in the *De Finibus,* the relationship of the good to external things.

The first twenty sections state the need to review the whole question although the demonstration in the first four books of the power of virtue to override mundane factors might be regarded by some as sufficient vindication of Antiochus' definition of virtue. Cicero says that they must not proceed like the mathematicians taking for granted facts previously demonstrated but must review the whole question, 'for philosophers collect together all that is applicable to any inquiry on which they are engaged, even if it has already been discussed elsewhere (*T.D.* v. 18). This part includes a panegyric of philosophy which might be drawn from any one of a number of available sources, but the review of the position of the argument makes it reasonable to suppose a fair amount of original composition by Cicero himself.

Some guidance is needed in interpreting the structure of the main argument because certain views on the mastery of emotions by reason might equally well support Stoics and Antiochus, and hence their relevance to the main discussion will be debatable. For whereas the Stoics held that the ideal Wise Man eradicated all emotions, some of their statements on this might be used by the other school in its attempt to show not that emotions must be eradicated but that they can be mastered. The following analysis is intended to reveal the course of the argument as Cicero intended to present it.

(a) STOIC CRITICISM OF ANTIOCHUS (SECTIONS 21-34)

This part opens with the statement of the disagreement of Brutus (here following Antiochus) with the Stoic conception of virtue absolute, 'for he thinks that happy life lies in virtue even if there should be some good besides virtue.' Cicero then states that on this view he challenged Antiochus frequently and more recently Aristus (Antiochus' brother) when returning from Cilicia in 50 B.C. He criticizes the admission of degrees of hap-

piness and the claim that 'happy life, even though it should
in some part be maimed, yet gets its name from that which
forms the greater part of it.' Similar arguments were observed
in the *De Finibus*. Next, in sections 24-5, he reveals divisions
in the Academico-Peripatetic tradition itself: especially had
Theophrastus denied the possibility of happiness in one sub-
jected to tortures and the blows of fate.[28] Nor does Epicurus'
demonstration of the ability of his ideal man to overcome pain
and misfortune give much help to the thesis of Antiochus. This
is all leading to a vigorous statement, in sections 28-31, of the
Stoic view that virtue cannot ensure happiness if there is any
good beside itself and if such things as poverty, obscurity, pain
and slavery are allowed to be evils. The Stoics will not allow
that other goods or evils can affect their Wise Man. If such
things are allowed any degree of influence then the perfection
of virtue is impaired. Thus Cicero's intention is obviously to
state the case which Antiochus must meet.

There follows a conversational interlude which is open to
misinterpretation. Cicero's interlocutor reminds him that this
argument is inconsistent with the theory advanced in *De Finibus*
IV that the difference between Zeno and the Peripatetics was
purely a matter of terminology. Cicero's reply does not do him
justice: 'I live from day to day; I say anything which strikes my
mind as probable.' This might suggest that he had no serious
purpose: yet my general interpretation of Book V is that he
intended seriously to examine the Antiochean case for the
sufficiency of virtue. It was part of Antiochus' case that, while
allowing some weight to things, he could nevertheless establish
the perfection of virtue and that accordingly his difference from
the Stoics was purely a matter of terminology. By raising this
question here Cicero accordingly forces attention to the problem
whether Antiochus can in fact maintain this perfection of virtue
while allowing the persistence of such influences so strongly
repudiated in the vigorous Stoic statement.

But having stated the conflict of the two schools Cicero
proposes first to examine the Stoic conception of the absolute
happiness of perfect virtue. However, he states his intention
obscurely in the lines, 'Let us grant Brutus that the Wise Man
is *always* happy. . . . Let us hold fast to the view that the
Wise Man is also *supremely* happy.' I take this to mean that
he will not for the present follow up the question whether

28. *Fin.* v. 77, 85.

the Antiochean case, represented by Brutus, by allowing the existence of external goods diminishes the perfection of virtue and happiness, thus leaving the Wise Man *always* happy but not *perfectly* happy: for the present he will disregard that question and will give his attention to the view which asserts the *supreme* happiness achieved by perfect virtue. Accordingly I interpret the next part, sections 34-72, as a general statement of the Stoic case. But Cicero does not keep his objective clear and mingles various criticisms of the allowance of other goods.

Because of his mention of his discussion with Antiochus this part might be taken as an expression of Cicero's own views and it might be said that he personally accepted the Stoic case against Antiochus. But this would be inconsistent with his admission at the end of Book v. The proper interpretation, I think, is that Cicero stated the Stoic case for the purpose of the argument and that it does not represent his own view.

The critical attitude in these sections again has the mark of original composition and need not be referred to any source.

(b) VIRTUE AND ABSOLUTE HAPPINESS (SECTIONS 34-72)

The first few sections state the general support of the Platonic tradition, which Cicero obviously esteems above the Stoic, for the identification of happiness with virtue. But in sections 37-9 we have a theoretical justification of the Stoics' claim of the attainment of perfection by man. This is based on principles already familiar in the *De Finibus*—the goodness of nature and the consequent perfection of each creature after its own kind. Then what can be wanting to make life happy for man who feels assured of his own appropriate good? There follows the Stoic description of absolute happiness, which is declared unattainable if there are such goods as bodily and external goods.

From this point the argument mingles the Stoics' arguments on the sufficiency of virtue to ensure happiness with further criticism of the Antiochean allowance of 'other goods' against which sections 40-2, with their condemnation of 'the man who makes a three-fold division of good', are obviously directed. In sections 43-54 there is some typically Stoic syllogistic reasoning on the ability of virtue to ensure happiness. From section 54 to 67 the dependence of happiness on virtue is supported by popular argument with examples. Such are the illustrations of temporal success, such as tenure of the consulship, to show that external advantages have no relation to goodness and true happiness. Thus the wealth and power of Dionysius did not make him happy, because he was not virtuous: but virtue entitled Archimedes to be considered happier than the tyrant, though he lacked worldly benefits and had not even an honoured tomb. Such an argument might be taken as support for Antiochus' doctrine of the mastery of virtue, as he conceived it, over external advantages. But in its essence it is Stoic argument and from its position here it must be considered as part of the Stoic case. Especially is this so since sections 68-72 offer a very full statement of the Stoic ideal of the Wise Man which strengthens our view that the whole part from 34 to 72 is intended as a declaration of the Stoic attitude, culminating in this statement of the ideal and the assertion that virtue in the Stoic sense ensures perfect happiness.

In this part Cicero appears again to be working out for himself the treatment of a topic which on his own evidence he had discussed with Antiochus and Aristus. Therefore we may reasonably suppose that in the main he relied on original composition without drawing directly from Greek sources. Of course these topics were discussed by men like Chrysippus, Posidonius and Philo, and Cicero was no doubt in debt to them for his ideas. But probably he did not need to translate them here, except that the 'chain-arguments' used to support the pre-eminence of virtue by logic, may be translations or close copies of some Stoic writer.

(c) ANTIOCHUS ON THE SUFFICIENCY OF VIRTUE
(SECTIONS 73-118)

The transition to the case for Antiochus is made in sections 73-6. Again Cicero's intention is not clearly expressed. Immediately at the end of the Stoic statement he asks the question whether the Wise Man is happy even on the rack and this suggests an intention to examine the Stoics further. But I do think that, as in other parts of this book, the asking of a question by the character A marks a transition. Then in section 75 Cicero's intention is confirmed: 'let the Peripatetics also and the Old Academy make an end at last of their stammering and have the courage to say openly and loudly that the happy life will step down into the bull of Phalaris.' This has been preceded by argument about Epicurus and the purport of this may now be seen: it asks, 'if the Wise Man of Epicurus is always happy, what ought to be expected of those who consider nothing desirable, nothing worth reckoning as good, which is devoid of moral worth?' Now this again might be taken as a reference to Stoicism. But it is also consistent with the Antiochean view and its connection is confirmed by the immediate exhortation of the Peripatetics and the Old Academy. Section 76 then clearly asks if Antiochus's theory justifies the claim of virtue to ensure not only happiness but supreme happiness.

It is not hard for the Antiochean school to establish the Wise Man's ability to endure pain. The whole argument of Books I-IV has supported it and in sections 80-2 Cicero states their confidence that even pain and torture cannot separate happiness and virtue: that is to say, virtue according to the Antiochean definition, allowing the real effect of pain, can achieve happiness. But the question remains whether it can achieve supreme happiness. Even yet there has been no solution of the crucial problem of this whole book, whether the allowance of other goods impairs the perfection of virtue and of happiness. Again the brief lapse into dialogue at this point stresses Cicero's desire to emphasize the point at issue. Cicero's interlocutor says that he has been offered a good deal of Stoic criticism of the 'Academico-Peripatetics': he now wishes to hear their positive case for attainment of perfect happiness.

Cicero's method of stating the case for the 'Academico-Peripatetics' is first to state the general testimony of the various schools of philosophy to the power of virtue to ensure happiness (sections 83-7; note the strong statement of the Peripatetic view in 85-6) and then to give in detail the testimony of Epicurus (sections 88-96). The effect of this is to argue that if even Epicurus can uphold the power of mind to judge for itself and rise superior to mere appearances, surely the more reputable philosophies can do so too.

From section 97 to section 116 the argument degenerates into general testimony, with popular illustrations, of the power of mind to triumph over material factors and to alleviate even the worst blows of fortune such as blindness and deafness, for even Epicurus can alleviate the emotions by diverting thoughts to pleasure.

In section 117 we have what at first sight might be taken as an admission of failure to rise superior to material influences. For suicide is advocated as a last way out. But even this is intended as a vindication of the power of the mind to choose freely and to triumph over evils.

J

In the main Cicero himself must have composed the argument of these last two parts of Book v. References near the beginning and at the end show that the general line of criticism was probably suggested to him by discussion going back to Carneades. A very large part of the argument obviously implies Cicero's acquaintance with Epicurus and the Epicurean apologists. But again these would be so well known to him that he could well rely on his general knowledge of them rather than on translation.

7. Cicero's Conclusion and its Significance

The argument of Book v does not amount to much more than a contrast of the two definitions of virtue, the reiteration of the question whether the Antiochean demonstration of the power of virtue to override inferior factors was adequate to establish the perfection of virtue, and certain rather shallow testimony to the power of virtue as conceived by Antiochus. Now while Antiochus, rejecting as ridiculous the Stoic doctrine that the Wise Man felt no pain, and substituting the view that the Wise Man's virtue was so great that the effect of pain was microscopic and entirely negligible, had made a case for the power of virtue to ensure happiness, it did not follow that the happiness was absolutely unimpaired. Accordingly the question raised at the end of the *De Finibus*, 'whether virtue could be so great as she is if anything outside virtue be classed as a good', still stood at the beginning of the fifth book of the *Tusculan Disputations* and now after the inadequate examination in that book it is time for the New Academy to make its comment. The comment is that which Carneades made upon the dispute on the same problem between the Old School and the Stoics and it is applicable to the case of Antiochus. Whereas the Academico-Peripatetics said that 'the superiority of the goods of the soul was so marked that they eclipsed goods of the body and external goods' and the Stoics thought that 'such things were not goods at all and made all good rest with the soul', Carneades saw no vital difference:

All that the Peripatetics regarded as goods were also regarded as advantages by the Stoics; the Peripatetics nevertheless did not ascribe more value to wealth, good health and other such things than the Stoics did. Therefore he said that since the determining factor was the thing, not the words, there was no cause for disagreement. (*T.D.* v. 120.)

This means merely what Antiochus claimed all along, that the differences between himself and the Stoics were a matter of terminology and that there was no substantial difference between them on the relation of the good to external things since to allow other goods did not detract from the perfection of virtue. Thus at the end of the *Tusculan Disputations* Cicero was willing to do no more than to say that Antiochus claimed to have established a system of morality as perfect as that of the Stoics. That he felt the need of further study of this claim is shown by his argument in the *De Officiis* where the detailed examination of the Panaetian case for the compatibility of expedient action with pure morality raises the same issue as Antiochus' reconciliation of the good with external things. Finally in *De Officiis* III Cicero proclaims the Stoic and the Antiochean definitions of the good as alternatives either of which satisfies him and besides which no other definition is acceptable. Since he cannot grant their first assumption of valid perception, both ethical systems must remain for him hypothetical but he does end by recognizing Antiochus' claim to have established by hypothesis a morality as perfect as that of the Stoics. Thus we may observe the continuity of Cicero's examination of the Antiochean case from his starting point in the *Academica* where he set out to examine the thesis that the right way to re-establish the true tradition was to correct the Stoic aberrations from it. Now without himself admitting the actual superiority of Antiochus' definition of the good—since he allows the Stoic definition to stand as a reasonable alternative—Cicero shows sympathy with his case by his sustained examination of it in the *De Finibus* and the *Tusculan Disputations* and again by the examination of the Panaetian case in the *De Officiis* where the same issues are involved. For the New Academy, deeply concerned with problems of practical morality because of its interest in the theory of calculation of probability, there is an obvious appeal in Antiochus' attempt to construct a system of ethics upon a theory of human nature, and the theory of the development of the virtues from the impulses and of man's own mastery of the emotions within him must seem to the Academy more true to normal experience than the Stoic doctrine of an absolute good and the complete excision of emotions in the Wise Man.

Ciaceri[29] suggests that in choosing the topic of the *Tusculan Disputations* Cicero had the practical purpose of offering advice

29. E. Ciaceri, *Cicerone e i suoi tempi*, vol. ii, p. 324.

for the control of grief to meet the troubled political scene during the summer of 45 B.C. when the work was composed. And certainly the slaughter of the civil wars, the frequent exile, the loss of money and the prevailing uncertainty must have put the contemporary Romans and Cicero himself in need of comfort as great as that of the later French Stoics who in similar circumstances turned for consolation to Epictetus. However, I do not find any urgent reference to the immediate political scene: there is hardly any reference closer to 45 B.C. than the discussion of Pompey's final misfortune,[30] which does seem remote if the purpose were to give immediate consolation. I think that the choice of the topic was really determined by the development of Cicero's philosophic programme. After the *De Finibus* it became necessary to state Antiochus' case for a perfect morality. This the *Tusculan Disputations* did but they made only a further stage and not the end of Cicero's study, since the relation of perfect morality to expedient action was to be reviewed again in the *De Officiis*.

30. *T.D.* i. 86.

CHAPTER V

THE COSMOLOGICAL AND THEOLOGICAL WORKS

1. THEIR PLACE IN CICERO'S PROGRAMME

IN the cosmological and theological works the main theme is a sceptical examination of the Stoic theory of divine nature and activity described in *De Natura Deorum* II. This was the Middle Stoic theory of Posidonius. It was very different from original Stoicism, being a compound of Stoic, Aristotelian and Platonic elements. Indeed the Academic influences were so marked in this phase of the Middle Stoa that Schäfer proposed to call it the 'Platonizing Stoa' and its system may reasonably be called 'Stoic-Platonic'.[1] Its account of divine nature is not consistent with the materialist doctrines of original Stoicism yet traces of that materialism linger in an assumption of physical determinism. This combines with a theory of detailed providential control to deny to man any freedom of choice. It is this denial of freedom that the New Academy attacks, though in the main it accepts the Stoic-Platonic account of divine nature.

After the *Tusculan Disputations* Cicero's mind would be disposed to consider human freedom. For there the problem was man's ability to act rationally despite the forces that assail him from within such as pain, fear, and the emotions, and this would naturally suggest the problem of man's ability to make his own decisions despite the forces that assail him from without such as divine influence, fate, and physical causes. The New Academy with its doctrine of calculation of probability must uphold the ethical decision as a free act of the man himself. Then again the sustained interest in Antiochus was bound to lead to an inquiry into the Posidonian physics with which he must have had much in common since the account of the Academico-Peripatetic theory which Antiochus probably accepted for himself presented it as a conglomerate of Stoic, Platonic, and other doctrines, while the description of Posidonius' system as 'Stoic-Platonic' shows its composite nature. It is not surprising that Antiochus should share common ground with the Stoics in physics despite their differences in the other divisions of philosophy. As we have seen, he proclaimed a broad

1. M. Schäfer, 'Diogenes als Mittelstoiker', *Philologus*, xci (1936), 174 ff.; cf. van Straaten, op. cit., p. 55.

affinity with those Stoics whom he sought to correct in the *De Finibus* and the *Tusculan Disputations*. His professed aim was to modify their system so as to bring it back to the true 'Academico-Peripatetic' tradition, as he understood it. At the same time, since he claimed to be head of the contemporary Academy he could consider those members of the New Academy who opposed him as, errants in details of doctrine, who would nevertheless accept the broad physical system. Cicero was one of those who could accept this and so the dispute on the questions of detail does not prevent his general agreement with the fundamentals of the Stoic-Platonic theology. That is why the account in *De Natura Deorum* ii is particularly important in our assessment of Cicero. Although he differs from it in many points it does furnish the key to his conception of divine nature and to his outlook in religion. In fact the New Academy's criticism in *De Natura Deorum* iii addresses itself to details of the proof of providential control, and does not seek to subvert the essential basis of the Stoic-Platonic theology: the spokesman for the New Academy makes a point of declaring his belief in the gods, while Cicero himself has a warm personal concern in the religion of the Stoic-Platonic system. For it provides the sanction for the social theory which is the part of philosophy about which he cares most sincerely and which in the end proves to be the most valuable part of the morality which he commends. Both at the beginning and the end of Book i he expresses concern lest the loss of religion subvert the principles of society: 'in all probability the disappearance of piety towards the gods will remove loyalty and social union among men and justice herself, the queen of all the virtues.'[2] Thus the general position in theological and cosmological theory was that Cicero professed a broad adherence to the Stoic-Platonic system of the Middle Stoa but attempted to modify its doctrines of mechanistic determinism and detailed providential control.

I am convinced that the translation of the *Timaeus* was intended as an introduction to the other three works: my reasons will be given below. The continuity of the *De Natura Deorum, De Divinatione* and *De Fato* is clearly indicated in Cicero's catalogue of his works in *De Divinatione* ii. 3 f. and the development of the argument through the group as a whole can be traced more easily than in the other divisions of his philosophy. The scheme of the argument is this:

2. *N.D.* i. 4; cf. ibid. i. 121.

(a) The translation of the *Timaeus* explains Platonic elements in the composite Stoic-Platonic cosmology.

(b) The *De Natura Deorum* first upholds the Stoic-Platonic attitude against the Epicureans, then expounds the composite system and then debates the degree to which the gods interfere in human affairs: the extreme Stoic view that the gods interfere in every detail of man's life is here opposed by the New Academy which ascribes to man some freedom of choice.

(c) The *De Divinatione* expounds and then criticizes the arguments based on divination by which the Stoics supported their doctrine of detailed interference by the gods.

(d) The *De Fato* criticizes both the extreme Stoic doctrine of the inexorable control by fate and the inadequacy of the attempt of a more moderate Stoic like Chrysippus to reconcile determinism with the allowance to man of some freedom of choice, and advances a stronger case for freedom.

The arrangement of this group of works refutes those critics who have said that Cicero's plan in his philosophical works was simply to treat the divisions of philosophy one after the other, stating the doctrines of the main schools in each division. For one can detect, both in the development of the argument and in its relation to the previous works, a connection that would hardly be there if his purpose were merely that. The presentation of the Epicurean case in the first book of the *De Natura Deorum* leads up to the main criticism of the Stoic account. The *De Divinatione* and *De Fato* derive from problems raised in the *De Natura Deorum*. The group as a whole provides the basis for assumptions made in the earlier works whose clarification is necessary. The discussion of the problem of human freedom follows aptly upon the demonstration in the *Tusculan Disputations* of man's power to control the forces that might affect him within himself, by considering the forces that affect him from without, namely the gods and fate. All this gives a coherency to the group and a connection with the other works. Now to ascribe the credit for this to Cicero himself might be going too far and attributing to him a perspicacity which he did not possess. He was heavily indebted to his Greek authorities. He took his topics in the order which they laid down. But these were topics which they had discussed in great detail for many years: the order of their treatment was not fortuitous.

The remains of the translation of the *Timaeus* are fragmentary. There are a few lines of the introduction and then the main part of Plato's account of the creation of the world by intelligent purpose, roughly Plato's sections 27-47, with two lacunae of one and three pages respectively, i.e. Plato's sections 37c-38c and 43b-46a. Whether Cicero translated the introductory myth we do not know: it would not serve his purpose and he may have started his translation at section 27.

The relation of this translation to the rest of the group has not generally been understood and must be examined in detail. Some explanations of Cicero's purpose in making this translation have not been more penetrating than that of Hermann,[3] who held that it was intended to be incorporated in a larger work on the origin of the world. However, Reid observed the relation of the doctrine of the *Timaeus* to the general position of Antiochus[4] and it is by developing this suggestion that we may best see the significance of Cicero's translation. In the introduction Cicero refers to his dispute in the *Academica* 'contra physicos'. By this he means the preliminary survey of the Old School's physics and the final survey of physical doctrines apparently shared by the contemporary Stoics and Antiochus. Intertwined with these were various doctrines from the *Timaeus*. We have also observed the influence of the *Timaeus* in a part of the *Tusculan Disputations* apparently based on Posidonius. Thus the *Timaeus* translation forms a link between the earlier discussion of the Antiochean physics and the projected study of the Posidonian Stoic physics which Antiochus must have accepted in part.

Thus the first service of the *Timaeus* is to assist the explanation of the Old School's physics. For example there is the underlying substance of the Old School like the matrix of the *Timaeus*. With this both the Old School in the preliminary survey in the *Academica* and Plato in the *Timaeus* reconcile the admission of the four elements, earth, air, fire and water. The *Timaeus* also is the source from which are drawn various doctrines mentioned in the final survey in the *Academica* of the Antiochean and Stoic physics: compare (a) *Ac. Pr.* ii. 118: the construction of the universe out of 'a material substance which admits of all modifications', i.e. the 'matrix' of the *Timaeus*;[5]

3. K. F. Hermann, *De Interpretatione Timaei*, 1842; see Mayor, ed. *N.D.*, vol. i, p. xlii.
4. Reid, ed. *Academica*, p. 18.
5. *Timaeus* 49a.

(b) ibid. ii. 119: a Stoic description of the universe 'instinct with wisdom and intelligence' and a description of the heavenly bodies as gods: this is consistent with the *Timaeus*;[6] (c) ibid. ii. 120: the provision of things for the sake of men;[7] (d) ibid. ii. 123: the acceptance by the school which Lucullus is championing, i.e. the school of Antiochus, of 'Antipodes' and a discussion of Plato's meaning in the *Timaeus* concerning the revolution of the heavenly bodies and the earth; (e) ibid. ii. 124: Plato's tripartite division of the soul.

Besides these particular points of agreement the *Timaeus* was admirably suited to provide a broad cosmological basis for various physical assumptions in the earlier works. There the Stoics and Antiochus were shown as assuming the existence of the created world as the sum total of the physical reality, asserting its essential goodness and the ability of perception to grasp it with complete validity. But as yet there had been no statement of the composition of the physical world, no description of the mechanics of sensation on which perception of it rested, and no justification of the assumption that the created world was good. The *Timaeus* offers an explanation of all these points. In the first place with its account of the created world which 'has come to be', which can be seen and touched and has body,[8] it justifies the assumption of real existence as the object of perception. This is the world made by the creator on the model of the complete and fairest of intelligible things, the eternal model. The *Timaeus* offers a detailed description of the mechanics of sensation according to which sensation is produced by the interaction of physiological mechanism with external physical factors.[9]

In its explanation of the creator's purpose as the justification of the goodness of the world, the translation of the *Timaeus* would both look back to the *De Finibus* and anticipate arguments of the *De Natura Deorum*. In the *De Finibus* the source of the virtues was the principle of self-preservation and self-love. This principle rested on the assumed goodness of the world and of men and now in the *Timaeus* we find the basis of this assumption. The world is necessarily beautiful because it is fashioned on the model of 'the ever self-same',[10] and the creator purposed to make it 'most nearly like the in every way perfect and fairest of intelligible things'.[11] The world is the most

6. Ibid. 40a.　　　　　7. Ibid. 77a.　　　　　8. Ibid. 28b.
9. Ibid. 45d. ff., 62-8.　　10. Ibid. 28a.　　　11. Ibid. 30d.

beautiful of things that have come to be and its maker is the best of causes.[12] The creator was good, not grudging, and he desired all things to be as like as might be to himself.[13] He that is best may not effect anything but that which is most beautiful.[14]

Now with this assumption of the goodness of the created world we may link the goodness of man from which was derived the principle that it is good to preserve each part according to its natural constitution because that agrees with the desire of the creator. For the creator desired man to be: otherwise his heaven would be imperfect.[15] The gods have a purpose in granting man endowments of the senses[16] just as sources of food are created for the preservation of man.

The inclusion of Platonic doctrines in a composite system must of course denote a certain laxity of theory and we may observe that there were some differences which the eclectic spirit of the age could gloss over and others whose significance was probably not even realized. Of the first kind was the problem arising from the Stoic view, described in the preliminary survey of the *Academica,* that no result can be achieved by an incorporeal substance so that a thing which exerts force or is acted upon must be corporeal. The Stoics implied that soul is physical and they even regarded such things as virtues as physical.[17] Now the doctrines of the *Timaeus* that the soul is partly compounded of 'the same' introduces a non-corporeal conception which, if pressed, would render Plato's view of the soul incompatible with the Stoic denial of force to the non-corporeal. However, there is some obscurity. The *Timaeus,* in describing the creation of the human soul, says that the creator used the same materials as before but mixed them differently 'in the second and the third degree'.[18] This appears to leave some difference between the human soul and the realm of pure being wherein lay the creator's original copy. And again the Stoics, on their side, for all their insistence that everything is corporeal, yet distinguished two kinds of matter, τὸ ποιοῦν and τὸ πάσχον.[19] So it is possible that even here the contemporary schools because of the obscurities glossed over the differences.

Since not only is there this connection between the *Timaeus* and the physical doctrines already discussed but also there are

12. Ibid. 29a.   13. Ibid. 29e.   14. Ibid. 30a.
15. Ibid. 41b.   16. Ibid. 47c.
17. Reid, trans. *Academica,* p. 96.   18. *Timaeus* 41d.
19. Diog. Laert. vii. 134; cf. Reid, ed. *Academica,* p. 124.

many points of agreement between the *Timaeus* and the Posidonian theology, as will be explained in the next section, it may be concluded that Cicero felt that by translating the *Timaeus* he was explaining Antiochus and also giving a suitable introduction to the so-called Stoic but really composite system of Posidonius which, despite differences on the extent of the gods' providential control over man and the universe, the New Academy and Antiochus accepted in the main.

2. THE *De Natura Deorum*

The discussion in the *De Natura Deorum* is supposed to take place between the chief Roman adherents of three schools, Velleius for the Epicureans, Balbus for the Stoics and Cotta for the Academy. Cicero says in i. 17 that he himself has come not as an ally for Cotta but as an impartial listener 'under no obligation to uphold some fixed opinion' and at the end of the whole work he gives the verdict that Balbus the Stoic seems to 'approximate more nearly to a semblance of the truth' than Cotta. But this does not mean that Cicero here deserts the Academy. We have to assess his meaning from a general survey of his presentation of the Academy's case against the Stoics in this work and in the supporting works, the *De Divinatione* and *De Fato*. What he really means to say is that the Academy, to which he adheres, after raising objections to many points of detail in the Stoic arguments and while insisting that the Stoic assertion of the universality of divine providential control must be modified, does not claim to have overthrown the Stoic-Platonic theology as a whole, and in fact is willing to accept its fundamentals. This interpretation of his purpose as an attempt to vindicate human freedom rather than to subvert the main structure of the Stoic theology is supported by the prominence given in the *De Natura Deorum* and the related topics of the *De Divinatione* and *De Fato* to the Academy's criticism of the Stoic doctrines of divine providential control and fatalism. This interpretation is not shaken by the sceptical tone of the introduction to the *De Natura Deorum,* where in section 11 Cicero praises 'the purely negative dialectic which refrains from making a positive pronouncement on anything', nor by the assertion, which he puts in the mouth of Cotta at the start of the Academy's reply to the Epicureans, in i. 57-62, that though he admits his belief in the existence of gods it is impossible to arrive at any

certainty about divine nature. It is a device of Cicero's to
repudiate as unworthy of consideration a topic which he really
intends to investigate and so the preliminary denial in the *De
Natura Deorum* may be regarded as a means of focusing attention on the main question to be raised: 'What theory of divine
nature seems likely?' And at the end of this work his verdict
means that, with modification of its doctrine of providential
control, the Stoic theory seems likely.

The structure of Book I supports this interpretation fully. Its
purpose is not primarily to give a survey of the Epicurean
theology, as some have supposed, but to use the Epicurean
criticism to throw into relief those doctrines of the Stoic-Platonic
theology on which the main argument of the work as a whole
must turn.

There are four main divisions in Book I. The first (sections
18-24) is an Epicurean attack on the theology and cosmology
of the contemporary Stoics and Academy treated as 'a composite
Stoic-Platonic system despite points of difference, as between the
Platonic doctrine that the world is everlasting and the Stoic
belief in its mortality[20] or between the assumption of the
five regular solids as the basis of all other forms of matter
and the Stoic description of the world as *ardens,* derived from
Heracleitus. There are affinities with the *Timaeus,* which is
significantly mentioned at the start of this division; for example
the Stoic view that the world is endowed with mind and senses
may be compared with the view in the *Timaeus* that the world
has soul and is 'one visible living creature', while there are
similarities in the account of its shape and composition as
spherical, with its elements formed into five regular solids.[21]
Most significant of all is the confession (section 20) of a difficulty in distinguishing between the Stoic Providence ($\pi\rho\acute{o}\nu o\iota a$)
and the Platonic God who fashioned the world according to
the description in the *Timaeus.* The vigour of a large part
of the Epicurean criticism directed against the conception of
providential activity of the deity in creation shows that it is
largely on the question of divine providential activity that the
future argument of the *De Natura Deorum* will turn.

The source of this part is not certain. It is different from the
source of the next part. It is undoubtedly Epicurean since it
is similar to the argument of Lucretius v. 110-235. Now during

20. *N.D.* i. 20.
21. Cf. *Timaeus* 30-1, 33 b, 34 b-c, 53 c.

the probable time of preparation for writing the *De Natura Deorum* on 5 August 45 Cicero in a letter to Atticus (xiii. 39) asked for some treatises of Phaedrus the Epicurean. Whence it is quite likely that Phaedrus is the source of this part.[22]

There follows a survey of the theology of most schools other than the Epicurean (sections 25-43). Cicero appears to have lifted it from Zeno the Epicurean, who taught him; for a manuscript of Philodemus discovered at Herculaneum derives from the same source as the Ciceronian passage and Philodemus was also a pupil of this Zeno.[23] Here again the purpose of this Epicurean criticism is to reveal the nature of the Stoic system; this is shown in the phrase by which the survey is introduced: 'Such is a general statement of the Stoic doctrines: I will now proceed to show how they are related to the older philosophies.'[24] In short this is an Epicurean survey of the background of the contemporary Stoicism. The faults of Cicero's method of composition can be seen in the lack of relation of the discussion of the Platonic and Stoic doctrines, here treated separately, to the opening criticism of the composite Stoic-Platonic system.

Even the exposition of Epicureanism (sections 43-56), which also probably derives from Zeno, seems intended not so much to provide a positive account of the Epicurean theology as to reveal the salient points of the rival schools. By contrast with the Epicurean gods, free from passion and care, the deity of the Stoic-Platonic system is full of care and trouble. And again the attack on the conception of god as a 'prying busybody, grievously overworked,' points to a theory mainly concerned with divine activity in creation and detailed control (sections 52-6). This part is significant also for its statement that the Stoic case raises two topics (which will be developed in the next two works), the doctrine of fate as an unbroken sequence of causation and its allied doctrine of divination.

The last half of Book I is a detailed refutation of the Epicurean theology which attacks in particular its argument of universal consent, the doctrine of atomism and the argument in favour of anthropomorphism. Cicero here goes into much greater detail than his purpose requires. For his purpose was to clear the way for the examination of the Stoic-Platonic theology whose distinctive doctrines had already been stressed by the Epicurean

22. Cf. van Straaten, op. cit., pp. 240 ff.
23. Cf. Mayor ed. of *N.D.*, vol. i, pp. xlii ff.
24. Mayor's interpretation of a corrupt passage, op. cit., vol. i, p. 101.

criticism. The case against the Epicureans is assigned to Cotta, the spokesman of the Academy, but it is quite possible that Cicero's source was Posidonius. This would be reasonable since the Academy, while it will criticize Posidonius vigorously in Book III, accepted a large part of his Stoic-Platonic system and would make common cause with him in rejecting the Epicurean theology as a preparation for the examination of his case. However it is not certain that Posidonius was the source and Clitomachus has been suggested.[25]

There can be no doubt that Cicero's source for Book II was Posidonius. For it is an elaborate presentation of the contemporary Stoic theology, the Stoic-Platonic system of Posidonius, and there are many points of resemblance in this account to what we know of him from Galen and Strabo.[26]

The Stoic case is divided into four parts to prove (a) the divine existence, (b) the divine nature, (c) providential government of the universe, (d) providential government of man. Cicero arranged Book III in corresponding sections to state the criticism by the New Academy but its third part and the beginning of the fourth are now missing. This loss however is repaired by our ability to reconstruct the Academy's attitude with the aid of the *De Divinatione* and *De Fato*. The source for the New Academy's arguments in Book III was probably Clitomachus, who recorded the views of his master Carneades and wrote, of course, in reference to an earlier stage of Stoicism and not with reference to the system of Posidonius, who was a young man when Clitomachus died in 110 B.C. This causes some lack of connection between certain parts of Book III and parts of Book II to which they should relate. For example in Book III it is assumed that the Stoics denied the extension of divine care to individuals: this is a flat contradiction of the Stoic doctrine of Book II.[27] However in broad structure the two books did have four main divisions corresponding to each other, and Cicero himself would no doubt feel that by arranging Academic passages, even of an earlier period, in order of topics corresponding to the Stoic divisions he was performing his self-appointed task with diligence and in detail even if all the details did not precisely correspond. It was the comprehensiveness of the argument and

25. Cf. Rackham, ed. *N.D.* (Loeb), p. xvi; and Mayor, op. cit., vol. i, pp. lii ff.

26. Mayor, op. cit., vol. ii, pp. xviii f.; but cf. van Straaten, op. cit., pp. 243 ff., for a review of theories about the sources.

27. Cf. *N.D.* iii. 93; ii. 164.

the orderliness of its arrangement that caused Mayor to pay Book II a tribute as 'perhaps the most important contribution to theological thought which has come down to us from classical antiquity.'[28]

The composite nature of the Stoic cosmology in Book II fully supports the theory already advanced that there was a broad agreement between it and the cosmology of the 'Academico-Peripatetic' tradition as interpreted by Antiochus, while it has obviously adopted various Platonic doctrines of the *Timaeus*. It differs from orthodox Stoicism in many ways.[29] As regards physical details, in the course of a wide treatment of almost all the sciences known to the ancients, the Ciceronian account states views on the size of the sun and moon and the position of Venus and Mercury which differ from the views of the older Stoics.[30] It mentions doubts about the orthodox Stoic theory of cyclic conflagration.[31] It differs from the older Stoics in the stress that it puts on the influence of climate upon human temperament;[32] while in its arguments from the scale of existence, which state that certain plants approach towards animal life and which adopt Aristotle's view that each higher function of the soul involves the lower, it combines all the functions with rationality in men and so recognizes an irrational element in human nature, which again was unacceptable to the older Stoics. These arguments were an important part of the Antiochean case in the *De Finibus* for the continuous development of the creature as a whole with retention of all its functions, as against the Stoic abandonment of the lower faculties as each higher stage was reached.[33] Finally the acknowledgment of Plato as '*deus philosophorum*' would offend orthodox Stoics.

As for its relations to the *Timaeus* the Stoic cosmology of Book II is in broad agreement with Plato in its conception of the control of the universe by intelligence, the status of man within the universe and various details of physical structure, as may be seen in the descriptions of the divinity of the heavenly bodies and their orderly movements determined by intelligence[34] or the spherical shape of the world and the descriptions of the regular solids.[35] Naturally there remain differences, as in their

---

28. Mayor, op. cit., vol. iii, p. xviii.
29. Cf. Mayor, op. cit., vol. ii, pp. xviii ff.
30. *N.D.* ii. 52, 92, 103.   31. Ibid. ii. 85, 115, 118.
32. Ibid. ii. 17, 42.   33. *Fin.* iv. 38; v. 39; cf. *N.D.* ii. 33 f., 85.
34. Cf. *N.D.* ii. 39, 43 f. and *Timaeus* 37, 39 f.
35. Cf. *N.D.* ii. 47 and *Timaeus* 33, 53 c.

accounts of the composition of the soul.[36] This is a difference that may have been overlooked because of the difficulty of the relevant part of the *Timaeus*.

The most important similarity of the Posidonian account to the *Timaeus* is of course the broad resemblance of the Stoic Providence to the Platonic Demiurgus, which we have already observed. This could not be achieved without some blurring of distinctions and there are traces of confusion in the passages that discuss them.[37] The fact is that in the Posidonian account there is an unresolved antithesis between the materialist view of Stoicism and the spiritualist view of Plato.[38] In the original Stoic materialism intelligence was the purest and subtlest form of matter so that Zeno could even conceive of 'thinking matter' and the universe, instinct with intelligence, was a divinity capable of creative, artistic and providential activity. This may have been wrong but it was consistently based on the assumptions of pantheistic materialism. Accordingly a justification for the doctrine of providence could be rested on a conception of 'world-mind' according to which the nature of the all embracing world was 'not merely "craftsmanlike" but actually a craftsman whose foresight plans out the work to serve its use and purpose in every detail.'[39] This materialist account Posidonius partly relied upon, but then he went on to describe divine power as if it were something separate, ruling the world in the Platonic sense: 'And yet if there are gods . . . they must be animate beings, and not only animate but possessed of reason, united by a sort of social community and fellowship and ruling the one world as a united commonwealth and state.'[40]

And in many points the description of divine providential activity suggests a free and rational deity: men should 'infer the presence not merely of an inhabitant of this celestial and divine abode, but also of a ruler and governor, the architect as it were of this mighty and monumental structure.'[41]

Now this Platonic conception of the free rational deity, supported in other respects by the general description of providential activity, is not reconcilable with the materialism of which the traces linger. Nevertheless it was not on this confusion that the New Academy seized. Its criticism, which Cicero gives in Book III, concerns rather the proofs than the essential nature

36. Cf. *N.D.* ii. 18 and *Timaeus* 42.
37. *N.D.* i. 20; ii. 73 f.
38. Cf. Mayor, op. cit., vol. ii, p. 103.
39. Cf. *N.D.* ii. 57 f.
40. Ibid. ii. 78.   41. Ibid. ii. 90.

of the Stoic theology and it goes on to direct its main attack at the Stoic account of the extent of providential control. For it says that the Stoics go too far when they assert detailed control of every aspect of human life which deprives man of any freedom at all.

We observed above that at the beginning of the Academy's criticism of the Epicureans in Book I Cicero took pains to assert that the Academy did in fact believe in gods though it had doubts about their nature. Similarly he is careful at the end of the Academy's examination of the Stoic description of the nature of the gods to make Cotta disclaim any pretence of having overthrown the Stoic case. So in iii. 93 Cotta ends his speech by saying: 'This in general terms is what I have to say about the nature of the gods. My purpose has not been to disprove it but to make you realize how obscure it is and how difficult to explain.' And again in section 95, he makes Cotta say: 'On my side I only desire to be refuted and in my arguments I sought to discuss the doctrines rather than to pronounce judgment on them: I am sure that you can easily defeat me.'

In keeping with this attitude the Academy's argument on divine existence and nature is inconclusive. It abounds in syllogistic reasoning and is intricate, but substantially it is shallow. To students of religious theory it is interesting as an examination of the logical grounds of various proofs of divine existence and nature, but in the end it does not subvert the Posidonian cosmology.

Cicero's own verdict we have already observed: he thought that the Stoic discourse 'approximated more nearly to a semblance of the truth.' This verdict he repeats later, in the *De Divinatione* (i. 8 f., ii. 148). It is no casual and insignificant utterance. It means that Cicero himself accepted the fundamentals of the Posidonian cosmology; as we have seen, it incorporated various Platonic elements which Cicero, as a member of the New Academy, could accept and he did not admit that the sceptical arguments in Book III sufficed to overthrow it. But Cicero could reasonably say that he accepted the Stoic theology in general without committing himself to the doctrines which the Stoics carried to the extreme. The *De Divinatione* and *De Fato* are intended to qualify his acceptance by rejecting the doctrine of detailed providential control which, as they show, would result in the complete negation of human freedom.

K

Accordingly it is to the Stoic-Platonic system of Book II that we must turn to assess the conception of divine nature held by the New Academy and by Cicero himself. Here the debt to the *Timaeus* is great, although lingering influences of original Stoicism prevent the identification of the Stoic Providence with the Platonic Demiurgus from being complete. For example the old pantheistic identification of God with the world causes uncertainty in the Posidonian account as to whether God is supposed to be in the world or out of it, although our decision on this point makes a great difference to our conception of God and the world.[42] Cicero's classification of the Peripatetics with the Stoics in theology might be taken as evidence that the predominant conception was of a God separate from the universe which he creates; for in Aristotle God lives apart from the world, directing his activity upon himself and influencing the world only in so far as it is drawn to him by desire. But this evidence is inconclusive because of the degeneracy of Peripateticism in the era of Posidonius. As for the *Timaeus* there are limitations in the conception of the Demiurgus which prevent it from attaining the conception of the perfectly free creator of Christian doctrine, although it has implications in regard to creation and providential control that are lacking in the rest of Greek theology.[43] In the first place Plato may not have really meant a creator god distinct from the universe he is represented as making: this is the implication of Cornford's view that the account in the *Timaeus* may be mythical.[44] In any case it imposes limitations on the creator. Plato's Demiurgus is not an omnipotent creator: he has two restrictions: the material on which he works already exists, so that his task is not to create it but to 'inform' it; and in the task of information he must be guided by the eternal model. Neither forms nor matter are products of the creator's will.[45] Thus although the *Timaeus* exceeds the rest of Greek theology by attributing to God a power of efficient causation[46] and does anticipate the Christian doctrine of creation, it falls below the Christian conception in which creation is free from limitations.

42. Cf. M. B. Foster, 'Christian Theology and Modern Science of Nature', *Mind*, xliv (1935).
43. Cf. M. B. Foster, *Political Philosophies of Plato and Hegel*, p. 136.
44. Cornford, *Plato's Cosmology*, p. 38; cf. *Timaeus* 29-30.
45. Cornford, op. cit., p. 37; Foster, *Political Philosophies of Plato and Hegel*, pp. 137 ff., 180 ff.
46. Foster, ibid., p. 139.

Nor is the doctrine of the *Timaeus* free from elements of paganism if, with Foster, we regard paganism as the failure to distinguish God from nature.[47] For Plato confuses the conceptions of God as artificer and God as father of the world: in so far as God is father of nature, it must exhibit his nature. By contrast the Christian God is the artificer who makes the world and, since he is not its father, it does not exhibit his nature.

It is possible that Cicero, who accepted doctrines without probing into their metaphysical grounds, did not realize all these implications of the *Timaeus* and formed for himself a conception of an independent deity that was even more free than the Platonic conception and so, while the Platonic theory made some advance towards the Christian conception of a free and benevolent creator but still fell short of it, Cicero from sentiment, but without metaphysical justification, went beyond Plato. But even so his broad acceptance of the Posidonian system would impose limitations which would make his conception of God different from the Christian conception. In so far as he accepted the Posidonian doctrine Cicero was not a monotheist. Providential control, as he describes it, is the activity not of one supreme God but of 'the gods'. This is consistent with the *Timaeus* in which first the 'created gods' have the specific task of making man but then merge into the general divine activity so that the difference between them and the Demiurgus is obliterated.[48] Now so far as the created gods are intermediaries between man and the supreme deity—before the difference is obliterated—their function is very different from that of Christ in Christianity. Christ was sent to redeem the world and to rescue man from the sin implanted by Satan. But in the *Timaeus* the Demiurgus specifically employed the created gods in the making of men because 'if they are made and endued with life by my own hands, they will be the equal of the gods.'[49] And then he went on to mix the soul of man 'yet not in the same purity, but in the second and third degree.' By contrast Christianity supposes that God made man in his own image and used Christ as an intermediary not to implant imperfection but to redeem man by grace. Hence the emotional warmth of Christianity which is lacking in Plato, and in Cicero who followed him.

47. Foster, 'Christian Theology and Modern Science of Nature', *Mind*, 1935.
48. Cornford, op. cit., p. 38.   49. *Timaeus* 41 c.

Certainly Cicero attributes a certain degree of providential control to divine benevolence. But we must beware of reading into this the Christian conception of 'overflowing love' and it is again in the *Timaeus* that we must seek the key of Cicero's meaning. We find it in the reason for creation: 'So, being without jealousy, he desired that all things should come as near as possible to being like himself.'[50] Now to be 'without jealousy' is a very different thing from feeling 'overflowing love' and one must here resist the influence of Christian thought: 'It is not fair either to Plato or to the New Testament to ascribe the most characteristic revelations of the Founder of Christianity to a pagan polytheist.'[51] Thus for the most part Cicero's argument has the coldness of a theological system rather than the warmth of religious acceptance. His supreme deity is an intelligent power which has constructed the world. But this God is not an object of worship and man is bound to him by an intellectual relationship, not by emotional bonds.

As for the relation of man to God, the Platonic elements in this system which Cicero accepts support his revulsion against the Stoic doctrine that imperfect man can have no participation in the divine life except that uncomprehending participation that comes from blind submission to fate. Although Plato's God acts from intellectual motives and without the warmth of divine grace, the essence of his ethics is that man's reason is divine and that men can rise by intellectual progress and come close to the divine.[52] Man has defects—may 'err of his own will'[53] and, to remedy emotion, must 'correct the orbits in the head which were corrupted at birth'[54]—yet he has motions within him akin to the divine, and 'God gave us vision in order that we might observe the circuits of intelligence in the heaven and profit by them for the revolutions of our thought.'[55] Thus in Plato man may aspire to divine excellence. But it is doubtful if Cicero fully appreciated the significance of the Platonic epistemology. As we have seen in the *De Finibus* and *Tusculan Disputations* he did not envisage a human intelligence able to comprehend the intelligible world although he sympathized with Antiochus' view that the mortal with the highest attainable wisdom can grapple with external factors and achieve happiness. Thus although Cicero might claim less than Plato for man's ability

50. *Timaeus* 29 e.   51. Cornford, op. cit., p. 35.   52. Ibid., p. 34.
53. *Timaeus* 42 e.   54. Ibid. 90 d.   55. Ibid. 47 b.

to reach the divine level, he did conceive of an approach to divine activity which in itself was more truly free than the divine activity of the Stoic theory. For even though the perfect Wise Man of Stoic theory (if he anywhere existed) might reach the divine level by virtue of the kinship of the human soul with the divine, yet the Stoic god was bound by the limitations of pantheistic materialism. By contrast the god of Plato could act with greater freedom, though not without some restrictions, and accordingly the human freedom envisaged by Cicero, since it approached the divine, was greater. God being free, a man who approaches his wisdom is likewise free. Thus Cicero, following the Antiochean theory of the *Tusculan Disputations,* makes morality very much a matter of man's own efforts: he raises him from the submissiveness of the Stoic to a reliance on his own power. Even Chrysippus saw the need to introduce some element of freedom into Stoicism as the *De Fato* shows and Cicero showed that it was necessary to go beyond him.

But Cicero still lacks the sense of aspiration of the Christian. In Christianity man is made in the image of God and hopes for personal immortality: hence an ecstatic acceptance of faith. Cicero had no hope of personal immortality: if the soul survived it was not a personal survival: and the approach to God was intellectual. Man's imperfections were intellectual and were to be remedied by reason. Cicero's conception of God was certainly an advance towards the Christian conception. It may be compared with the view of Philo of Alexandria. But it fell short of Philo and he again belonged to philosophy as well as to religion.[56] Cicero knew none of the ecstatic strivings of the soul to free itself from the conditions of present life and return to God. His denial of divination would reject revelation which in Christianity is an important means of divine assistance to man.

The Posidonian account accepted the doctrine of the goodness of the world and of man. For this it had the authority both of Stoicism and of the *Timaeus.* In the *Timaeus* the fact that the world is created by intelligence and pervaded by intelligence explains why all its parts are combined as is best for beauty and utility and why nature exhibits a skill 'infinitely beyond the reach of art'.[57] Its goodness derives from the eternal model and from the creator's purpose. But for the perfection of the universe the existence of man is also essential, for 'if mortal creatures are

56. Lebreton and Zeiller, *History of the Primitive Church,* pp. 21-4.
57. Mayor, op. cit., vol. ii, p. 198; *N.D.* ii. 86.

not born heaven will be imperfect, for it will not contain every sort of living creature, as it must if it is to be sufficiently perfect.'[58] Hence are sanctioned the provision of food and other measures for the preservation of men. In fact while mechanistic and materialistic doctrines in modern science suppose an essential conflict of religion and science Plato will have none of it nor does he assert a fundamental enmity between man and the natural cosmic order such as is assumed in theories of evolution.[59] Now in Posidonius some of the restrictions of Stoicism still lingered but Cicero, refusing to allow a completely determined chain of causes and effects, here followed Plato. Thus he does not teach submissiveness as did the strict Stoics but from his belief in man's goodness, coupled with his insistence on man's ability to make free decisions, upholds human dignity.

3. The *De Divinatione* and *De Fato*

There is no doubt that Cicero intended these two works to be linked closely with the *De Natura Deorum*. As early as *De Natura Deorum* i. 55, he mentioned the doctrines of divination and fate as necessary corollaries of the Stoic theology. The catalogue of works at the beginning of *De Divinatione* ii expressly stated the intention to complete the discussion of the gods and divination by an examination of fate. There are various references which interlink the three works.[60] But more important as a proof of Cicero's intention is the continuity of the argument. One of the main proofs that the Stoics could advance of detailed divine intervention in the affairs of man was divination, for divination was supposed to be rendered possible by communication by God to man of knowledge otherwise beyond his ken. Then if it could be proved that divination was authentic and frequently occurred the Stoic case for providential government, advanced in the second book *De Natura Deorum*,

58. *Timaeus* 41 b.
59. Cf. Foster, op. cit., *Mind*, 1935; and Huxley's view in *Evolution and Ethics, 1893-1943*, 1947.
60. *N.D.* ii. 162; iii. 93; *Div.* i. 9, 117, 127; ii. 19. I attach no importance to the objection of certain editors to the validity of *Div.* i. 127. They argue the inconsistency of putting in the mouth of the Stoic speaker the promise to show 'that all things happen by fate' with the actual treatment in the *De Fato* where we find no such positive demonstration. But surely it is reasonable to expect that at this stage Cicero would be satisfied to note the agreement of the various schools on the need to examine the topic of fate, without binding himself to the form of treatment.

would be strengthened. If on the other hand Cicero, by using
the arguments of the New Academy, was able to refute the
authenticity of the alleged instances of divination, he would
be qualifying his general acceptance of the Stoic theology by
refusing to support its extreme claims. That is to say, while
still accepting the Stoic belief in the nature of the gods he would
not grant that they interfered in the details of human life.

But Cicero needed to do more than challenge alleged instances
of divination. He had to attack also the theory of determinism
that underlay the Stoic account of divination. Here we see the
effect in the Posidonian system of the unresolved antithesis
between the lingering materialist influences of original Stoicism
and the spiritualist elements adopted from Plato. For although
this late Stoic account of divine providential activity suggested
a free and rational deity it persisted in holding that all things
are held under the universal control of fate. Thus divination,
said to be valid by virtue of revealing the divine plan, was
really valid only by virtue of interpreting part of the inexorable
chain of fate. Accordingly Cicero passed on in the *De Fato* to
consider the doctrine of determinism. But his treatment of the
problem there is complicated by the fact that Chrysippus, in an
endeavour to make some concession to common sense, had tried
to modify the Stoic determinism in such a way as to allow some
power of choice to man. Therefore much of the argument
of the *De Fato* will deal with the logical indefensibility of
Chrysippus' attempt but it does also reveal Cicero's challenge
to determinism and his belief in some degree of human freedom.

The main part of the *De Divinatione* is taken up by debate
on the authenticity of instances of divination. But we can detect
the underlying Stoic theory which consistently with the composite Stoic-Platonic system of *De Natura Deorum* II rests partly
on the assumption of benevolent divine intervention and partly
on the doctrine of a physical system in which everything is
determined by physical causes. Thus divination will be in part
a matter of revelation and in part a process of interpretation of
natural signs. These two divisions are called natural divination
(prediction by the soul's inherent power, as in dreams or states
of inspiration) and artificial (prediction based on observation
of phenomena, as in soothsaying and augury).[61] Together they
assume the most intricate interconnection of physical causes

61. *Div.* ii. 26.

and the most detailed intervention by divine power in human affairs. Cicero's first concern is with that view which presents divination as one form of the working of providence: according to this view the demonstration of successful divination is taken by the Stoics to support the general case for providential government of the world. This part of the Stoic case rests on the doctrine of the diffusion throughout the universe of an intelligent force which may be described variously as the will of the gods or the force which controls all things:

> If we take as granted this assumption that there is a divine power which pervades the lives of men, we can readily understand the principle directing those premonitory signs which we see come to pass.[62] For the choice of a sacrificial victim may be determined by an intelligent force (*vis quaedam sentiens*) diffused throughout the universe.[63]

Here this supreme force is supposed to intervene in a matter so small as the choice of a victim. This force is assumed to be good because of the Stoic doctrine of the perfection of the universe: it follows that the gods' attitude is benevolent and that they grant some power of divination to man as a blessing to enable him to interpret part of the divine will.[64]

The explanation of this communication lies in the Stoic doctrine of the kinship of the human soul with the divine. Outside the human soul is the divine soul from which it is derived.[65] 'Since the universe is wholly filled with the eternal intelligence and divine mind, it must be that human souls are influenced by their contact with divine souls.'[66] In those passages where there is discussion of the requisites for communication there is some admixture of Platonic doctrine: we meet the familiar view that communication will take place most easily when the soul is in its purest state and this may well occur during sleep since, when men are awake, their souls are subject to the demands of everyday life and are withdrawn from divine association, being hampered by the chains of the flesh. There is a good deal of Platonic argument of this kind but the basic theory of the kinship of the human soul and the divine is essentially Stoic.

62. Falconer's trans. of '*non difficile est, quae fieri certe videmus, ea qua ratione fiant, suspicari*', in his edition of *Div.*
63. *Div.* i. 118.
64. N.B. *Div.* i. 117, 120, and the very full Stoic account of divination as a form of providence in section 82, repeated verbatim in ii. 101 f.
65. *Div.* i. 70.
66. Ibid. i. 110.

Now alongside the view of divination as a form of revelation is the other view of it as interpretation of natural causes. Within the original Stoic framework of pantheistic materialism these views could be reconciled because the divine plan meant nothing more than the physical operation of the whole system of the order of things, and traces of the original attitude persist:

> Nothing has happened which was not destined to happen and likewise nothing is destined to happen unless nature contains the efficient causes of it. From this we realize that fate is that which is called, not ignorantly but scientifically, the eternal cause of things—the cause of things past, things present and things to come. (*Div.* i. 126.)

The intellect which could discern the links that join each cause with every other cause would never be mistaken in any prediction: it would in fact have the knowledge which is proper to a god. Man, denied this knowledge, must presage the future by means of certain signs which indicate what will follow them. Thus divination implies the ability to interpret some part of the chain of causes, controlled as they are by fate.

From this account it can be seen that the doctrine of divination is based in part upon a theory of determinism and implies ultimately the negation of human freedom. For Cicero and the New Academy, and likewise Antiochus, if he upheld a doctrine of freedom, it was important to challenge it. But in his answer to the Stoics, in Book II, Cicero deals superficially with matters of theory. He shows that he is willing to admit a certain measure of interconnection between things and a general divine control but he says that the soothsayer's art claims a fantastic degree of interconnection and of detailed intervention. Thus he concedes a wide natural connection between things apparently unrelated,[67] but thinks it ridiculous to suppose a connection between 'that divine system of nature whose great and glorious laws pervade all space and regulate all motion' and changes in the heart and lungs of a sacrificial ox.[68] Similarly it is going too far to suggest that the divine will will intervene at sacrifice to provide appropriate omens in individual cases.[69] Thus when no heart was found in the bull which Caesar sacrificed it is wiser to suppose that it was overlooked because disease had robbed it of its resemblance to a heart than to suppose that at

67. *Div.* ii. 34.   68. Ibid. ii. 29.   69. Ibid. ii. 36.

the moment of sacrifice the gods removed the heart—for it could
not have lived to the moment of sacrifice without one.[70]

The effect of such argument is to give general support to the
New Academy's limitation, in the *De Natura Deorum*, of the
Stoic claims for detailed providential government. But it rests
on opinion rather than on demonstrated proof. Cicero adds a
repudiation, step by step, of the syllogistic proof of the Stoics
which linked belief in divination with belief in benevolent and
provident gods and which is repeated verbatim in this book.[71]
In addition to that he has some theoretical arguments of a
slight and sophistical nature, for example the argument of the
superfluity of divine communication to man (since the Stoic
system in any case would deprive man of free choice), or the
argument that, if gods did intend to send messages, they would
make them clearer. He is able to attack Stoic arguments on
interpretation of portents by showing that to assume such
uncaused phenomena is inconsistent with their whole theory of
interconnected causes. And the opening discussion of the consistency of the Stoics' allowance of divination is similar. This
is a sophistical argument which requires explanation. It says
that either things are in the sphere of an expert who can trace
causes and make predictions from an established body of knowledge (in physics, ethics, logic, politics, etc.)—in which case there
is no place for divination—or else things happen by chance. But
if the Stoics suppose that divination operates in the field of
things that happen by chance (*res fortuitae*), their definition
rules out the possibility of valid prediction. Now this argument
supposes a definition of '*res fortuitae*' which the Stoics could not
accept. To the Stoic all things are bound by the series of causes:
they are determined and cannot happen by chance. But there
will be many things whose causes man cannot trace: to man
they appear fortuitous, but strictly, in Stoic theory, they should
not be so called since divine intelligence understands them and
uses divination as the means to let man know of them as things
beyond his ken. Cicero's argument would not shake the Stoic
case unless it extended to a more serious examination—not here
attempted—of the doctrine of the universal chain of causes.

From the superficial nature of these arguments it can be seen
that Cicero's purpose is not seriously to tackle the Stoics in the
details of cosmological theory but rather to rely on a general

70. Ibid. ii. 37.   71. *Div.* i. 82; ii. 101 f.

repudiation of alleged instances of correct divination and a broad denial that divination is sufficiently established to afford proof of detailed divine intervention. Thus apart from these rather trivial incursions into theory Cicero's case consists almost entirely of assaults on the credit of the various forms of divination. It is easy to discredit predictions from lightning. For natural phenomena are due to natural causes and happen without regularity. Then why should we look to them for signs of future events? 'It is passing strange, if Jupiter warns us by means of thunderbolts, that he sends so many to no purpose.'[72] Many prophecies of soothsayers don't come true, and when they do how can we show that the agreement of an event with prophecy was not due to chance? Then again what good would it be for the gods to warn us of things we cannot understand without an interpreter and which in any case we cannot avoid?[73]

A similar argument applies to auspices and astrology. They are not reliable and if in any case a prophecy is fulfilled we should look for natural causes rather than suppose some subtle, inconceivable force.[74] In the course of this discussion Cicero has to justify his own acceptance of the post of augur. In part he urges expediency: the Romans maintain augural practices out of respect for the opinion of the masses. In short, augury is a practical means of influencing popular opinion. But he goes further when he claims that augury as practised officially in Rome is in some degree an art depending on long and systematic observation. By contrast other nations reduce augury to superstition rather than to art because they base it on divination, understood in the Academic sense as the 'power to predict things whose causes cannot be traced': 'What then is the nature of an art which makes prophets out of birds that wander about—now here, now there—and makes the action of man depend on the song or flight of birds?'[75] Moreover the other nations ascribe the power of augury not to dignified men, like the members of the Roman college, but to people devoid of learning: the Etruscans ascribed the whole origin of their system to an elfish boy ploughed up out of the ground. Again there is inconsistency among augurs since in some countries favourable signs are said to be on the left but in others they are said to be on the right. To sum up, Cicero thinks that although the Romans raise

72. Ibid. ii. 44. 73. Ibid. ii. 49-55.
74. Ibid. ii. 94-5. 75. Ibid. ii. 80.

augury to a degree of respectability and have reasons of state
for practising it, it cannot justly claim to be a valid source of
information from the gods.

As for the 'natural' forms of divination—dreams and inspiration—Cicero asserts that the fulfilment of prophecies can be
ascribed to the intervention of luck and, as regards the claim
that man in frenzy may give correct prediction, asks the pertinent
question how a man who has lost human intelligence can be
invested by frenzy with the intelligence of the gods. Even such
supposedly established works of frenzy as the Sibylline books
can be shown to be works of deliberate art, for 'throughout the
entire work each prophecy is embellished with an acrostic so
that the initial letters of each of the lines give the subject of
that particular prophecy. Such a work comes from a writer who
is not frenzied, who is painstaking, not crazy.'[76] We have already
observed in Book I the use of the Platonic argument that in
sleep the body may be in a state of purity and better disposed
to act in communion with other souls: that is to say, the purest
state of sleep should facilitate communication between human
souls and the divine. But even so it does not follow that dreams
are in fact communicated from a divine source. It is possible
to show that many dreams could not possibly come from such
a source, and if occasionally one does dream something that
turns out to be true, may this not be like the shooter who shoots
at a mark all day long and just occasionally hits it? Surely if
the gods desired man to foresee the future they would grant him
that power or at least would send him messages when he is
awake. In short, obscure messages by means of dreams are
utterly inconsistent with the dignity of the gods.[77] Finally after
a long discussion Cicero decides that dreams cannot be used
as evidence of divine communication to man in support of the
general Stoic theory of providential government.[78]

It is important to observe that what Cicero is challenging
throughout the discussion is the Stoic theory of detailed interference by the gods and not their existence. In the *De Natura
Deorum* the relevance of the doctrine of divination to the theory
of the existence of the gods has been raised several times and
at the beginning of the *De Divinatione* he has taken pains to
stress his belief that the gods do exist.[79] He repudiates the Stoic

76. Ibid. ii. 112.   77. Ibid. ii. 121-6.
78. Ibid. ii. 147.   79. *N.D.* ii. 7-11; iii. 14; *Div.* i. 9 f.

claim that belief in divination is essential to belief in the gods.[80] At the end of this work he makes his attitude very clear. He has directed his argument against superstition which 'has taken advantage of human weakness to cast its spell over the mind of every man':

> But I want it clearly understood that by destroying super- stition one does not destroy religion. For it is the function of wisdom to preserve the institutions of our forefathers by preserving their sacred rites and ceremonies. Moreover the celestial order and the beauty of the universe compel me to confess that there is some excellent and eternal being com- manding the respect and admiration of the human race.[81]

Having conceded the existence of gods while limiting the extent of their intervention in human affairs, Cicero must next examine the other aspect of the Stoic theory of detailed provi- dential government, the doctrine of universal control by fate. One would expect that on this subject, so intimately related to the whole problem of man's freedom, Cicero would speak out freely. But he presents his argument in a manner so complicated that it is only by examining it in detail that we can interpret his general purpose.

The *De Fato* has come to us in a fragmentary state, so much so that some editors have thought that what we have is the remains of two books. Their theory is based on: (a) an apparent promise in two passages of the *De Divinatione* (i. 127; ii. 19) to give an exposition of the Stoic doctrine of fate: since this does not appear in the work as we have it, they suppose it was in a missing part: but it is not right to suppose that at the time of writing the *De Divinatione* Cicero had a precise plan for his arrangements of the *De Fato*; (b) a phrase in section 40, '*in adsensionibus, quas prima oratione tractavi*'; now '*prima oratione*' means the 'beginning of my argument' and it is going too far to suppose that it implies a missing 'Book i'. We can reconstruct the plan of the work quite well on the assumption that it was written in one book from which parts have dropped out.

The interpretation of the work will be aided by a knowledge of what the schools called the 'dominative argument'.[82] It turned upon three propositions which asserted: (a) that everything

80. *Div.* ii. 41.   81. Ibid. ii. 148.
82. Levin, *Six Lectures Introductory to the Philosophical Writings of Cicero*, pp. 76, 88 ff.

which has happened has occurred in conformity with a fixed law; (b) that all nature *either* acts in conformity with immutable law *or* it does not; (c) that what neither has occurred nor will occur yet might happen. Now to admit two of these implies the rejection of the third and thus the Megarian school, represented in the *De Fato* by the views of Diodorus, which accepted the first two, was the main proponent of the doctrine of absolute necessity. By rejecting the third proposition it ruled out the discussion of possibility. For a true proposition must state a necessity and can imply only one possibility—what inevitably must happen. Thus 'that alone is possible which is or will be true; whatever will be he says to be necessary; whatever will not be he calls impossible.'[83]

It is clear that the case for freedom must turn upon the acceptance or modification of certain of these propositions and that is why Cicero's discussion deals mainly with problems of logic. Now the first part of the *De Fato* was probably a criticism of the first proposition. For after the fragmentary introduction we retain, in sections 5-11, what appears to be the end of a discussion of divination as proof of universal control by fate based on the Stoic conception of συμπάθεια as the necessary physical interaction of all things. This consists first of a refutation of alleged instances of the intervention of fate. Many of these can be explained by mere coincidence while others are flimsy to the point of fiction; for example the killing of Philip by a sword on whose handle was the figure of a quadriga could only by a flight of fancy be taken as vindication of the prophecy that he would be killed by a quadriga. In short, why should one assert the intervention of fate in happenings attributable to luck or to natural causes? There follows a more serious examination of the question whether one may admit general causality without admitting control by fate. Here the critic of fatalism admits that interconnection between things is demonstrable but denies that it entails control by fate: to use the Latin terms, *contagio naturae* does not imply *vis fatalis*. Thus although natural causes must be allowed some modifying effects, they do not have the final determining influence upon action:

> If we granted that, then nothing would be in our power. Certainly it does not depend on us that we are bright or dull, strong or puny. But a man who accordingly thinks that we

83. *De Fato*, 13.

don't have the power to decide whether we are to sit down or walk does not realize the true sequence of cause and effect. (*De Fato, 9.*)

Such refutation of fatalism on behalf of the champions of freedom would well suit Cicero's general plan. He needed to consider more fully the implications of the admission which he had made in the *De Divinatione* that there is some degree of interconnection between things. The theoretical discussion from the New Academy's side in the *De Divinatione* was slight, as we saw. It would be appropriate for him to follow it with a more serious investigation of the theory of fate and his inquiry has now passed beyond the mere topic of divination as such to the wider question of universal government. We must observe that the acceptance, in this part, of physical interconnection without admitting control in every detail is similar to Cicero's admission of benevolent divine control without detailed intervention.

But the New Academy did not have to argue the case entirely by itself for on the Stoic side an attempt was made to modify the extreme rigour of the doctrine of fatalism so as to allow 'something in the power of man'. This was the attempt of Chrysippus. Cicero's plan was to criticize Chrysippus so as to show that he himself both rejected the strict Stoic determinism and went beyond Chrysippus' modification of it.

From the equation of true, possible and necessary Diodorus argued that the contrary of a true prediction was an impossibility. Consider the proposition 'If a person is born at the rising of the Canicula, he will not die in the sea.' If this proposition is true then Diodorus argues that the contradictory of its second part—'he will die in the sea'—is impossible. For in a valid proposition, i.e. one whose consequent cannot be denied without contradiction of the antecedent, the necessity of the antecedent implies the necessity of the consequent.[84] In short, every false utterance about the future expresses an impossibility. Hence the Megarians maintain what is called the 'principle of contradictories': 'every proposition must be true or false'. According to them there could be no variation of what is possible. If the proposition was true it must be necessary and any variation was impossible.

For the Megarians, who derived from the Parmenidean logic, there was no question of causality because things did not act

84. Yon, *Du Destin*, p. xx.

one upon another and a given essence contained in itself its whole future. But when the Stoics superimposed on this logic their doctrine of the physical interaction of all things they were bound, in strict theory, to a complete physical and logical determinism. Then from the Megarian identification of real necessity with logical necessity it came to be accepted that the doctrine of fate had its rational explanation in the logic, so that in the *De Fato* the Stoics say that the doctrine of fate is imposed by the principle of contradictories: if the principle of contradictories is conceded then, say the Stoics, one must grant the chain of causality. That is why the main argument of this book—whose purpose is the vindication of human freedom—turns upon a logical problem.

Now granted that a given prediction is true, Chrysippus desired to find some way of retaining its validity while allowing the variability of its consequent or, to refer it to the terms of the 'dominative argument', he wanted to uphold the third proposition which the Megarians rejected. This is the point of the statement in the introductory section that discussion of the axioms of the present topic involves the question of the 'possibles'.

The first step was to attack the first proposition and to separate the 'true' from the 'necessary'. The sympathy of the Academy with such an attempt has already been shown in our interpretation of the purpose of the incomplete early sections. But it did not feel convinced of the validity of Chrysippus' argument. For he first attempted to separate 'true' and 'necessary' by changing the form of the proposition: 'There is no person who is born at the rising of the Canicula and who must die in the sea.'[85] By this means he sought to avoid positive statement of a condition whose fulfilment would necessitate the stated consequence. But the dissatisfaction of the Academy is revealed in a very full discussion of the logical possibility of making a distinction between 'true' and 'necessary'. Here Cicero shows that for one who does not accept determinism the distinction is permissible, but that Chrysippus is inconsistent in making the distinction while maintaining the chain of causality. This part of the argument opens with a statement of the extreme implications of the view of Diodorus. If true, possible and necessary are synonymous, then all the petty details of a happening are

85. *De Fato*, 15.

determined just as surely as the main event: it will be equally true to say 'Scipio will die' and to say 'Scipio will die a violent death, in bed, at night.' Against this there is set the view which the New Academy wished to establish, that there *is* a difference between 'true' and 'necessary'. The argument runs thus: we may grant that it is true to say 'Carneades goes to the Academy', but surely that does not imply that the event is determined by an extended series of causes:

> It has always been true to say that Epicurus will die, after living 72 years, in the archonship of Pytharatus: yet there were no causes fixed by fate why that must happen so: but because it happened it was certain to happen as it did. Those who say that the future is immutable, that what is true in the future cannot become false, do not establish the necessity of fate. They only say what the words mean. (*De Fato,* 19 f.)

The suggestion is that, if the truth of a future proposition is granted it is just as true as if it expressed a past event: but we cannot conclude from this that it must be considered necessary. The New Academy accepts the principle of contradictories that every proposition is true or false. But this does not bind it to the acceptance of necessity.

On the other hand Chrysippus uses the principle of contradictories as the justification of causality. 'A true future thing cannot be a thing which has not causes determining its happening; therefore what is true must have causes; so when it happens it will happen by fate.'[86] He clings to the doctrine of fate and the chain of causality but at the same time tries to separate fate from necessity. The attempt is logically indefensible.

Cicero's case requires an examination of causes. First he quotes Carneades' distinction of internal and external causes. Carneades was willing to grant that there is no uncaused movement. But he did not bind himself by this to admit that every happening results from external prior causes. Thus it is only a manner of speech to say that an event is uncaused. Just as we say that a vase is empty, meaning 'empty of water, but not empty in an absolute sense', so, when we say that an event is uncaused, we may merely mean 'without external cause'. Thus voluntary movement is within man's power and has internal causes, but is free from external causes.

86. Ibid. 26; cf. 20.

L

By this expansion of the conception of *cause* Carneades thought it possible to free the doctrine that every proposition must be true or false from the implications of determinism, asking in effect why every proposition should not be true or false without implying that everything happens by fate.

The argument for the distinction of 'true' and 'necessary' is supported by a demonstration that there are 'fortuitous' causes. Cicero argues that, while upholding the principle of contradictories, one may allow that every proposition is true or false without insisting that, if past, it has been determined by an immutable chain of causes or that, if future, there exist immutable causes to prevent it from happening in a way different from that in which it will happen. In short, the true is that which has happened or will happen, but that does not mean that it must happen by necessary causes. As an example he takes a proposition, 'Cato will come to the Senate', of the same order as that used previously, 'Carneades will go to the Academy.' He says that the causes which make the truth of the proposition are fortuitous, not being inherent in the natural order of things; that is to say they stand outside the chain of fate.

The doctrine of fortuitous causes is further supported by close argument whose purpose is to overcome the dilemma proposed by Chrysippus: 'Either you must admit that everything is controlled by fate or you must allow that something can happen without cause.' Carneades was able to admit that everything has a cause without admitting that that cause must be derived from eternal causes. Hence further support for the distinction of 'true' and 'necessary'; for some events are true from all eternity yet their causes are not 'founded in the order of nature'. For example there was no reason in nature why Oedipus should kill his father and consequently even Apollo could not predict it. Prophecy can only be of those events which have their efficient causes in the order of nature. This argument brings in the distinction between the effective and necessary cause (*cum quo*) and that without which a thing could not be (*sine quo*), e.g. the sum of circumstances which precede it. From all eternity it was true that 'Philoctetes will be abandoned on an island.' But, says Carneades, all the series of past events was not the cause for his abandonment on Lemnos: it was only when the effective cause occurred—when he was bitten by the serpent—that he was abandoned. Here then is a true proposition that was not necessary because its fulfilment depended on a fortuitous cause.

In the New Academy's case there have been four main assertions: (a) there is something in the power of man, (b) truth
may be distinguished from necessity, (c) there is a distinction
between internal and external causes, (d) there are fortuitous
causes. These assertions cannot be said to have been established
adequately by proof; for even the distinction of truth and
necessity, to which great attention was given, depends on the
denial of determined causes rather than the disproof of them,
while a thorough-going determinist would contest the separation
of the so-called 'fortuitous' causes from the others. Nevertheless
these four assertions show clearly that the New Academy upheld
the doctrine of freedom however incomplete its demonstration
of it may have been.

Now although it is their bearing on the problem of freedom
that constitutes the real importance of these assertions, Cicero
maintains his pre-occupation with the logical inquiry. That is
why he ends this part of the *De Fato* with an emphatic statement that he acknowledges the principle of contradictories
according to which every proposition is either true or false
without admitting the identity of 'true' and 'necessary'; 'Logic
herself will force us to admit that there are things which are
true from all eternity and that they are not fastened to eternal
causes and are free from the necessity of fate.'[87] On the other
hand Chrysippus, who tried to do the same thing and to take
a stand mid-way between fatalism and free choice, could not
legitimately separate truth and necessity because from the principle of contradictories he inferred the chain of causality.

But although Chrysippus was proved inconsistent in the argument on logic, the third part of the *De Fato* shows that in the
discussion of 'assent' he came very close to the other philosophers
who upheld free will and maintained a distinction between fate
and necessity which he had not established by his logic.

He achieved this by advancing a doctrine of 'auxiliary causes'
or 'confatalism' derived from the view of every event as the
resultant of compounded causes. Thus there are 'auxiliary and
proximate causes' which fall within the chain of necessity. But
in addition there are 'principal and perfect causes' which lie in
the nature of the thing on which the others act. For example,
a cylinder needs an impulse to set it in motion: but, granted
the impulse, the real cause of its rotation is in its own nature.

87. Ibid. 38.

If its shape were not cylindrical its reaction to the impulse would be different. Thus the nature of the principal implies a certain tendency (*adpetitus*) but this is not to be included in the chain of fatal and necessary causes.

By thus distinguishing classes of causes so as to avoid necessity while retaining fate, Chrysippus was introducing a modification into the second proposition of the 'dominative argument'. He advanced a category of cause which lies outside the scope of mechanistic determinism. By means of this distinction he held that a free act might be described as determined and predictable by virtue of the external causes but nevertheless not necessary, because of the element of spontaneity in the principal.

There might appear to be little difference between this and the Academy's conception of 'fortuitous' causes which Chrysippus condemned. But his explanation would be that what he objected to was the intrusion of a fortuitous element in the external causes, for it was to them that Stoic theory assigned the chain of necessity. He would say that his conception of the internal cause was a different matter, and that by virtue of it he could maintain that an action could be fated without being necessary.

This separation of fate and necessity was Chrysippus' peculiarity. His explanation of it is not satisfactory; but the important thing was that by it he arrived at a final position close to that of the positive supporters of free will. They granted that perception preceded assent but not that it was a necessitating cause. Chrysippus said that perception was a cause of assent but likewise agreed that it was not the necessitating cause. Both schools declared that there was something in the power of man. The difference was that Chrysippus reconciled this element of freedom with his doctrine of fate. He did this because by his peculiar doctrine he separated fate from necessity.[88]

Yon considers that the *De Fato* achieves a reconciliation with Chrysippus, and by its sympathy with Stoicism shows independence from the normal Academic attitude after Carneades. He seeks the source in a philosopher 'tending to eclecticism and independent of the pure doctrine of Carneades.'[89] This source he finds in Antiochus because 'among the philosophers of the Academy Antiochus best represents the development favourable to Stoicism.' Now the case in the *Tusculan Disputations* for man's ability to grapple with adverse factors suggests that

88. Cf. Yon, op. cit., p. xxxii.   89. Yon, op. cit., p. xl.

Antiochus would want to reject complete dominance by fate much in the manner of Chrysippus. Accordingly we might expect him to uphold some measure of human freedom.[90] Nor is it unreasonable to suggest that it was from his attention to the Antiochean case in the earlier works that Cicero became convinced of the need to develop the case for freedom by criticizing the Stoic theology. But Cicero could not be satisfied with the position of Chrysippus and his purpose in the *De Fato* was to show the need to go beyond him. Hence if Chrysippus' approach towards freedom could satisfy Antiochus, Cicero, while profiting from the suggestion of Antiochus, really wanted to show the New Academy's criticism of Chrysippus.

We are now in a position to review Cicero's achievement in the *De Divinatione* and *De Fato*. The direct statement that one might expect from a philosopher seeking to establish a doctrine of freedom was impeded by the critical method that he adopted and the nature of his sources. In the *De Divinatione* Cicero probably used Posidonius for the Stoic case, taking from Chrysippus the section on man's origin from God; the Academic source was probably Clitomachus, reporting his master Carneades, with ten sections on portents from Panaetius.[91] Now Posidonius and Clitomachus were also the probable source of the Stoic and Academic cases in the *De Natura Deorum*. But Clitomachus was prior to Posidonius: hence a certain lack of directness in both works in the Academy's reply to the Stoics. Nevertheless Cicero's attitude was quite clear in the *De Divinatione*: he rejected the claims of divination as a proof of divine intervention. But that left him with a more serious problem. There are some grounds for thinking that in the first part of the *De Fato*, which we have in fragmentary form, he dealt fairly directly with the Stoic theory of an all-pervading fate. But the main part which we have left devotes itself to the examination of the intricate and unconvincing case of Chrysippus. Nevertheless there are sufficient hints of the attitude which Cicero wished to proclaim. He opposed the determinism suggested by the Stoics in the *De Natura Deorum* because it was incompatible with man's sense of spontaneity and his sense of moral obligation. He was glad that Chrysippus, the great systematizer of Stoicism, found it necessary to modify the determinism: but he was not

90. Despite the phrase in *Ac.* ii. 126. Cf. pp. 36, 145, 195.
91. For sources see van Straaten, op. cit., pp. 257 ff.; and K. Hartfelder, *Die Quellen von Ciceros Zwei Büchern de Divinatione.*

satisfied with his proofs. There is no doubt that he wanted to pass beyond Chrysippus to a positive demonstration of freedom. But his method of criticism impeded him. His proclamation of freedom has the quality more of an act of faith than of reasoned conviction.

But although Cicero criticized the Stoics he did not seek to subvert their whole system. We may detect in him the admission of a certain measure of interconnection between things apparently unrelated, just as in the *Timaeus* we may detect the recognition of the operation of 'brute necessity'. Thus Cicero allows the operation of fate in a broad controlling sense. He concedes also the benevolence of the gods and their general providential control over man's life. His difference from the Stoics is that he will not allow that these forces intervene in details and so he insists on the freedom of man to make decisions, limiting the intimacy of the intervention of both gods and fate.

CHAPTER VI

THE *DE OFFICIIS*

1. Its Philosophic Function and Structure

THE *De Officiis* is a treatise on duties—those arising from virtue, those arising from expediency and those which may be in dispute when expediency and moral rectitude seem to clash. The source of the first two books is generally admitted to be Panaetius, περὶ τοῦ καθήκοντος with various additions and Roman illustrations by Cicero himself, while the third book is Cicero's own discussion of the conflict of the right and the expedient composed by him with considerable independence but drawing various arguments from Posidonius, Hecaton, Diogenes and Antipater.[1] The work has usually been treated as if it were an independent moral treatise, not closely connected with Cicero's other philosophic works but written from motives directly relating to his own problems as a citizen and a father—for the general guidance of the Romans in their time of distress and for the particular exhortation of his son, whose conduct as a student in Athens is alleged to have worried Cicero in the summer of 44 B.C. Thus Holden suggested that it was immediate political circumstances that determined Cicero's choice of a subject and his method of treating it[2] and that in the conditions of late 44 'it was natural that his thoughts should be diverted from abstract discussions and questions "on the chief good" and "the being of the gods" to those of practical interest.' Hence the *De Officiis* was supposed to be 'the last farewell to family and country'.

But the real motives for the *De Officiis* may be found in its connection with Cicero's earlier programme. The topic of 'duties' would follow naturally after the argument of the cosmological and theological group: since there Cicero had agreed that man has some power to choose, he would now want to discuss the principles that guide man's choice. In the *De Officiis* he follows the procedure we should expect for he first sets up the Panaetian theory and then examines it from the viewpoint of the New Academy: in the first two books he states the theory

1. For reference to the use of Panaetius see *Att.* xiii. 8; xvi. 11, 4. For a recent discussion of the sources see van Straaten, op. cit., pp. 276 ff.
2. In his edition of *Off.* iii. p. ix.

of Panaetius on pure morality and the 'expedient' activity which is compatible with pure morality: then in Book III he discusses the ordinary man's difficulties in reconciling the right and the expedient. Now in this section of philosophy there was agreement between the position of Panaetius and the Antiochean account of natural morality in *De Finibus* IV and V in (a) the theory of the development of the virtues from the primary impulses, (b) the description of the primary impulses, and (c) the theory of the relationship of purely virtuous conduct to the practical conduct subsidiary to it which in *De Officiis* II is classed as 'expedient' activity. As regards this last point, the Panaetian account attempts a final explanation of a theory of pure morality which takes account of the natural advantages. For it advances the belief that expedient action can be reconciled with pure morality, that ethical significance may be ascribed to the former without detracting from the perfection of the latter and that expedient action is subsidiary to, but essential for, the full realization of purely virtuous conduct. Since this was the problem which remained over after the examination of the Antiochean case in the *De Finibus* and *Tusculan Disputations* it seems reasonable to suggest that one of Cicero's main motives for the topic of the *De Officiis* was his desire to tackle from another point of view this problem of the Wise Man's ability to maintain pure virtue unimpaired even though he must allow external factors some significance and grapple with them.

The key to the bearing of the work on this problem is to be found in an explanation of the several meanings of the term *officium*. We have already met its true Stoic sense in *De Finibus* iii. 58, where it means 'appropriate action which is neither good nor bad'. This was part of the Stoic denial of ethical significance to all practical activity. Now the Antiochean theory quarrelled with the Stoics on this point for it insisted that some ethical significance should be ascribed to practical activity. By accepting *officium* as a 'mean' thing—an intermediate something which is neither good nor bad but which may be performed in such a way that 'a reasonable account can be rendered of its performance'—Panaetius advanced the suggestion that activity directed towards such 'mean' things was quite compatible with purely moral conduct and was in fact requisite for the full realization of moral conduct. This is the sense in which the 'expedient actions', the *utilia* of *De Officiis* II, must be understood. They are appropriate for the development of man to his full perfection as a moral creature and should not at all be understood in Book II in the sense in which expediency is sometimes taken, as a sort of inferior morality which conflicts with the good. We shall however detect some inconsistency in the treatment of them in Book II.

Up to this point then we have the two conceptions of *officium* as 'mean' activity—the Stoics denying, and Panaetius insisting that when performed with full understanding it has positive ethical significance. But Panaetius went further, for he upheld the essentially practical nature of purely virtuous conduct itself and he extended the meaning of the term to embrace not mere 'mean' activity but such forms of activity as are an essential part of the exercise of pure morality (*honestas*). This is the sense in which *officium* is used in Book I. The conception of the practical nature of purely virtuous conduct is explained in a passage in the introduction which states that 'no phase of life whether public or private . . . can be without its moral duty (*officium*): on the discharge of such duties depends all that is morally right and on their neglect all that is morally wrong in life.'

The present interpretation is further supported by a passage at the beginning of Book I, whose difficulty however requires it to be examined in detail:

> Every discussion of duty (*officium*) has two parts. One part relates to the ethical end: and the other is concerned with the practical rules (*praecepta*) by which daily life in all its bearings may be regulated. Under the first part come questions such as these: 'Are all duties absolute?' 'Is one duty more important than another?' and so on. As for the duties for which practical rules are laid down, *they do relate to the ethical end* but this fact is less obvious because they seem rather to concern the regulation of everyday life. It is these that I must explain in these books. (*Off.* i. 7.)

This shows an intention to deal with the practical rather than .the theoretical. But the statement that the duties which must be explained *relate to the ethical end* shows that it does not mean the practical as a sort of inferior morality. It means the practical activity which is essential for purely virtuous activity. Now this practical activity has two divisions which the argument goes on to distinguish in section 8. The first division is that which is itself an essential part of purely virtuous activity: this is 'absolute' duty (*perfectum officiium*) which the Greeks call κατόρθωμα: it is this that is to be discussed in the account of the virtues in Book I. The second division is 'mean' duty (*medium officium*) which the Greeks call καθῆκον ; it is duty for the performance of which an adequate reason may be rendered; in itself it is neither good nor bad, but as performed by the truly Wise Man it is quite consistent with the good; this is the expedient activity (*utile*) of Book II.

For this division of duties we should compare the Stoic division of goods in *De Finibus* iii. 55: these goods are divided into three classes, (a) those which are 'constituents' of the final end: the Greeks call these τελικά and Cicero's phrase is '*ad illud ultimum pertinentia*', (b) those which are 'productive' of the end, in Greek ποιητικά, and (c) those which are both: for wisdom is both constituent and productive. This last division recognizes the compatibility of the practical with pure morality.

In the first two books then Cicero has given us the Panaetian theory which involves two sorts of *officia*. First is that which in its own nature is virtuous activity and is performed with full understanding. Second is that which is neutral but is appropriate for the exercise of virtuous activity provided it is performed with full understanding. In this sense there is no clash between moral action and expediency (*honestas* and *utilitas*). The expedient is completely reconcilable with the good. The Wise Man can engage in practical activity, that is to say, interest himself in things, without impairing the pure state of virtue. As performed by the truly Wise Man a 'mean duty' may be thoroughly correct; in this sense the expediency of Book II must be marked off from the inferior morality of imperfect understanding which is the concern of Book III. In Book III we meet a second sense of 'mean duty' for there it implies the conduct appropriate for the man who is not truly wise.

But although the first two books advance a theoretical conception which could support the Antiochean attitude on the relationship of the good to the 'natural advantages' they also reveal a woeful weakness in the justification of that conception. The good is shown as the resultant of the complete development of the structure of the virtues, so that here the Panaetian account at least explains in detail just how the full self-realization of man, on which Antiochus insisted, was supposed to take place. But the description of the virtues is little more than an account of various duties sanctioned by them and the foundation of the whole structure is most insecure, while its completeness is asserted but not proved. Then the attempt to justify the theory of a distinction between purely virtuous conduct and 'expedient' conduct—i.e. between the *perfecta officia* and the *media officia*— which is to support the ascription of ethical significance to the 'natural advantages' without impairing the perfection of virtue, fails to establish a clear distinction. Instead of pressing on with a theoretical investigation of such a distinction, the discussion of the virtuous man's ability to engage in 'expedient' activity without impairment to his virtue degenerates into a survey of the means by which a man may enlist the aid of other men to help him resist the power of fortune and thus maintain control over external factors. In the end the case is found to rest on a confidence in its ability to sustain a theory of complete wisdom— a confidence which is not supported by adequate proof—and in the ability of that wisdom to deal unerringly with particulars.

2. Purely Virtuous Conduct and the Relation to it of 'Expedient' Action: Books I and II

There are two aspects of the explanation of purely virtuous conduct. First is the account of the structure of the virtues of which purely virtuous conduct is supposed to be the resultant. Second is the description of the duties in the performance of which it is made manifest.

The account of the structure of the virtues, taken by Cicero from Panaetius, agrees with the theory of Antiochus in the *De Finibus*. Just as in the *De Finibus* Cicero had shown the insistence by both Stoics and Antiochus on the origin of the virtues in the primary impulses and their efforts to define those impulses, so now the Panaetian structure of the virtues is shown to rest upon man's 'natural endowments'. These are described in sections 12-14, more succinctly than in the Antiochean account, as (a) the instincts which man shares with other creatures— the instinct of self-preservation, the reproductive instinct and parental affection; (b) the endowment which marks him off from the beasts, i.e. reason, by which he perceives causes and effects and guides the conduct of his life with high regard for truth and justice; and (c) the other impulses to social behaviour in its several aspects. 'It is from these elements,' says the argument, 'that is forged that moral goodness which is the subject of this inquiry.'

There is a close correspondence between these divisions and the several functions of reason which may be detected in the system of the the virtues. Panaetius describes the virtues as

Fortitude, Temperance and Justice under the general presidency of Wisdom. In this classification Bréhier[3] says that the functions of reason are (a) intellectual activity in general, guiding the whole conduct of life; (b) the control within man of the passions, the moderative function; and (c) the social function: this is derived from the fact that reason is universal and thus forms a link between men, expanding the social inclination which in animals goes no further than care for the young. Thus Bréhier regards the three significant functions of reason as Wisdom, Temperance and Justice; Panaetius' fourth virtue, Fortitude, he relegates to a subordinate position and in fact it does not appear in some of its aspects indistinguishable from Wisdom as the guide of life and in others is subordinate to Justice. Panaetius describes it as something much wider than physical courage: it is the virtue which enables a man to decide the course of his life with indifference to outward fortunes; under this aspect of it are discussed the rival merits of a life of public service or a life of retirement. As for its relation to Justice, Courage exercised without regard to the common interests of men is mere brutality and savagery.[4] Bréhier then correctly assesses the Panaetian account—which as yet we should beware of ascribing to Cicero, who at this stage has it under examination— as implying a well-integrated structure of reason closely related to the several aspects of man's natural endowments and directed towards the control of life viewed as the life of a creature essentially social. The full self-realization of man implies the unity of reason under these three forms.

This is consistent with the Antiochean doctrine that the good implies man's perfection and that this perfection is to be attained through correct development of the virtues from the activities sanctioned by the primary impulses. Of the primary impulses Antiochus had said: 'We are so constituted from birth as to contain within us the primary instincts of activity, of affection, of liberality and of gratitude.'[5] He held that the germ of the virtues is contained in the impulses of childhood but in their full development the virtues are the characteristic activities of man's highest nature—in short they are activities implanted by nature and subsequently developed by reason.

3. E. Bréhier, 'Sur une des origines de l'humanisme moderne, le *De Officiis* de Cicéron', *Report of the Amsterdam Conference,* 1948, p. 777.
4. *Off.* i. 157.
5. *Fin.* v. 43.

It is clear enough then what ideal conception Panaetius, and Antiochus too, had of the man who should attain perfect morality. But the justification of the doctrine in the *De Finibus* depended on the theory of the continuity of development upwards from the impulses and this was not adequately sustained. Here the greater conciseness of the Panaetian account does us the service that it clarifies the diffuse arguments of the *De Finibus*. But at the same time it reveals a weakness in the account of the primary impulses on which the whole structure of the virtues is supposed to rest. As an analysis of human instincts the enumeration of various impulses such as self-preservation, parental affection and the mutual attraction of men, is arbitrary and incomplete. Even if one were to admit the possibility of establishing a valid ethical theory upon such a basis—and this possibility may be doubted—surely the account of the impulses would have to be much more penetrating than this arbitrary classification by Panaetius or Antiochus. As compared even with McDougall and the psychologists at the turn of the century, who sought an ethical basis in a detailed examination of the instincts, this account which Cicero hands down is jejune.

One would expect that such impulses would have an inherent tendency to conflict with each other and in fact there does arise an unresolved conflict of self-regarding and altruistic impulses. This persists in the account of the duties imposed by the several virtues, manifesting itself in an opposition of individual interests and social obligations. The result is an indecisiveness in the treatment of problems where interests clash.

In such problems—which arise time and again in the discussion of the duties imposed by the virtues—Panaetius, in Book I, cannot rise beyond an attitude of pious exhortation, with the plausible advice that man 'must observe the universal laws of nature while safe-guarding the bent of his particular nature.'

For example private property is made out in a vague way to be compatible with the interests of society but there is no precise examination of how such reconciliation is possible. On the one hand man's interest in private property might be traced back, according to the theory of the impulses, to the instinct for self-preservation which would make him want to surround himself with things which will increase his security as an individual. But on the other hand the impulse of natural affection should impel him to desire to hold things in common with his fellows.

Whence one would expect a conflict of private and social impulses and a difficulty in reconciling private property with a man's interests as a member of a community. Yet the whole treatment of the problem of private property implies a weak assumption that somehow the reconciliation of individual rights and universal obligation is possible. But there is no precise discussion of the possibility of conflict between them nor any clear attempt to state a criterion supposing the question of priority should arise. Thus in Book I private property is described as a thing which it is reasonable to recognize when it has been acquired by law or by conquest and when the tenure of it is confirmed by long duration. That is to say, property is represented as something which man should reasonably maintain, if it has fallen to his lot. However, it must be reconciled with the claims of the community in general, so that it would be wrong for anyone to go to excess in the acquisition of property and the individual should only maintain his private rights provided they do not impair the bonds of society by hurting others. Thus in Book I the Panaetian argument recognizes individual rights; no doubt they can be sanctioned theoretically by the doctrine of self-preservation. But at the same time great importance is attached to the common bond of mankind which also derives from a basic impulse, namely the impulse of mutual affection.

On the other hand the discussion of property in Book II lays much greater stress upon the rights of the individual and makes us aware that what is really fundamental in this ethical theory is the conception of the attainment of the good by the development of man's essential nature. But again, because it does not altogether solve the problem of the conflict of individual and universal rights, it reveals that the conception of man's essential nature, involving as it does the rivalry of the impulses, may in itself be inadequate as the basis for a structure of ethics. Thus in Book II private property is treated as something essential for man's full development and as a thing which the statesman must uphold if he is to help the citizen to maintain his influence and so bend fortune to his will. Hence it is necessary that the condition of property in the state should be well ordered and the prime consideration is 'that everyone should have what belongs to him and that private citizens suffer no invasions of their property rights by action of the state.'[6] Here then is

6. *Off.* ii. 73.

the emphasis of the rights of man as an individual 'for the chief purpose in the establishment of constitutional state and municipal governments was that individual property rights might be secured',[7] so it was that nature guided men to form communities and when they had made acquisitions they banded together in cities in order to protect them. Similarly it is laid down that statesmen must

> make every effort that everyone shall possess his own property by the fair administration of the law and the courts, that the poor shall not be oppressed because of their low degree, and that envy shall not handicap the rich, to prevent them from keeping or recovering possession of their property. (*Off.* ii. 85.)

A similar acceptance of individual rights is shown in the discussion of agrarian laws: they are criticized because of their infringement of the rights of property. This is said to do away with equity for 'it is the peculiar function of the state and the city to guarantee to man the free and undisturbed control of his own particular property.' But despite the strength of this plea for private rights the discussion of property in Book II ends with the admission that, while observing their own interests, men must strive in every way to advance the state 'in power, in territory, and in revenues.'[8]

Now I do not say that a reconciliation of individual and general interests is impossible but I do say that Panaetius did not offer a serious theoretical justification of it. If the highest appeal is to man's essential nature and if that essential nature in itself includes the rival impulses, we reach an impasse. Or, if it is not an impasse, yet the theory of Panaetius did not offer a satisfactory solution. In a similar position Butler appealed to the power of conscience.[9] Now it may be that likewise Antiochus and Panaetius would feel that the social function of reason, to which Bréhier draws attention, would regulate the conflict, and in fact the Panaetian account of the virtues clearly considers man as a social creature. But my point is that, though undoubtedly he claimed to establish the structure of the virtues as a system of control by reason in its several aspects, the argument in support of this claim was deficient. When he derived the virtues from the natural endowments he did not investigate

7. Ibid. ii. 73.
8. Ibid. ii. 78, 85.
9. Cf. W. J. Norton, *Bishop Butler*, 1940, pp. 99 f.

the possibility of conflict among impulses. Nor did he specifically consider how the social function of reason could be reconciled with the fact that on the whole the doctrine of the attainment of the good by the full development of man's essential nature stressed the development of man as an individual, as the discussion of property tends to show, albeit inconclusively.

The general intention, however, is clear. Somehow man's interests as a social creature were supposed to absorb his self-seeking impulses. The assumption of social bonds natural to man may be seen in the discussion of duties under the heading of Fortitude. It is man's duty to place the public welfare above his own. Those who enter public life must maintain the good of the whole people regardless of their own interests. Thus the virtue of fortitude is seen to manifest itself in a courageous conception of social duties. The truly courageous man should dedicate himself without reserve to his own country and should have the valour to master passion, conducting his life without self-seeking, without vindictiveness or harsh temper and with due disregard of material rewards.

Elsewhere we detect the assumption of the essential nature of man as a social creature with the duty 'to respect, defend and maintain the common bonds of union and fellowship subsisting between all the members of the human race.'[10] The result may be seen in Cicero's own attitude in Book III in his unexamined assumption that somehow individual interests may be reconciled with the common bonds that bind mankind.

The next stage in the argument for the development of complete morality from the impulses is to pass beyond the inadequately examined basis of man's essential nature to the account of the development of the virtues themselves. In the *De Finibus* this development was maintained with insistence rather than by demonstrated proof and the Panaetian account therefore comes to supplement Antiochus by showing what it means by the correct development of the virtues according to the requirements of human nature.

A distinctive doctrine in this part of the argument, whose importance Bréhier stresses,[11] is the function it assigns to 'propriety' (*decorum*). 'Propriety' is declared to be inseparable from the several virtues: it is essential to moral rectitude in general and to each particular virtue. So that it may be achieved it is

10. *Off.* i. 149.
11. Op. cit., p. 778.

necessary that the several virtues should develop in the way that is appropriate for the attainment of the full perfection of that essential nature which was revealed by the analysis of man's natural endowments. Only if they accord with 'propriety' can the duties prescribed by the several virtues be consistent with the true moral nature of man. Thus this doctrine emphasizes that the Panaetian view of ethics is that which Antiochus proclaimed, the attainment of the good by man's full self-realization.

But here again the ideal of the harmonious integration of man's whole nature is proclaimed with inadequate attention to the problem of the unresolved conflict of the self-regarding and altruistic impulses. It is admitted that there are diversities of individual character and in accordance with these man must hold fast to his own peculiar gifts. He should choose his career in accordance with his individual endowments and one must determine what is proper for him from each man's native disposition. But at the same time individual interests must be reconciled with those of the community. But how this can be done is not made clear and the significance of the problem is not realized. As before, pious exhortation takes the place of demonstration. It is recognized that different duties are appropriate to different individuals so that each may attain perfection by the development of his own true individual nature in accordance with the requirements of 'propriety'. But it is supposed that somehow the individual may conform with the general interest. Thus a young man should show deference to his elders, guard against sensuality, inure himself to toil. On the other hand the old should endeavour to give service by their counsel and to guard against luxury and idleness. Similarly men in different stations have special duties: the magistrate must be conscious of his duty to the state; the private citizen must preserve right relationships with his fellow citizens; and the alien must refrain from meddling in politics. Again it is propriety which must determine modesty and behaviour, self-control and performance in oratory and conversation. In remonstration, reproof or in self-praise or again in the conduct of the home and the choice of occupation propriety must be guarded. In other words, from the doctrine of the need to develop the individual endowments we arrive at a conception of duties appropriate to varying circumstances, character and age, with the general assumption that in all these man's 'individual' nature may be reconciled with his 'universal' nature.

M

As for the structure of the virtues, in arranging Justice, Fortitude and Temperance under the presidency of Wisdom, this theory proclaims the ideal of a completely rational morality attainable by man. But one must ask whether this plausible account of the system of the virtues is adequate to establish the perfection of reason. It does not attempt any justification on metaphysical grounds nor does it venture on an epistemological investigation of the nature of the pure reason whose attainability is assumed. What Panaetius probably envisaged was the Antiochean conception of a sum-total of knowledge developed continuously from perception and directing itself, not in the Platonic sense towards pure being, but towards the practical life. This interpretation of his meaning is borne out by the nature of his description of purely virtuous conduct. For this is purely and simply a description of the various duties which the several virtues prescribe for a man in his practical life as a member of society. Thus under the heading of Justice are discussed such topics as a man's social relationships and duties, which may require him to curb his personal ambition, to fulfil his promises or to observe justice in the requital of wrong-doing; or his proper attitude as a member of society towards a hostile society, which involves a discussion of a nation's duties towards the vanquished and the fulfilment of international obligations. This gives Cicero a chance to insert into the Panaetian account a statement on the humanity of Rome's laws of war and to quote the case of Regulus as a supreme example of loyalty to a promise. In short, the whole discussion of the duties prescribed by justice constitutes a statement of the principles of human society and of relationships between societies as sanctioned by the comprehensive bond which 'unites together men as men and all to all' (*Off.* i. 51).

Similarly under the virtue of Fortitude are discussed such topics as man's attainment of moral courage by indifference to outward fortunes and control of passions. But since man's personal perfection also depends on his conduct as a member of the state, the discussion also deals with the manifestation of courage in a citizen's life of public service. This leads to a comparison of the services of warriors and of statesmen and thus affords Cicero the opportunity, dear to him, to work in a description of his victory over Catiline as an 'instance of civic courage' (Ibid. i. 78).

From this discussion of man's duties as a social creature, under Justice and Fortitude, we pass, under Temperance, to a review of the precepts by which man's individual perfection may be assured. Here it is still a question of practical morality, for the argument deals with such topics as the need of self-control and modesty and the choice of occupation that will enable a man to realize himself fully.

From all this it can be seen that purely virtuous conduct is conceived as the right conduct of man as a member of society and acting with full understanding. It rests on an insecure foundation. For in the first place it assumes that the supreme goal in ethics is the full development of man—whereas in our earlier discussion of Antiochus and the Stoics we have exposed the insufficiency of this 'subjective final end'. In the second place it, rests on an imperfect view of human nature, with an inherent conflict of self-regarding and altruistic impulses which is never solved. In the third place it assumes the completeness of understanding without other justification than the unproved assertion of the perfection of the system of virtues. Nevertheless the influence of this conception of virtuous conduct has been very great, both on humanistic and social theory in general and on Cicero in particular. His social theory presented in Book III is largely influenced by it and it caused him to adopt the high ideals of decency in private and public conduct which he handed on. Admittedly neither he nor his sources were able (or felt the need) to overcome in theory the basic conflicts of man's 'individual' and 'universal' nature. This produced a certain vagueness in the social thought which we shall detect in his third book. But it is probable that he and they were not aware of the fundamental nature of the conflict, did not feel the need to tackle it in theory, and thought that their plausible explanations of the reconcilability of 'individual' with 'universal' nature were adequate. Thus the pronouncement with which Cicero ends the Panaetian account of the duties prescribed by Fortitude implies that Panaetius accepted the compatibility of individual excellence with universal obligation: 'By observing these rules one may live in magnificence, dignity and independence, and yet in honour, truth and charity toward all' (Ibid. i. 92).

My view that the Panaetian account of the structure of the virtues implies the assumption which Antiochus also made, that human reason, if perfectly developed from perception, can attain completely rational morality needs to be defended against a possible misinterpretation of a passage concerning the priority of Justice or of speculative reason. If this passage were not understood correctly it might seem to imply that Justice challenged the supremacy of Wisdom, which was asserted at the beginning of the account of the system of the virtues. It occurs towards the end of Book i, where, in section 152, Cicero commences a discussion of the possible conflict of perfectly moral actions—a point which, as he says, Panaetius 'overlooked' and which others might feel no need to discuss. Miller's marginal note in the Loeb edition suggests that Cicero contemplated a conflict between Justice and Wisdom. Now the whole point of the passage depends on the particular meaning of 'wisdom'. Here it means inactive contemplation. What Cicero is really comparing is the claim of the practical life against the life of contemplation. Basing his argument on the nature of man and his gregariousness and the general rightness of society derived from this and other natural impulses, Cicero decides that according to the Panaetian theory man's highest activity should be that which is directed towards the maintenance of society. Accordingly the virtue of Justice, which is particularly fitted to satisfy the claims of humanity, is pre-eminent. Thus he says 'the duties prescribed by Justice must be given precedence over the pursuit of knowledge (*scientia*) and the duties imposed by it, for the former are necessary for the interests of men and nothing ought to be more sacred in man's eyes than those interests' (Ibid. i. 155). In this sense it is right for Wisdom to devote itself to the service of Justice, for if Justice, which centres in the safe-guarding of human interests did not accompany the pursuit of knowledge, then that knowledge 'would seem isolated and barren of results . . . . Hence it follows that the claims of human society and the bonds that unite men together take precedence over the pursuit of knowledge' (Ibid. i. 157).

In all this Cicero is not contemplating the conflict of Justice and the true virtue of Wisdom as the president of the virtues, but is trying to say that the Panaetian view is that Wisdom directed according to the principles of Justice to the service of humanity is more important than speculative knowledge. Thus 'every duty that tends to maintain and safe-guard human society should be given preference over that duty which arises from speculation and science alone' (Ibid. i. 158).

This explanation shows that the Panaetian account can be reconciled with Cicero's account of the order of the virtuous activities according to the system of Antiochus in the *De Finibus*. For in *De Finibus* v. 58 philosophic inquiry is rated first and political theory and practice next. It is reasonable to suppose that there Antiochus by 'philosophic inquiry' meant Wisdom in the sense in which it occurs in the Panaetian account as the presiding virtue. Nor can the precedence ascribed to Justice over speculation in the last sections of *De Officiis* be construed as a challenge to the supremacy of true virtue of Wisdom.

The effect of the last part of Book I is to clarify the Panaetian conception of the presidency of Wisdom over the other virtues and to clarify also the conception of virtuous conduct under the control of Wisdom as essentially practical. As was said in section 19, 'the whole glory of virtue is in activity.' Now this is precisely the conception of virtuous activity which Antiochus must have had in his theory of natural morality. For in the *De Finibus* and *Tusculan Disputations* we saw that the Antiochean ideal was that wisdom which considered every aspect of man's life rather than the arid wisdom which the Stoics thought they could attain by making their transition to their realm of pure morality.

This being so, we should expect to find in the Panaetian account a theoretical solution of the main Antiochean problem, which was the need to reconcile purely virtuous activity with everyday practical conduct. It was required to show that the virtuous man, though he must grapple with adverse factors and must be affected by them (for example, by pain), can still maintain his virtue unimpaired and act according to the principles of pure morality. This is what the Antiochean argument had upheld, particularly in the *Tusculan Disputations*. Now the solution should really be a matter for metaphysical inquiry directed towards the problem, which Plato faced, of relating perfect intelligence to the world of the senses. But, as we have said, Cicero does not show that Antiochus made any serious attempt to investigate the epistemological problems involved. Nor does the Panaetian account address itself directly to this task. However, we can infer from Book I the sort of conception of perfect understanding which both Antiochus and Panaetius must have held. They probably thought that the way in which the perfect system of knowledge must be developed, if the Wise Man were to attain it, would be by systematically building up from the facts of perception. There are certain features in the

Panaetian account which support this interpretation. For, it being assumed that the ethical end is to be attained by the full development of man, and the structure of the virtues under Wisdom being supposed to provide for the development of the whole man, and not of mind alone, then it might plausibly be supposed that the rule of reason is demonstrated, if not established metaphysically, by the account of the completeness of the system of virtues. Moreover, since the Panaetian description of the duties made virtuous conduct out to be essentially practical, there would seem to be no obstacle to assuming the full ability of the virtuous man to cope with practical life while maintaining his perfect virtue unimpaired.

But inconsistencies are discernible in the Panaetian account which imply hazy thinking and a failure to realize the issues involved, and so lead in Book II to a facile treatment of the main problem. Whereas the theory of the practical nature of purely virtuous conduct should produce a reconciliation between that and the forms of activity described as 'expedient', so that really there should be no difference between them, there persists a sense of antithesis between them. There is still that hankering after the transcendental nature of pure virtue and that denial of respectability to 'things', which we remarked in the *De Finibus*. This is partly due to the inability to shake off entirely the influence of the Stoic conception of the absoluteness and remoteness of the good. Partly also it is caused by that tendency to separate external things from the truly good, which results from the theory that the good is attained by man's own full development. Hence, since there seems to be an inferiority in that practical activity which is directed to things not intimately part of the man's self, it is lightly assumed that the right way to show the compatibility of such practical activity and pure virtue is to show simply that virtue can dominate it, which was the Antiochean argument in the *Tusculan Disputations*. But of course the criticism still applies that to show the power of virtue is not the same thing as to show that its purity remains unimpaired.

The influence of this assumption of the inferiority of that sort of practical activity can be seen when the Panaetian account, having described the duties which derive from moral rectitude, proceeds in Book II to discuss the duties of expediency. By this it means the activity which is subsidiary to and requisite for the realization of purely virtuous conduct. This is first said to consist of the duties 'which have to do with the arrangements necessary for life (*vitae cultum*), with the means of acquiring the things which men use, with their substance and their wealth' (*Off*. ii. 1), and the description is expanded in section 11 to show that these duties embrace control over inanimate things like gold and silver and the fruits of the earth as well as relations with gods and men. Here the Panaetian account expands the Antiochean distinction (in *Fin*. v. 67 f.) between the goods that constitute the ultimate good and the external goods. In the first class Antiochus had placed the goods of 'mind and body' which achieve the perfection of the self: the external goods were those which belonged neither to the mind nor to the body such as 'friends, parents, children, relatives and one's country itself'. That is to say, the Antiochean argument in the *De Finibus* classed as external goods the relation of friendship and relations to family and others, with obvious implications for the theory of man's attainment of the good by his full development as a social creature. To this the Panaetian account adds man's need to deal with inanimate things. In both Antiochus and Panaetius one may discern the influence of the doctrine of the good as man's self-realization in this allotment of the goods of 'mind and body' to the first class.

Now the Panaetian account strongly insists that concern with the external goods is completely reconcilable with moral rectitude and that it is only a perversion of terms that declares expedient action of this kind to be incompatible with the good. Thus there could be no more pernicious doctrine than to say that a thing may be morally right (*honestum*) without being expedient (*utile*) or that it may be expedient without being morally right. But this view is not established by theoretical argument and the sense of inferiority of the external goods which are not goods of 'mind and body' persists.

Consequently the Panaetian account develops in a manner unpenetrating and disappointing. So far from grappling with the metaphysical problems or investigating the epistemological principles which must be implied in the assumption of purely rational conduct, it degenerates into a survey of the practical means by which a man may enlist the aid of his fellow-men to ensure his dominance over things.

The way in which the argument develops is this. After admitting the necessity of expedient things—the external conveniences of life, means, wealth and influence—and their compatibility with the life of pure morality, Panaetius (as recorded by Cicero) reflects that the right way to control them is by man's effort. For without that there would be no provisions for health, no navigation, no agriculture. Moreover without the efforts of men —and especially their mutual helpfulness—there would be no houses to keep out the cold, nor aqueducts, canals and other useful works. Then man being the source of the greatest help to man, it becomes the peculiar function of virtue to 'win the hearts of men and attach them to one's own service.' In short, it is admitted that in order to control the power of fortune, i.e. to bend external factors to his will, man must win the affectionate co-operation of his fellows and from that point the rest of the book is a study of means of winning this support—in short, a survey of social conduct.

In the discussion of the means of influencing one's fellow citizens the argument passes from the disadvantages of tyranny and intimidation—in which Cicero works in his own censure of recent conduct in Rome—to the advantage of friendship (which is only lightly touched on since it has been discussed fully in the *Laelius*) and such means of attaining glory as winning goodwill, confidence and admiration or again the various ways of winning a good name (a) by a military career, (b) by personal character, (c) by association with the great, (d) by eloquence and by service towards friends in the courts.

Similarly the discussion of kindness and generosity as means of maintaining influence involves all sorts of practical topics such as the right standards to be observed in making gifts of money or in performing public services such as giving games for the people, or again the proper attitude in personal service to inferiors. The statesman's duties in matters of practical policy, such as taxation, agrarian laws and private property, are also discussed as the means by which he may, by proper administration, enable citizens to maintain influence within the state and so bend fortune to their will. Here we find that greater emphasis on the function of private property as a requisite for the individual's self-fulfilment upon which I remarked earlier in this chapter.

It is clear that this survey contains none of that theoretical discussion of the relations of universals to particulars which we would expect to find in a serious attempt to establish pure morality and to determine the relation to it of practical conduct. What Cicero has given us from Panaetius is no more than a demonstration of the power of wisdom, with practical aids, to triumph over adverse factors. This is an argument of the same order as the *Tusculan Disputations,* and it is open to the same objection, that to demonstrate the power of virtue is not the same thing as to establish a theory of pure morality. Plato endeavoured in the *Republic,* from his use of the figure of the Line, to show that pure intelligence, once established, may be supposed able to survey the subordinate divisions of the Line, while itself remaining unimpaired. But in the Panaetian argument there is no more serious proof that concern with external factors will not impair the perfection of virtue than just this empirical demonstration that virtue can in fact triumph.

As for the justification of the attainment of pure morality, the whole case for it is weak. There is confusion about the interpretation of purely virtuous and expedient conduct. Whereas the theory of the reconcilability of expedient conduct with purely virtuous conduct was based on the assumption that expedient conduct was subsidiary to the purely virtuous but distinct from it, much of the description of virtuous activity in Book I includes forms of activity which do not really differ from those classed as expedient in Book II. In fact the whole conception of purely virtuous conduct remains deficient. Just as the *De Finibus* and *Tusculan Disputations* abounded in claims for the efficacy of *honestas* but without any clear statement of what it was, while the criticism in the *De Finibus* was rather a criticism of the details of the account of the establishment of the conception than a criticism of the conception itself, so now the justification of purely virtuous conduct rests on an arbitrary assertion of the completeness of the structure of the virtues while the description of it is nothing more than a description of various forms of activity which seem to be sanctioned by the virtues. As for any valid proof of the completeness of the structure of the virtues or any epistemological argument to prove the attainment of perfect understanding, such is entirely lacking. And although Antiochus agreed with the Panaetian conception of perfect wisdom and the examination of Panaetius was probably intended to supplement the examination of Antiochus, there is no attempt to consider how this perfect wisdom could derive from Antiochus' starting point, the doctrine of perception.

Thus we have found weakness in the theoretical attempt to solve the knotty problem of the relationship of the good and the natural advantages within the theory of pure morality. That

Cicero himself had no proper appreciation of the issues which should be involved in such a problem is shown by the anecdote which he appends as his own addition to the argument from Panaetius. For he uses it to illustrate the comparison of expediencies and it shows that he thinks that they are to be assessed by comparison of their practical advantages and not by reference to an ideal standard. He says that Cato, asked about the comparative merits of various forms of expedient activity, ranked first 'raising cattle successfully', next 'raising cattle with fair success', and after that 'raising cattle with but slight success' and fourthly 'raising crops'. But when his questioner asked 'How about money-lending?' Cato replied, 'How about murder?'.

3. THE ETHICAL STANDARD FOR THE ORDINARY MAN: BOOK III

At the end of the *Tusculan Disputations*, after examining Antiochus' case for the perfection of his pure morality which concerned itself with particulars, Cicero was willing to do no more than to state that Antiochus was claiming perfection no less than that of the Stoics. Now, after examining the case of Panaetius which likewise claimed that pure virtue was unimpaired though it engaged in the practical life, Cicero in *De Officiis* III at last gives his verdict. He distinguishes two theories of ethics, (a) that which upholds the *honestum* as the *sole* good, i.e. the Stoic theory, and (b) that which holds that the *honestum* is the object *most worth seeking for its own sake* (*maxime propter se expetendum*) : by this he means the theory which allows that 'expedient' activity (in the Panaetian sense) or 'other goods' (in the Antiochean sense) are reconcilable with pure morality. Of these he says 'either alternative satisfies me; now the one and now the other seems more probable and besides these no other definition seems probable at all' (*Off.* iii. 33).

This is his decision despite an earlier statement which, if wrongly interpreted, might suggest that he upheld the Stoic definition alone:

> Therefore we must establish some general rule to make possible unerring decision in any apparent conflict of what we call the expedient with our conception of the morally right; if we follow that rule in comparing courses of conduct we shall never swerve from the path of duty. Now this rule will be in full agreement with the system and doctrines of Stoicism. That is what we are following in these books because

—although the Old Academy and your Peripatetics (who once were the same as the Academy) rank the morally right above seeming expediency—yet the discussion of these problems is more inspiring when it is conducted by those who consider that whatever is morally right is also expedient and nothing expedient which is not morally right than when it is conducted by those who think that something not expedient may be morally right and that something not morally right may be expedient. (*Off.* iii. 20.)

Now I do not believe that Cicero intended to throw the rival theory over. What he wanted to say was: 'I acknowledge that the right standard—if it could be attained—would be perfect morality unimpaired by contact with things: I shall accept it in the Stoic terms because I want no ambiguity: I shall not permit any possible conflict of right and expedient.' Here he did not mean to admit that the rival theory allowed such a conflict. But he thought it best to say it in the Stoic way because that excluded ambiguity. His attitude was very like that adopted in *Tusculan Disputations* ii. 46, when Cicero showed that Antiochus would prefer to say that moral worth was the *only* good (the Stoic view) rather than to say that it *was not the greatest*. By this Antiochus meant that he was so certain that the allowance of other goods (in the Antiochean sense) did not detract from the perfection of the good that, rather than admit any doubt about it, he would even declare for the Stoic definition. But he did not mean that he really felt any doubt.

Cicero's verdict means only that he finally admits that the theoretical case for perfect morality reconciled with practical activity is as sound as the Stoic case. But he himself cannot accept either since he maintains the sceptical attitude of the New Academy. He does however regard them as ideal, if unproven, systems to which he may turn for guidance in the task which he attacks next, the task of giving rules of conduct to men of imperfect understanding. For them there is the constant problem of conflict between the good and the expedient. This is a task which Cicero is a fit person to attempt since by virtue of his original rejection of the Stoic doctrine of perception he must insist that human understanding is imperfect. He would obviously be a better person to discuss the conflict of the good and the expedient than Panaetius who had presented the case for their compatibility. Accordingly in Book iii we are concerned with the inferior morality which deals with '*secunda quaedam honesta*', what we might call 'second-class goods'. And the first task is to establish an ethical standard. For among ordinary men there are worthy ones who have a disposition to virtue, but because of the lack of perfect knowledge cannot attain it in its perfection. Thus national heroes like the Decii may provisionally be called brave but they cannot be accepted as perfect models of courage. For these men we must find a high standard to guide them. Now this cannot be perfect but it must be as sound as possible. For example this provisional morality of the men of imperfect understanding (*quod communiter appellamus honestum*) must not be outweighed by considerations of profit (*emolumenta*) any more than true morality may be outweighed by expediency. By finding such a standard we must help these worthy men to maintain such progress towards virtue as they have made. Here we should observe Cicero's recognition of the allowance of progress in the προκόπτοντες which the Stoic intransigence denied and Antiochus upheld. In short, Cicero proposed in Book III to make his own final statement on the ethical standard for the man whose imperfect understanding allowed a confusion of the right and the expedient.

Throughout this book the debt to Panaetius is obvious. One superficial evidence of it is that in reviewing the conflicts between seeming expediency and the right—for which purpose he classifies them according to the virtue involved—Cicero observes the Panaetian order of Wisdom, Justice, Fortitude and Temperance. But more significant are (a) his recognition of the complete compatibility of the expedient with the good if perfect understanding were granted, (b) the basing of the rule of conduct upon the assumption that respect for the bonds of human society is enjoined by the law of nature. Since in both these points Antiochus agreed with Panaetius, Cicero's acceptance of them here shows that he must have had considerable sympathy with the Antiochean case during his prolonged examination of it in the earlier works.

On the first of these doctrines he was influenced by Panaetius' case in Books I and II where the *utile* was reconciled with the *honestum* and this involved the same view as Antiochus' case for the compatibility of the 'natural advantages' with virtue. According to this Cicero recognizes that it is only where the understanding is imperfect that conflict between the expedient and the good is possible. But since, if correctly understood, it

merges with the good the expedient must be completely opposite
to the base and can never be compatible with it. Hence it can
never be expedient to profit by baseness even secretly, as Gyges
profited by using the magic ring. Accordingly it is stressed
throughout this book that in the practical life of worthy men,
who have not perfect knowledge, any plea for the expedient
as against the right must rest on error. Thus 'it is never
expedient (*utile*) to do wrong, because that is always immoral
(*turpe*); and it is always expedient to be good, because that
is always morally right (*honestum*)' (*Off*. iii. 64). So far the
rejection of baseness rests upon the Panaetian and Antiochean
theories of the relationship of the true *honestum* to the *utile*,
but it also rests in part on the view that by performing a base
act a man detracts from his own true nature as a good man.
That is why Cicero condemns actions of Gratidianus, Pompey,
Caesar and other Romans who for seeming expediency incurred
the moral loss that comes from wrong ambition. Here Cicero
reflects the theory which Panaetius upheld but which can be
traced in greater detail in the study of the Antiochean case that
man's true development should be towards ethical perfection.
It rested upon the original doctrine of the goodness of nature
and the consequent goodness of the primary natural impulses
which were the basis on which the structure of the virtues was
erected. Now the special feature of this theory was that because
of the stress it placed upon the altruistic impulses it suggested
that man's right development was as a social creature. It is this
that determines the nature of the rule of conduct which is that
a man must not for his own private gain do a thing which will
harm a fellow-man. Cicero now maintains that to profit by a
neighbour's loss is against the law of nature because it breaks
the bonds of society which 'are most in accord with nature's
laws'. This assumption was implied in the Antiochean case. It
supposes that it is only as a member of good society that man
will fulfil himself; this is supported by the argument of the
dependence of a limb upon the whole body, so that only if the
body is in a healthy state will each limb be truly strong, while
an attempt to strengthen itself at the expense of the rest will
involve a limb in the common destruction. Thus Cicero proclaims a very high standard of conduct based on a genuine belief
in the universal brotherhood of mankind. And this he thinks
he can trace back to nature's laws. Accepting man as a creature
essentially social, he thinks that man's full perfection—and con-

sequently the attainment of the ethical end—is to be achieved as
a member of a sound society. But between societies there must
be mutual consideration, for the universal law (*ius gentium*) is
wider than the civil law (*ius civile*) : it is sanctioned by the
natural law (*naturae lex*) which implies a bond of fellowship
between all men. Thus the civil law is not necessarily the
universal law, but the universal law ought also to be the civil
law (Ibid. iii. 69). For example it would not matter if a Roman
civil law for free distribution of grain were not accepted uni-
versally: but a universal law, 'don't harm a fellow-man for
private gain', ought to be acceptable to all civil codes.

Now this supposed identity of the interests of individual and
community rests ultimately on the acceptance of mutual affection as the primary impulse and makes no due allowance for
the fact that the other impulse of self-preservation supports
equally well the conception of man as a creature essentially
selfish. This was a difficulty in the Antiochean position and
produced a conflict of individual and universal rights in the
Panaetian case in Book I. But Cicero does not recognize it as a
problem. He is convinced that private and common weal are
interwoven because the perfection of man is attainable only in
a community and he does not contemplate a clash of interests.
The attitude is like that of Book I where the somewhat plausible
advice was given that man 'must observe the universal laws of
nature while safe-guarding the bent of his particular nature.' In
all the cases he examines he rates respect for fellow-men and the
interests of a community above narrow selfishness as when he
quotes from Hecaton: 'We do not seek to be rich for ourselves
alone but for our children, relatives, friends, and, above all, for
our country. For the private fortunes of individuals are the
wealth of our country' (Ibid. iii. 63). The main part of the book
is taken up by discussion of apparent clashes between expediency
and right in the everyday life. In all such problems—questions
of family and civil life, problems of business and politics—Cicero
enjoins a high standard of decency and consideration of man
for his own sake. Cruelty as a matter of political expediency
must be rejected: the Athenians must be condemned for cutting
off the thumbs of the Aeginetans to end their sea-faring skill
and their commercial rivalry; against the claims of common
humanity such seeming expediency must not prevail. Nor should
a citizen body debar foreigners from enjoying the advantages of
its city, because that would be altogether contrary to the laws

of humanity. To cheat in business is wrong because it injures the common bonds of society. In the relations of nations with one another also there must be due regard for the law of nature. An oath given even to an enemy must be observed since to violate oaths would make it impossible for nations to observe the rules which have enabled them to live together with the mutual respect due to fellow members of the human race. Thus for Regulus, whose case is discussed at length, there was no real conflict of personal expediency with duty. It was his duty to Rome and to himself as a citizen of Rome to observe his oath and return to Carthage.

The copiousness of Roman examples in Book III shows that Cicero intends his discussion of morality to be regarded not as a mere philosophic exercise but as something which has practical application. He recognizes that his denial of valid perception debars him from proclaiming perfect axioms of moral conduct: in fact he has expressly stated that this book is intended to give a guide to men of imperfect wisdom, therefore the rules cannot be more than provisional rules for practical conduct. Nevertheless they are based on high ideals. In his solution of the various problems one can detect constantly the reference to the principle of refraining from harmful and selfish conduct and this principle is sanctioned by the acceptance of the essential goodness of humanity which implies the brotherhood of men. Although he has insisted on the traditional liberty of the New Academy to choose the doctrine which seems most probable, this has resulted not in a random eclecticism nor a policy of narrow expediency but in a reasoned system of ethical conduct in which he has an obvious debt to the conception of human nature and its place in the world which had to be considered in the examination of the ethics of Antiochus and Panaetius.

4. THE PRACTICAL PURPOSE OF THE *De Officiis*

After this discussion of the philosophic function of the *De Officiis* we are in a better position to review the general purpose of the work with particular attention to Holden's view that Cicero's choice of subject was determined by immediate political circumstances.

It will help us first to consider the date of the composition of the work in relation to Cicero's political activity. In the months of despair and ineffectiveness that followed the murder of Caesar, Cicero gradually made up his mind to go to Greece in order to keep out of harm's way. He set sail on 17 July 44 but at Leucopetra on 7 August received news which made him see a glimmer of hope. Therefore he turned back and, although later news dimmed this hope, persisted in his journey to Rome, which he reached at the end of August. There followed Antony's attack in the Senate and the first *Philippic* in reply, on 1 and 2 September. Antony's next violent speech came a fortnight later but Cicero had kept away from the Senate, sensing the gathering storm, and early in October he withdrew to Puteoli where he composed the second *Philippic*. During all this time he was negotiating for support for the republican cause, especially with Octavianus. In October the violent conduct of Antony in his massacres at Suessa and Brundisium made a break inevitable and he continued his stormy manoeuvres in November until he went, late in that month, to encounter Decimus Brutus. On Antony's departure from Rome Cicero returned early in December and delivered the third and fourth *Philippics* on the twentieth. The break was now complete.

The main work of composition of the *De Officiis* fell in the period September-November 44. It is mentioned in a letter to Atticus (xv. 13) dated at Puteoli on 25 October. Here he says: 'I am philosophizing here (what else can I do?) and am getting on splendidly with my *De Officiis* which I am dedicating to my son. A father could not choose a more appropriate subject.' This, says Holden, is the first intimation of his being engaged on a treatise on ethics. But he does say elsewhere that the work was interrupted by the attempted journey to Greece, which would mean that it started in July. In *Att.* xvi. 11, dated 5 November at Puteoli, he says: 'The *De Officiis*, so far as Panaetius is concerned, I have finished in two books.' He then goes on to discuss the divisions of the subject and the need to deal with the third topic, omitted by Panaetius: 'Posidonius took up that topic. I have ordered his book and have written to Athenodorus Calvus. I have asked him to send me a summary of it and am expecting it. I wish you would spur him on and beg him to let me have it as soon as possible.' He then discusses the suitability of the title in relation to the meaning of the Greek καθῆκον. From this it is clear that, even if the work were started before the departure for Greece, the important period in its composition was precisely the three months leading to the final break with Antony.

If then the work was written for direct application to the immediate political scene and as a call to arms one would expect it to be fired by the spirit of urgency of the *Philippics* and to abound in direct illustrations. There is indeed a passage in one of the letters which has been taken as proof that Atticus felt the writing of the work to be so dangerous for its political implications that he tried to divert Cicero to history as a safer occupation. This is the letter of 11 November[12] in which Cicero says, 'I have a burning passion for history—for your suggestion has had a wonderful effect on me—but it is not easy to begin or carry it out without your assistance.' But this is most inconclusive, especially when one considers the remoteness of nearly all the historical illustrations. For example Cicero goes back to Crassus to illustrate the dangers of ambition.[13] In discussing the humanity of Roman warfare he refers to the wars of the third and second century.[14] For performances of statesmanship he quotes Africanus, Gracchus, Pompey and his own victory over Catiline.[15] In Book II there is strong criticism of the tyranny of Caesar.[16] Similarly in Book III the discussion of honesty in business and of the principles governing legal decisions, while drawn from the Roman scene, goes back to earlier generations— to Cato, to the Fimbria about whom Cicero's father used to speak, to Gratidianus' selfish manoeuvre with the coinage in the era of Sulla. The great example of fidelity to an obligation is Regulus in the Hannibalic war. This is all far away from the troubles with Antony. Apart from several references to Antony in the early part of Book III the latest ones are the scathing indictment of Pompey and Caesar in Book iii. 82 and the approval of the killing of the tyrant in Book iii. 19. As for the references to Antony they display regret at the flouting of republican institutions and the virtual downfall of the Republic, but so far from prescribing immediate action they even given a hint of acquiescence and desire to keep away from trouble.[17]

Compare the vehemence of the *Philippics,* e.g. in the second, composed in September 44: 'one single man was found bold

---

12. *Att.* xvi. 13 (arranged by Winstedt as 13c) ; cf. Syme,
    The Roman Revolution, p. 145.
13. *Off.* i. 25 f.
14. Ibid. i. 37 ff.
15. Ibid. i. 76 ff.
16. Ibid. ii. 23 ff.
17. *Off.* iii. 1, 2, 4.

N

enough for that from which the anxiety of all beside had shrunk appalled' (ii. 64), or in the fourth, in December:

> Romans, you have no contest with an enemy with whom any terms of peace are possible. It is not, as formerly, for your enslavement, it is for your blood that his anger has driven him to thirst; no sport seems to him more joyful than bloodshed, than massacre, than the butchery of citizens before his eyes. (Ibid. iv. 11.)

In the *De Officiis*, written just before, there is no language of this kind.

It is a fair conclusion that Cicero's choice of topic was determined by the development of his philosophic programme and not by immediate political circumstances. We have already observed the connection of the argument with that of the earlier works. As for their relation in time, we know that he was still engaged on the *De Divinatione* at the time of Caesar's death and may assume that the *De Fato* was hastily thrown together soon after the completion of the *De Divinatione*. That is to say, the group of cosmological and theological works was finished in the early summer of 44. The following months of indecision were not free from philosophic writing: to them belong the *De Senectute* and *De Gloria*. In the normal development of his programme Cicero would be ready to start the *De Officiis* about the end of the summer.

Syme, who holds that the delineation of the ideal state in the *De Re Publica* was Cicero's reaction to his sense of failure in the years just before 51 B.C. (having been ineffective in politics he wanted to display his conception of the ideal), considers that the *De Officiis* resulted similarly from an impulse to 'demonstrate his conception of a well-ordered state and to corroborate it in the light of the most recent history.' Thus 'the *De Officiis* is a theoretical treatment of the obligations which a citizen should render to the Commonwealth, that is, a manual of civic virtue.'[18] Now I by no means intend to eliminate practical motives. The philosophical programme had reached the stage at which Cicero needed to define his own practical morality and political circumstances enhanced the need for clarification. But I do think that the real reason why the *De Officiis* was written at this time was that the plan of philosophic works required it. Political

18. R. Syme, op. cit., p. 145.

considerations certainly reinforced the choice but they were of secondary importance.

It will be observed that I am attaching no significance to the dedication of the *De Officiis* to Cicero's son, which has some-times been taken as proof of an urgent personal motive. It has been suggested that young Marcus was behaving so badly in Athens as to furnish his father with a pressing reason for writing a moral treatise in the hope of reforming him. There has been gross exaggeration. The theory rested on the assumption that Cicero's anxiety was prolonged for some months. But this came from confusion about the dates of correspondence. My view is that there was a short period of annoyance which occupied about a week at the end of April and early May of 44 B.C. and which provoked Cicero to swift action and the summary dismissal of the tutor Gorgias. As for various allegations of the son's extravagance, they arise from misinterpretation of the father's normal precautions to ensure for his son an adequate supply of funds in troubled times.[19] In short I regard the dedica-tion of the *De Officiis* to the young Cicero as a normal gesture with no implication that the choice of topic was governed by parental anxiety.

Cicero's main purpose then appears to have been to round off his long programme of philosophical investigation by a final review of the conception of pure practical morality raised in his study of Antiochus. In clarifying his attitude he must at the same time touch on issues important in political theory. With-out attaching so much importance as does Syme to the impulse to demonstrate the conception of a well-ordered state, one may agree that Cicero must have felt that his demonstration of decency and high ideals in private and public life and inter-national relations, though they might not sound an immediate call to arms against Antony, must help to bolster the morale of men of good will and enhance their respect for the republican ideal.

19. The relevant letters of Cicero are *Att.* xiv. 13, 16; xv, 16 f.; *Fam.* xii. 16; xvi. 21.

CHAPTER VII

THE HUMANISM OF CICERO

FROM the series of works there have emerged four propositions which Cicero did accept: (a) man, having a limited understanding because of the impossibility of indubitably valid perception, may rely on calculation of probability as a reasonable guide to what is true, (b) man can make decisions without detailed interference by gods or fate, (c) in decisions of practical conduct man's guiding rule must be respect for his fellow-men, (d) no ethical theory is likely other than the Stoic with its definition of virtue absolute or the theory of pure practical morality accepted by Panaetius and Antiochus with its reconciliation of virtue and the natural advantages. From these we may infer his acceptance of other doctrines. Thus the first implies a general agreement with the Stoics upon the process of perception since Cicero allows that true perceptions are mingled with the false, and so his conception of man as the agent and of the existing world of reality as the object to which his senses are directed must be like the Stoic conception: his scepticism is limited and he feels no doubt about the existence of the world of things. Similarly his case for freedom supposes the world order as it was conceived by Posidonius except that Cicero limits the extent of divine providence and physical determinism. The guiding rule of respect for man implies a general agreement with the basic doctrines put forward in the examination of the Antiochean case—the assumption that, because nature is good, man's first natural impulses provide the key to his ethical end, and the further assumption that one of the first impulses in man is affection for his kind. In fact the acceptance of the criterion implies a general agreement with the Stoic theory of human nature which is confirmed by Cicero's recognition of the natural rights of man for these derive from the Stoic theory of the first impulses.

Thus it seems certain that Cicero had a coherent system and it deserves the name of humanism because it was concerned with man first and foremost and with other things only in so far as they were relevant to man's position in the world. First it inquired into man's nature, the validity of his perception, the nature of his highest virtue, the condition of his happiness, the

degree of his freedom and his relation to the forces which control the world; it ended by asserting a theory of freedom and
a rule of conduct enjoining the highest respect for man and
systematically based on the theory of human nature. While the
later Stoics, relaxing the shackles of original materialism, made
progress towards a positive form of humanism with its ethical
sanctions based on the account of the primary instincts, Cicero,
starting with the advantage of the Academic theory of perception
and a sense of man's free choice, asserted a stronger case for
freedom and reached a conception of humanism more liberal
still. His system might be described as an attempt to adapt a
theory of human freedom to the general background of contemporary Stoicism, while maintaining scepticism in the field of
perception. The limited nature of his scepticism allowed him
to assume the existence of the natural order and he was in
general agreement with a large part of the contemporary Stoic
theory about this natural order. This interpretation is reasonable because the philosophy of Cicero's age was the product of a
process which had been continuous since early in the Hellenistic
era, a process of reaction and counter-reaction between Academy
and Porch with a gradual assimilation of their systems so that the
disputes occurred within the framework of a large body of common doctrine. This is well shown in the position of Antiochus
who, while claiming the headship of the Academy, devoted so
much effort to the modification of Stoicism and who maintained
the view, which Cicero did not query, that there was a common
tradition going right back to Plato and Aristotle of which
Stoicism was a divergent form, and not a separate system. The
assimilation of Academy to Stoicism in this era was aided by
their common lack of understanding of Plato's distinctive
position, especially in epistemology, and by the Stoics' readiness
to incorporate sundry elements of the Platonic cosmology, for
example the adoption by Posidonius and by Antiochus of doctrines from the *Timaeus*.

Now the spirit of humanism was at work in Stoicism, and,
under the impulse to adapt a severe philosophy to man's sense
of his actual experience, there were changes of doctrine. Cicero
far from being the mere transmitter of a static body of dogma,
was actively criticizing the modifications of Stoicism and was
watching developments which had an immediate appeal for him.

It was the nature of early Stoicism which determined the first
acceptance of the doctrine of the brotherhood of man. For

Stoicism was the philosophic expression of the two impulses of individualism and universalism, and in its first stages there were historical conditions which allowed these two apparently conflicting impulses to appear reconcilable with the result that objections which might have been made against the submergence of individual rights were never raised. The city state had imposed narrow loyalties, and individual freedom was almost completely submerged in the duties of citizenship. The wider horizons of Alexander's empire encouraged a sense of the unity of mankind and at the same time imposed on the individual the need to readjust his relations. He had to make his own way in a new world where the old standards had vanished. He was conscious of the need of free and personal decisions. He looked to philosophy to give him above all a guide for conduct. So it was that the interests of the early Stoics were pre-eminently ethical while in particular they gave attention to political theories which should recognize at once the equality of men and their ability to combine in society for a common end. To this period belong the Utopias with their insistence on equality and brotherhood and their imaginary descriptions of virtuous barbarians living according to nature. Such were the Utopias of Euhemerus (c. 300 B.C.) and Iambulus, of the third century; their descriptions were more realistic than the splendid and remote conception which Zeno had advanced. In the imaginary state of Iambulus the people were equal in every way: they shared in work, in production and in government in a communistic fashion. Rostovtzeff says that Iambulus was not actually Stoic. But at any rate his account does reveal the contemporary impulse to reconcile social organization for a common end with individual freedom and regard for the equality of man. Such was the sense of the identity of interests of individual and community that originally there was no thought of conflict between them. As for the doctrine of the equality of men it was greatly helped by the Stoic denial of mundane evils; for seeming inequalities could be glossed over if worldly things, wealth, pain and sickness were of no importance. The early physical doctrine too could support the reconciliation of individual and universal interests. This was the comparison of microcosm and macrocosm according to which man was an organic part of nature and indeed a miniature representation of the cosmos. In orthodox Stoic theory the human soul, as part of the divine soul, had it in its own nature to attain the level of divine understanding which was the condition of perfect morality. Hence the will of the perfect man could be raised to complete identity with the universal will. Such was the doctrine which the French Stoics adopted from Epictetus when they proclaimed that the way to happiness was to bring the individual will into agreement with the supreme will.

There resulted the uncritical conception of man as a social animal with private rights and universal obligations which persisted in the time of Panaetius and Antiochus and although the illustrations of virtuous action in the *De Officiis* revealed certain conflicts these were not investigated but we find them waved aside with platitudinous exhortation to man to 'reconcile the needs of his person with the universal nature.' This attitude reflects itself in Cicero's political theory. For in the *De Re Publica* he states the Stoic views, and apparently accepts them, on the reconcilability of individual rights with society and even shows reasons why kingship, provided the king be enlightened, is acceptable since man can be organized under a wise control with due regard for the natural interests of men.[1] While this refusal to see grounds for conflict prepared the way for the feeling of brotherhood there was also a positive argument based on the Stoic assumption of the essential goodness of human nature leading to the conception of the law of nature as an ideal of excellence standing behind the laws of states. It was here in particular that the Roman genius for legal forms was transformed by the humanizing and cosmopolitan spirit of Hellenism so that it prepared the way for that high ideal of humanity which has been characteristic of Western civilization in its true forms. Originally to the Romans '*ius gentium*' meant no more than the law common to nations. The Romans first found the need to detect it because in their dealings with the many communities in Italy they encountered a great diversity of usages. But among the diversity they could find particular usages common to separate communities. By codifying these they could arrive at rules commonly acceptable. But at this stage *ius gentium* was a convenience, an appendage to the *ius civile*, intended to facilitate dealings with foreigners for whom the practical Romans felt no warm sentiment. It was by no means a model standing behind the civil law. As Rome expanded she met the same problem in her dealings with the large and civilized nations of the Mediterranean world and continued to refer to

1. *Rep.* i. 53, 69; iii. 24, 45-7; cf. *Leg.* i. 35.

the category of *ius gentium* the common usages observed in commerce and general intercourse. Hence the term among the lawyers of the second century B.C. took on a quasi-technical sense which distinguished universal and informal usage from the *ius civile*. But in Cicero we find a new meaning for *ius gentium*: he speaks of it in the *De Officiis* as something wider than the civil law.[2] In the sense in which he uses it there the term may be translated 'universal law'. Now the passage in the *De Officiis* is very important because it does reveal the philosophic basis for this conception of universal law. He has just argued that dishonesty in private bargaining is wrong because it is forbidden by the law of nature since it injures the common bond which should unite men, although it might not actually be forbidden by civil law. 'Accordingly our ancestors distinguished *ius gentium* from *ius civile*.' But the basis of distinction here is moral: *ius gentium* derives its sanction from the law of nature, and the principle of the law of nature is respect for the common bond of mankind. So it is again from his acceptance of the Stoic doctrine of the goodness of human nature that Cicero derives his ultimate sanction for the law of nature by virtue of which the law of nations is transformed into a broad ideal which should be a standard for civil codes to guarantee their respect for men. For codes and their resulting rights were founded in order to protect man's essential nature. Moreover the law of nature applies not only to the relations of men within society but also to the relations between nations. There is a common brotherhood of mankind that transcends nations.

While the Stoic conception of human nature thus provided the grounds for Cicero's criterion of social conduct it also, through the doctrine of the derivation of the virtues from the impulses, involved him in the investigation of a form of naturalistic humanism which proclaimed man's perfection as the ethical end. Here he had to deal with the attempts of Panaetius and Antiochus to make the Stoic theory consistent. They argued that it started with the assumption that the examination of the impulses would reveal the essential nature of man as a moral creature, and that the ethical goal was to be attained by development of this nature to perfection; but that it then neglected the essential parts of the creature by attention to mind

2. *Off.* iii. 69. On the whole question of *ius gentium* and *lex naturae* see D. G. Ritchie, *Natural Rights*, pp. 35 ff., and H. Nettleship in *Journ. Philol.*, xiii (1885), 169 ff.

alone, discarded the humbler faculties, created a gap between
the impulses and the virtues, denied the emotions and proclaimed a definition of the good which was meaningless. In
short this phase of Stoicism set out to seek morality within the
stream of life but then diverged by the unrealistic account of
man's inward state and the excision of the emotions and by
exaltation of the transcendental ends. Panaetius and Antiochus
stressed the conclusions of experience. Observation convinced
them that reason does grapple with the emotions and is concerned with things. The argument which Cicero hands down
from them makes a sincere, if imperfect, attempt to arrive at
the primary impulses and proceeds to demonstrate the derivation
of the virtues from them. Thus it makes out a case for the
unity of man as a rational creature with reason in its three
aspects, intellectual, social and moderative,[3] consistently based
on the original elements of man's nature. And because of the
insistence that perfect morality is to be achieved by development
of the whole of man's essential nature and not of mind alone,
the intellectual control which it envisages is a unified rational
control of human life in all its aspects. The attention to the
essential parts other than mind does not prevent the triumph
of the highest attributes of humanity any more than it does in
Comte who likewise advanced in modern philosophy a purely
naturalistic idea of man.[4] The theory of the natural endowments as the basis of the structure of the virtues resembles some
attempts by modern humanists, for example Frère's survey of
the characteristic endowments such as curiosity, invention and
the fundamental impulse to seek rationality, which exalt man
above other animals, and a less effective attempt by Novak to
found a theory of humanism on a classification of human values
starting from the impulse of self-preservation and adopting
values in an arbitrary fashion with some attempt to reconcile
the altruistic and the self-seeking impulses.[5] However, there are
defects in this modified Stoic theory. The impulses are chosen
in an arbitrary fashion without regard for inconsistencies and
the demonstration of the development of the virtues from them
is not convincing. What Cicero offers us in the De Officiis is

3. Cf. Bréhier, 'Sur une des origines de l'humanisme moderne, le *De
Officiis* de Cicéron', *Report of the Amsterdam Conference*, 1948, pp. 777 ff.
4. J. Maritain, *True Humanism*, p. 15.
5. *Report of the Amsterdam Conference*, 1948, Frère, 'Bases positives de la
dignité humaine', p. 60, and Novak, 'Esquisse d'une théorie de l'humanisme',
p. 226.

Panaetius' assertion that the structure of the virtues is complete; but this is not a proof. Actually from the intrusion of practical activity into the descripion of purely virtuous conduct it appears that the classification is quite arbitrary. In fact we cannot feel that the perfection of virtue is established theoretically, and neither the demonstration in the *Tusculan Disputations* of its power to triumph nor the theoretical treatment in the *De Officiis* of the relations of *honesta* and *utilia* can be considered adequate. Nor can we be certain of the meaning of the Panaetian-Antiochean claim for perfection of human understanding. Apparently what they contemplated was complete knowledge of the material system—what we may call perfect natural wisdom.[6] But if, as seems likely, they agreed with the *Timaeus,* they would not equate this supreme human intelligence to the divine.

As for Cicero's attitude towards the theory, there is no doubt that he was sympathetic with the fundamental conception of human nature, with the account of the impulses and the general classification of the virtues, but he was bound by his assumption of the imperfection of human understanding. Accordingly he could not agree that man can attain perfect morality. But his idea of the nature of the ordinary man would not differ from the idea held by Antiochus.

From the strength of the Stoic interest in man it was inevitable that the problem of freedom should develop. At first no difficulty was apparent, for orthodox Stoicism implied the unity of God, man and the universe. God and soul were bodies, part of the complete material system organized by all-pervading, intelligent law. In such a system there was no difficulty in reconciling human reason with the divine because it was part of the divine reason and, in its full perfection, merged into the divine. Thus in a restricted sense under old Stoicism one might uphold the self-sufficiency of man: in his perfect development he lacked nothing. But the early Stoics in their enthusiasm for ethics and political theory and from their practical experience would have some sense of the unreality of a theory which denied man any power of decision and would have some reluctance to accept the complete determinism which must result from a theory of the universe as a physical plenum bound by universal 'sympathy' and an intricate interaction of all its parts. Chrysippus, as the *De Fato* shows, attempted to make concession to common sense with his complicated and unconvincing attempt to

6. Cf. Maritain, op. cit., p. 13.

find some loophole for independent action by man. This, while it may have been concerned primarily with the question of man's role in perception, would ultimately suggest some case for freedom in ethical judgment. Thus the Stoics came to recognize that they had on their hands the problem of reconciling a general doctrine of fatalism with the common-sense demand for freedom in ethical decisions and they realized that to deny some power of choice would remove all moral responsibility from man. Accordingly Antiochus was responding to a need which had developed within Stoicism, dimly discerned perhaps by Chrysippus. And Cicero, in investigating Antiochus, was attempting the next stage of the continuous process. But Cicero's case for freedom is complicated by obscurities in the account of the nature of deity. In the Posidonian account in *De Natura Deorum* II, while the retention of determinism implies that the deity is still partly conceived as a physical force in the old Stoic sense, there is also some evidence of a view of the god as a force outside the material world, endowed with the power to act as an independent creator. Cicero himself, who gave even less thought than the contemporary Stoics to the material composition of the world and who threw off the doctrine of determinism, seems to have gone even further towards the idea of a creator god if, as seems likely, he followed the *Timaeus*. For in the *Timaeus* all that is good is derived from the eternal model and the creator's purpose. He thus fell short of modern naturalistic humanism by denying the complete self-sufficiency of man and by deriving his moral order from a principle higher than man.[7]

On the other hand Cicero's retention of the Platonic confusion between the conceptions of God as artificer and God as father of the world prevents him from reaching the position of Christianity. Christianity has an answer to the naturalistic humanist. The criticism which the latter makes is that to suppose a god wholly other than man implies ends beyond time and raises an impassable barrier between man and God: for the means intended to achieve them, being temporal, cannot be linked by a causal or logical continuity with the ends. Against this Christianity can oppose the argument that its doctrine of incarnation implies a God who is not 'wholly other' but yet is above man: man shares the divine nature, and the divine part of him, the

7. Hook, 'Nature and the Human Spirit', *Report of the Amsterdam Conference*, 1948, pp. 774 ff.

soul, is different from the material. But the confusion in the Ciceronian theology makes it obscure whether his god is of the world or outside it and of a nature in which man can share or quite different, while the relationship is further complicated by the Platonic confusion according to which the created world may share the nature of both God and man, although this cannot be certain. Thus the whole assumption of the goodness of man is vitiated by the confused conception of the divine nature. Nor can Cicero base the assertion of man's essential worth, as Aquinas does, on the doctrine of the eternality and goodness of the individual soul.

Thus we can see that the Ciceronian case for freedom falls between the two modern theories. It is not entirely anthropocentric, nor is it altogether theocentric. It cannot agree with the modern naturalistic humanist's assertion of man's self-sufficiency in so far as it supposes a principle higher than man. Nevertheless it is confused about the nature of this higher principle and cannot therefore establish a clear relationship between man and God in the Christian sense nor assert the fulfilment of God's purpose in the immortal life of the individual soul. But despite these limitations Cicero's theory has made an advance beyond the orthodox Stoic position towards the Christian conception of God and has put forward grounds for human freedom though without fully vindicating them. In Cicero man has some share of divine essence, some ability to advance towards the highest level of intelligence and great freedom of action by his own efforts. There is certainly a loosening of the bondage of man's complete subordination to the universe, which has been supposed to characterize Greek thought, and there is a definite proclamation of the essential worth of man. In the end he achieved a sense of humanity which not only was far ahead of the old outlook of the city state but also had a vitality far greater than that which the traditional Stoic attitude could be expected to achieve. Certainly Cicero's system lacked warmth of feeling for the unity of human and divine purpose in the Christian sense and was not inspired by the Christian spirit of love. But it did reveal a real concern for the welfare of men and society and there was no little glimmer of emotion in the concern which he expressed in the *De Natura Deorum* that to deny religion would break the bonds of society. He adopted for himself a high ideal of conduct. Because of his reservation on man's attainment of perfection it was a working rule rather than a principle established with philosophic certainty. His working rule—that man must not seek personal gain by harming another—based as it was on recognition of the essential worth of man, showed some of the respect for universal obligation which Kant proclaims in his practical imperative: 'So act as to treat humanity, whether in thine own person or in that of any other, in every case as an end withal, never as means only.'[8]

But to say that Cicero is sincere does not establish his originality and I can find no support for Ciaceri's view[9] that in the political theory which he finally proclaims in the *De Officiis* there is a distinctively Roman quality. Certainly when the broad universalism of the first era of Hellenism narrowed before the more exacting demands of the Roman state a restatement of the theory which reconciled individualism and universalism was appropriate and more so when new forms of dictatorship began to threaten the Republican ideal, which, after all, in Cicero's view, did maintain an adequate respect for the individual. But there is no theory which cannot be traced back to Hellenism. Cicero makes no original contribution and his own most distinctive doctrine, the calculation of probability, is derived from the Greeks of the New Academy. But the political theory is certainly acceptable to the moderate Roman. That can be seen by the aptness of the many Roman illustrations in the *De Officiis*, while the sense of devotion to the state and fellow citizens and the condemnation of tyranny are thoroughly consistent with the true ideal of Republican Rome. In short the theory was not distinctively Roman in the sense that it had elements which the Greeks lacked but it did suit the Roman scene in the last few years of the Republic. That we are right in supposing that Cicero accepted the views which we have ascribed to him is shown by their consistency with the theory of the *De Re Publica* and *De Legibus*. He published the *De Re Publica* in 51 B.C. and a large part of the composition of the *De Legibus* coincided in time with the writing of the *De Re Publica* although it was not published until later and then probably in an incomplete form.[10] These works were written at a stage in his political career when, after the disappointments of the half-dozen years after his return from exile, he earnestly

8. Kant, *Fundamental Principles of the Metaphysics of Morals*, ed. Abbott, 1925, p. 56.

9. Ciaceri, *Cicerone e i suoi tempi*, vol. ii, p. 371.

10. Cf. C. W. Keyes, 'Did Cicero complete the *De Legibus*?', *Am. J. Philol.*, lviii (1937), pp. 403 ff.

desired to clarify his attitude.[11] They do consequently show what he regarded as the principles of political theory.

There is a slight difficulty in the interpretation of the *De Legibus* that must be cleared up in passing. He says 'Let the New Academy be silent' and for his political theory he expects the approval of—

> all who believe that all things right and honourable are to be desired for their own sake and that nothing whatever is to be classed as a good unless it is praiseworthy in itself, or at least that nothing should be considered a great good unless it can rightly be praised for its own sake. (*Leg.* i. 37 ff.)

i.e. of the Stoics and our old friends the 'Academico-Peripatetics'. Now it might be said that this repudiation of the New Academy, his own school, was inconsistent and that accordingly the doctrine of the *De Legibus* did not represent Cicero's normal view. But we cannot have come so far in our interpretation of Cicero without developing an ability to assess his meaning in passages like this. We met similar problems of interpretation in *Tusculan Disputations* II and *De Officiis* III. What he meant was that, whereas in general he accepted the New Academy's principle of keeping an open mind and surveying all possibilities, this did not debar him from making a decision where it seemed reasonable; thus on the issue in question in the *De Legibus* he was willing to decide for the theory accepted by the Stoics or the Old Tradition as he understood it.

There are several doctrines accepted by Cicero in the series of philosophic works which are treated in the *De Re Publica* and *De Legibus* so that we may turn to these works for amplification of them. One of them, the doctrine of the goodness of the order of nature as the starting point of morality, is explained more fully in the *De Re Publica* and *De Legibus* than elsewhere. Here the justification is traced right back to the Stoic conception of all-pervading reason, the highest principle in the universe. It is by virtue of this that the order of nature is good and this is the basis of true law: for law is 'right reason in agreement with nature'. Hence man's morality derives from his endowment of reason, which he shares with all men alike, and requires that he observe the true law which is an expression of right reason. Nowhere is this conception of the foundation of morality and true law better expressed than in this passage from the *De*

11. Cf. Syme, op. cit., pp. 148 ff.

THE HUMANISM OF CICERO

Re Publica which, in Last's opinion, deserves more perhaps than
any other passage in the literature of Western Europe to be
familiar to every educated man[12] for it is the source of the
absolute distinction between right and wrong and it was this that
confirmed Cicero's influence in political and moral philosophy.

> *Rep.* iii. 33: True law is right reason in agreement with
> nature: it extends to all men, is unchanging and everlasting;
> it calls men to duty by its commands and by its voice of warn-
> ing holds them back from deceit. Its orders and its prohibitions
> are not unheeded by good men, though they do not influence
> evil men. It is sinful to try to amend this law, nor is it right
> to try to repeal any part of it. It is impossible to abolish it
> entirely. Neither by senate nor by popular edict can we be
> freed from the obligations of this law. We need not seek the
> help of another to expound and interpret it. There will not
> be different laws in Rome and in Athens or different laws now
> and in the future but all nations at all times will be under
> the sway of one law, everlasting and unchangeable. And there
> will be one universal master and ruler, the God, who is the
> author of this law, its promulgator and its enforcing judge.
> Whoever disobeys him will be fleeing from himself and turn-
> ing away from the very nature of man and as a consequence
> of this he will pay the greatest of penalties, although he
> escapes what is commonly considered punishment.

Here is a conception of morality which has high regard for
man. Now in strictest Stoic theory this might bind man to the
kingdom of nature and conformity with the universal reason
might mean merely acquiescence. But Cicero's insistence that
man has some degree of freedom raises it to a form of morality
ennobled by the notion of man's responsibility.

It is important to observe that the doctrine of true law as
something wider than civil law, well expressed in the next
passage and based on the description of law as right reason in
agreement with nature, is the basis of the theory of *De Officiis*
iii. 69 on the priority of *lex naturae* to *ius gentium* and *ius civile*.
This law is conceived as a force founded on nature and prior to
rights established between men.

> *Leg.* i. 17: But in this discussion we must embrace the whole
> question of universal justice and laws while our own civil law,
> as we term it, is confined to a small and narrow corner. For
> we must explain the nature of justice, seeking it in the nature

12. H. Last, Presidential Address, *Proceedings of the British Classical
Association*, 1950.

of man; and we must consider the laws by which states should be ruled; and then we must deal with the laws and decrees of nations which are formulated and recorded: among these we shall not overlook what are termed the civil laws of our own nation.

Here again the high regard for man is shown in the thought that justice must be sought in man's nature. It is here and in the conception of man's common endowment of reason as the basis of morality that is to be found the ultimate sanction for the doctrine of human brotherhood. Its justification is stated with more precision in the *De Re Publica* and *De Legibus* than in the philosophic works:

Leg. i. 18 f.: Well then, the most learned men have decided to start with law; and probably their decision is right if, according to their definition, law is the highest reason, implanted in nature ordaining what is right to do and forbidding the opposite. This reason, when established and developed in the mind of man, is law. Thus they think that law is intelligence and that its natural function is to command right conduct and forbid transgression. . . . If this is right, as I think it to be in general, then the origin of justice is to be derived from law: for law is a natural force; it is the mind and reason of the intelligent man; it is the standard by which justice and injustice are measured.

Leg. i. 23: Therefore, since there is nothing better than reason and since it is found both in man and in god, the first common possession of man and god is reason; but those who have reason in common also have right reason in common. Since this is law then it must be assumed that we men share with the gods in law. Moreover those who share law together must share justice; now those who share these must be considered members of the same commonwealth. If they obey the same authorities and powers this is much more so: now they do obey this celestial system, the divine mind and the all-powerful god. The result is that this whole world must be considered to be one commonwealth of which gods and men are members.

Leg. i. 42: For justice is one. The whole of human society is under its sway. One law is its basis. This law is right reason applied to command and prohibition. The man who knows not this law, whether it has been recorded anywhere or not, is a man without justice.

While the *De Re Publica* and *De Legibus* advance this more fundamental justification of the doctrine of brotherhood, they also amply support the theory of the natural bond of affection between men which in the philosophic works is the main ground for the doctrine of brotherhood.

Rep. i. 39: Then a commonwealth is the property of a nation. But a nation is not any assembly of men collected by any means at all. It is an assembly large in numbers and bound together by a common regard for law and a partnership for the common good. The first reason why it gathers together is not so much weakness as a certain natural tendency in men to flock together.

Leg. i. 28 f.: But of all the material of learned discussions there is certainly nothing more important than the clear understanding that we are born for justice and that right is based not on opinion but on nature. This will immediately be obvious if you realize the fellowship and union that exists between men. For there is no single thing so like another, so closely corresponding to it as are all of us to one another.

Similar statements on men's bond of natural affection are found in *De Legibus* i. 16, 32, 35, e.g. 'How can I help being convinced when it has been proved to us that . . . all men are bound together by a natural feeling of kindliness and good will and also by their partnership in justice?'

We observed that a large part of the argument of the *De Officiis* discussed the relation of individual rights and universal obligation and concluded, though without precise proof, that somehow they were reconcilable. The *De Re Publica* deals more particularly with this problem because it has to discuss forms of political organization. It shows that Cicero himself favoured the rule of an enlightened aristocracy and that, since the test of enlightenment was due regard for the citizens as persons and for the common weal, he considered that such a form of government could adequately respect individual rights. The principle of all sound societies must be justice: 'For in the first place a people exists only when the individuals who form it are held together by a partnership in justice' (*Rep.* iii. 45).

Accordingly even kingship is an acceptable form of government if it is enlightened and can respect both the individual and the common weal. 'But I cannot admit that view of yours that aristocratic government is better than the rule of a king. For if it is wisdom that rules the state what does it matter if it is found in one person or in several?' (*Rep.* iii. 47).

o

In fact the right sort of government would seem to be an enlightened kingship allowing an adequate voice to aristocrats and commoners:

> *Rep.* i. 69: For I feel that there should be a supreme and royal power in the state, and that there should also be some recognition bestowed on the power of the leading citizens while certain matters should be left to the desires and wishes of the common people. In the first place such a constitution has a high degree of equality of which free men can hardly be deprived for any length of time, and then it has stability.

A final point of agreement between the theory of the *De Re Publica* and the *De Officiis* is the admission of the superiority over speculative wisdom of wisdom 'directed according to the principles of justice to the service of humanity'. Thus the Republic stresses the importance of political activity, as in Book iii. 4 f.

Since it is reasonable to suppose that Cicero himself accepted the political theory of the *De Re Publica* and *De Legibus,* the agreement on these points between them and the philosophic works confirms the view of his sincerity in the philosophic works. Moreover between the two groups there is a community of sources which is significant. For the *De Re Publica* and *De Legibus* the usually suggested source is Panaetius, who is the predominant influence in the *De Officiis.* But it is possible also that Antiochus of Ascalon was the main source for the *De Legibus.*[13] If this were established then the relationship between Antiochus and Panaetius in these two works would strongly reinforce our thesis of the interrelation of the Antiochean doctrines of the *De Finibus* and the Panaetian doctrines of the *De Officiis.*

We can now see that Cicero's fight for the Republic was inspired by principles in which he had a strong personal belief. He felt that his ideal of a stable and balanced state guided by an enlightened ruler or ruling body could be achieved by the existing system, with senate and people observing their separate functions in pursuit of the common good. In this system he saw the possibility of that blending of universal and individual

13. For discussion of sources see A. Schmekel, *Die Philosophie der mittleren Stoa*; Ioh. Galbiatius (= G. Galbiati), *De fontibus M. Tullii Ciceronis librorum qui manserunt de re publica et de legibus quaestiones,* 1916; R. Hoyer, *De Antiocho Ascalonita*; A. Laudien, 'Die Composition und Quelle von Ciceros i. Buch der Gesetze', *Hermes,* xlvi (1911), 108 ff.

obligations, and at the same time that respect for man, which were demanded by the theory of human nature which he accepted in his philosophy. He resisted Antony bitterly because in him he saw no possibility of an enlightened control. For the central theme of Cicero's ethical theory was that the attainment of the good required the full self-realization of man as a social creature. From this sprang the theory of human rights and an assumption that somehow the individual rights of man were reconcilable with the universal obligations of society. Respect for man determined the distinction between right and wrong: this implied that only that can be right which respects man and the effect of this assumption may be seen in the principle of practical morality which Cicero accepted in the *De Officiis,* that no man should harm another for personal gain. Further it implies that the state has a moral obligation towards the individual.

That Cicero must have had high principles to guide him is made more evident as, in our expanding understanding of Roman history, we develop an increased appreciation of the difficulty of his role. In his *Roman Revolution* Syme has revealed a greater complexity in the Roman political scene than has been suspected. In the old interpretation, with its stress on individual rivalries—as of Caesar and Pompey—the issues seemed clear-cut and the middle course fairly well defined. But now we are aware of conflicts of oligarchic groups behind the individual rivalries: Roman politics seem more complex, with more hidden violence, intrigue and antagonism than used to be suspected. Difficult as was the path of the moderate under the old conception, immeasurably greater entanglements would surround him in the complexity of the power politics of the groups. Our contemporary experience helps us to see this: we are aware of the concealed pressure groups; we detect the psychological maladjustments of the Hitlers and the Mussolinis who urge extremes of policy and scorn moderation. The result is that we feel greater admiration for Cicero as a man who stuck consistently to the course of moderation amidst extreme violence and whose moderation was not the middle course of inactivity; for he did try to influence events. Now in our time we see that it takes great moral courage to resist the extremes and that to resist consistently requires a firm belief in principles. And so we come to feel that with Cicero high principles did indeed guide his conduct for it does not seem that a man could maintain a consistent course, rally time and again after his rebuffs and at the end of his life lead a vigorous campaign against new threats unless he had a firm foundation of belief. That he should be a moderate in politics was inevitable because of the nature of his philosophy. But he was a moderate with a sense of purpose. The argument which we have been able to trace through his works led from a statement of man's inability to attain to perfect knowledge—with the resulting need to determine practical conduct by calculation of probability—to a search for a guiding principle that should make the decisions of practical life as good as possible. While his form of scepticism forced him to believe that man cannot know for certain in any particular case, it did not prevent him from accepting a general scheme of the nature of the world, of man's place in it and of an ideal morality which should be valid for man if only his perception could be free from error. And so his was the moderation which believes that man cannot know anything for certain and must on occasion determine his conduct by calculation of expediency but which believes nevertheless that there is a system of truth to which man, despite his imperfect reason, may approximate. His ethical enquiry was sincere and systematic. Going down to first principles—in epistemology to the nature of sense perception, in ethics to the fundamental impulses—he emerged with a doctrine of social obligation founded plausibly enough on parental affection, mutual attraction and the design of nature and with a doctrine of natural rights founded, if incompletely, on man's nature. Undoubtedly there were flaws in his doctrines and defects in his proofs. As a matter of fact in his whole ethical system and theory of social obligations very little was established adequately: brotherhood of man rested on an arbitrary and incomplete classification of natural impulses, and the right of private ownership on a deficient analysis. But at least the attempt was there and Cicero—or rather the Greeks whom he copied—appreciated the need to proceed by analysis.

Thus part of the value of the study of Cicero's philosophic works is that they advance some justification of the moderate. He deserved the title because it has been the traditional role of the moderate to uphold a form of government which has a fundamental respect for humanity and he was convinced that his ideal form of the Republic had that respect. It has also been characteristic of the moderate to demand proof rather than accept dogma, but to accept provisional standards based on sincere observation where certainty is lacking and to throw moral responsibility on man. All this Cicero did by virtue of his loyalty to the tradition of the New Academy. But he also drew from the modified Stoicism a body of positive doctrine about man's place in the universe which raised his humanism to the highest form attainable in the pagan world and which, as we have seen, placed him midway between the modern naturalistic humanist and the humanism which is based on Christianity.

APPENDIX

THE PHILOSOPHIC SCHOOLS WITH WHICH
CICERO WAS CONCERNED

1. *The Academy*

Since Cicero did not challenge the Antiochean account in the *Academica* of the developments in the Academic tradition in the immediate post-Platonic era, we may assume that he shared Antiochus' hazy understanding of the Academy before Arcesilaus. Presumably he accepted also the confused version of Peripateticism, for he did not assail the Antiochean account of the common origins of these two schools as the starting point from which the later schools were supposed to have diverged. The Academic doctrines with which he was directly concerned were those of what is sometimes known as the *Middle Academy*. Its main men were:

Arcesilaus (315-241 B.C.). He may be called the founder of the Middle Academy. He carried scepticism to a point beyond that developed in the now defunct school of Pyrrhonism and added the doctrine of suspension of judgment, termed $\dot{\epsilon}\pi o \chi \dot{\eta}$. Thus he maintained no positive thesis but excelled in refutation and, in this respect, his influence can be detected in the arguments in the *Academica*.

Carneades of Cyrene (214-129 B.C.). He gave the next important impulse to the Academic tradition by his endeavour to overcome the impasse imposed by Arcesilaus. This was his suggestion of the calculation of probability. No doubt it was the compatibility of this with the Roman mentality which enabled Carneades so instantly to capture enthusiasm when he visited Rome in 156 B.C. as one of the Athenian ambassadors. His teaching was predominantly oral and it appears that he left no written works. However his teaching was recorded by Clitomachus who succeeded him as president of the Academy and, without personal originality, wrote some four hundred books.

Clitomachus of Carthage (*c.* 180-110 B.C.), originally known as Hasdrubal. His main work was to record the teaching of his master Carneades, who was the last great figure of the Academy.

He, together with Philo, was Cicero's main source in those parts of the *Academica* where he dealt with the doctrines of the Middle Academy on perception, suspense of judgment and the calculation of probability.

The Middle Academy ended with Clitomachus and was followed by the *New Academy* of Philo and Antiochus, who were both teachers of Cicero. The dispute between them on the problem of perception was discussed in the *Academica* by Cicero, who then examined Antiochus' attempt to modify contemporary Stoicism so as to establish a system in conformity with the Academic tradition as he understood it.

2. *The Stoa*

In the doctrine of perception Cicero dealt with arguments that were consistent with the original doctrine of *Zeno* (*c.* 336-264), the founder of Stoicism. But he probably drew the arguments from contemporary sources: for example there is little doubt that Antiochus was his source for the arguments on perception in the *Academica*. There are other Stoic arguments such as the refutation of immortality or the account of the emotions in the *Tusculan Disputations* which, as Cicero gives them, are consistent with orthodox Stoicism and it is probable that here Cicero was indebted to *Chrysippus* (*c.* 280-206 B.C.) the great systematizer of Stoicism, or to sources derived from him. Chrysippus seems to have surpassed even Clitomachus in the number of his books and to have surpassed him in originality also. He was responsible, as Cicero's *De Fato* reveals, for the attempt within Stoicism to make some concession to man's power of choice. However it was mainly with the Middle Stoa that Cicero's argument was concerned and here the names of importance were:

Diogenes Babylonius, who visited Rome in the embassy of 156 B.C., and who really preceded the era of the Middle Stoa. It was his intransigent doctrine of absolute virtue, possibly accepted by some of the Middle Stoa, that was set up for Antiochus' criticism in the *De Finibus.*

Antipater of Tarsus, who was taught by Diogenes Babylonius and himself taught Panaetius. However his main importance was as a link in the tradition of Stoicism and Cicero used him only in *De Officiis* III. Another philosopher of the same order and to whom Cicero made scant reference was Hecaton, a pupil of Panaetius.

Panaetius of Rhodes (180-110 B.C.). He had an important influence on Rome through his friends Scipio and Laelius. Into Stoicism he introduced Platonic elements and abandoned orthodox materialism and the doctrine of periodical conflagration. However he did reject immortality of the soul, allowing only that the soul might live for a certain time after the death of the body. It is possible that he relaxed the Stoic doctrine of universal 'sympathy' and with it the determinism of which traces remain in other members of the Middle Stoa, e.g. in his pupil Posidonius; but whether there was such a division requires separate investigation.

Posidonius of Apamea in Syria (*c.* 135-51 B.C.). He was a pupil of Panaetius and actually taught Cicero in Rhodes. It seems certain that the Stoic theology of *De Natura Deorum* II came from him. Accordingly he accepted determinism and detailed providential control and represents the Middle Stoic cosmology and theology which Cicero criticized. He did however admit Platonic elements. In fact the Middle Stoa, of which he seems to be the main support, is called the 'Platonizing Stoa'. For example Posidonius accepted immortality.

We can see then that in the account of god, man and the universe, Cicero was trying to modify the doctrines of Middle Stoicism. The Middle Stoicism of Posidonius incorporated various Platonic doctrines but it still clung to the theory of determinism and detailed providential control and it was these that Cicero desired to overthrow, while accepting the general scheme of things.

3. *Peripateticism*

Cicero did not treat Peripateticism as a separate system. He did not challenge the Antiochean account of its original identity with the Academy. In theology he classed it under Stoicism. The only distinctive doctrine which he allowed it was its doctrine of emotions as 'desirable mean states' which he refuted in *Tuculan Disputations*.

4. *Epicureanism*

Cicero did not intend to give a positive account of Epicurean doctrine on the several topics but employed it in order to throw into relief the Stoic or Antiochean doctrines, as at the beginning of the *De Finibus* and the *De Natura Deorum*. Accordingly he

P

was content to draw on contemporary versions of Epicureanism, of which many were available, e.g. an epitome for the *De Finibus* or the works of his own teachers Phaedrus and Zeno for the *De Natura Deorum*. He did not advance any original point of view on Epicureanism and his account of it has little value except for the detailed description of the case for pleasure as the primary impulse and the chief good.

BIBLIOGRAPHY

1. Texts

The translation of passages is based on the text listed first in the relevant section.

(a) *Academica*, J. S. Reid, 1885; ibid. smaller edition, 1874; H. Rackham (Loeb), 1933.

(b) *De Finibus*, W. M. L. Hutchinson, 1909; J. N. Madvig, 1889; H. Rackham (Loeb), 1914; Books I and II, J. S. Reid, 1925.

(c) *Tusculan Disputations*, Books I and II, T. W. Dougan, 1905; Books III-V, T. W. Dougan and R. M. Henry, 1934; J. E. King (Loeb), 1927.

(d) *Timaeus*, Cicero's translation, C. F. W. Müller, 1879.

(e) *De Natura Deorum*, J. B. Mayor, 1880; H. Rackham (Loeb), 1927.

(f) *De Divinatione*, W. A. Falconer (Loeb), 1927; C. F. W. Müller, 1878; A. S. Pease, 1920.

(g) *De Fato*, A. Yon (*Traité du destin*), 1933; C. F. W. Müller, 1878.

(h) *De Officiis*, H. G. Holden, 5th ed., 1889; W. Miller (Loeb), 1913.

2. Other Relevant Classical Texts

Arnim, H. von. *Stoicorum Veterum Fragmenta*, 1905.

Cicero. *Epistulae ad Familiares*, W. Glynn Williams (Loeb), 1929.

Cicero. *Epistulae ad Atticum*, E. O. Winstedt (Loeb), 1918.

Cicero. *De Re Publica and De Legibus*, C. W. Keyes (Loeb), 1927.

Cicero. *De Re Publica*, G. H. Poyser, 1947.

Clement of Alexandria. *Stromateis*, vol. viii, in *Patrologiae Cursus Completus*, ed. J.-P. Migne, 1857.

Diels, H. *Doxographi Graeci*, 1879.

Diogenes Laertius. *Vitae Philosophorum*, R. D. Hicks (Loeb), 1925.

Epictetus. *The Discourses as reported by Arrian*, W. A. Oldfather (Loeb), 1926.

Fowler, H. N. *Panaetii et Hecatonis librorum fragmenta*, 1885.

Pearson, A. C. *Fragments of Zeno and Cleanthes*, 1891.

Plato. *Timaeus*, J. Burnet, 1905.

Ritter, H., and Preller, L. *Historia Philosophiae Graecae*, 1934.

Sextus Empiricus. *Hypotyposes*, ed. H. Mutschmann, 1912; R. G. Bury (Loeb), 1933.

3. Discussion of Cicero's Sources

In addition to the studies listed here there is considerable discussion of sources in the editions listed above of Reid, Hutchinson, Dougan and Henry, Madvig, Mayor, Yon and Holden.

Finger, P. 'Die beiden Quellen des III. Buches der Tusculanen Ciceros', in *Philologus*, lxxxiv (1928-9), 51 ff., 320 ff.

Hartfelder, K. *Die Quellen von Ciceros zwei Büchern de Divinatione*, 1878.

Heine, O. *Ciceronis Tusculanarum Disputationum libri V*, 1881.

Hoyer, R. *Die Urschrift von Ciceros de Officiis i-iii*, 1898.

Hoyer, R. 'Quellenstudien zu Ciceros Büchern *de natura deorum, de divinatione, de fato*', Rhein. Mus., liii (1898), 37-65.

Klohe, P. *De Ciceronis librorum de Officiis fontibus*, 1889.

Kühner, R. *Tusculanae Disputationes*, 1853.

Laudien, A. 'Die Composition und Quelle von Ciceros i. Buch der Gesetze', *Hermes*, xlvi (1911), 108-43.

211

Lörcher, A. *Das Fremde und das Eigene in Ciceros Büchern de Finibus Bonorum et Malorum und den Academica*, 1911.
Pohlenz, M. 'Das zweite Buch der Tusculanen', *Hermes*, xliv (1909) , 23-40.
Pohlenz, M. 'Das dritte und vierte Buch der Tusculanen', *Hermes*, xli, 321-55.
Poppelreuter, P. H. *Quae ratio intercedat inter Posidonii* περὶ παθῶν πραγματείας *et Tusc. Disp. Ciceronis*, 1883.
Reinhardt, L. *Die Quellen von Ciceros Schrift de Deorum Natura*, 1888.
Schiche, Th. *De fontibus librorum Ciceronis qui sunt de divinatione*, 1875.
Schwenke, P. 'Über Ciceros Quellen in den Büchern de Natura Deorum iii', *Jahrb. f. klass. Philol.*, cxix (1879).
Straaten, M. van. *Panétius*, 1946.
Wilsing, N. *Aufbau und Quellen von Ciceros Schrift de republica*, 1929.
Zietzschmann, G. *De Tusculanarum disputationum fontibus*, 1868.

4. *Particular Studies of Cicero*

Boissier, G. *Cicéron et ses amis*, 1879.
Boyancé, P. 'Cicéron et son oeuvre philosophique', *Revue des Etud. Lat.*, xiv (1936) , 288-309.
Bruwaene, M. van den. *La Théologie de Cicéron*, 1937.
Bruwaene, M. van den. *Etudes sur Ciceron*, 1946.
Carcopino, J. *Les Secrets de la correspondance de Cicéron*, 1946.
Ciaceri, E. *Cicerone e i suoi tempi*, 1939-41.
Conway, R. S. 'The Inner Experience of Cicero', *New Studies of a Great Inheritance*, 1920.
Conway, R. S. 'The Originality of Cicero', *Makers of Europe*, 1931.
DeGraff, Thelma B. 'Plato in Cicero', *Class. Phil.*, xxxv (1940) , 143.
Edelstein, L. 'Cicero de Natura Deorum ii', *Studi Italiani di Filol. Class.*, 1934, 131-83.
Finger, P. 'Die drei kosmologischen Systeme im zweiten Buche von Ciceros Schrift über das Wesen der Götter', *Rhein. Mus.*, lxxx (1931) , 151-200, 310-20.
Finger, P. 'Die drei Grundlegungen des Rechts im i. Buch von Ciceros Schrift *de Legibus*', *Rhein. Mus.*, lxxxi (1932) , 155-77.
Frank, T. 'Cicero', Annual lecture on a master mind, *Proc. Brit. Acad.*, xviii (1932).
Frisch, H. *Cicero's Fight for the Republic*, 1946.
Haskell, H. J. *This was Cicero*, 1942.
Hirzel, R. *Untersuchungen zu Ciceros philosophischen Schriften*, 1877-83.
How, W. W. 'Cicero's Ideal in his *De Republica*', *J. Rom. Stud.*, xx (1930).
Jeanmaire, H. 'Introduction à l'étude du livre II du *de Natura Deorum*', *Revue d'hist. de la philos. et d'hist. génér. de la civilisation*, i (1933), 12-57.
Jones, R. E. 'Cicero's Accuracy of Characterisation in his Dialogues', *Am. J. Philol.*, lx (1939), 307-25.
Jungblut, Chr. *Die Arbeitsweise Ciceros im i. Buche über die Pflichten*, 1907.
Keyes, C. W. 'Did Cicero complete the *De Legibus*?', *Am. J. Philol.*, lviii (1937) , 403-17.
Laurand, L. *Cicéron*, 2nd ed., 1935.
Laurand, L. 'Deux Mots sur les idées religieuses de Cicéron', *Cicéron*, volume complémentaire, 1938, pp. 351 ff.
Levin, T. W. *Six Lectures Introductory to the Philosophical Writings of Cicero*, 1871.
Masson, J. 'Cicero on the Epicurean Gods', *Class. Rev.*, xvi (1902) , 277.

Nelson, N. E. 'Cicero's *De Off.* in Christian Thought', *Univ. of Mich. Essays and Studies in Eng. and Comp. Lit.*, x (1933).
Newman, Cardinal J. H. *Historical Sketches*, vol. i, 9th ed., 1889.
Packer, Mary M. Porter. *Cicero's Presentation of Epicurean Ethics*, 1938.
Petersson, T. *Cicero*, 1920.
Plasberg, O. *De M. Tulli Ciceronis Hortensio Dialogo*, 1895.
Pohlenz, M. *Antikes Führertum: Cicero de Officiis und das Lebensideal des Panaitios*, 1934.
Pöschl, V. *Römischer Staat und Griechisches Staatsdenken bei Cicero*, 1936.
Richards, G. C. *Cicero*, 1935.
Rolfe, J. C. *Cicero and his Influence*, 1923.
Sprey, K. *De M. Tulli Ciceronis Politica Doctrina*, 1928.
Thiaucourt, R. *Essai sur les Traités philosophiques de Cicéron et leurs sources grecques*, 1885.
Trollope, A. *The Life of Cicero*, 1880.
Whitley, A. F. *The Tremulous Hero*, 1939.

5. *Other Relevant Works*

Alston, L. *Stoic and Christian in the Second Century*, 1906.
Arnold, E. V. *Roman Stoicism*, 1911.
Bailey, C. 'Roman Religion and the Advent of Philosophy', *Camb. Anc. Hist.*, vol. viii.
Bauer, E. *Vom Griechentum zum Christentum*, 1923.
Barker, E. 'Greek Political Thought in the Fourth Century', *Camb. Anc. Hist.*, vol. vi.
Barth, P., and Goedeckemeyer, A. *Die Stoa*, 1946.
Bevan, E. *Stoics and Sceptics*, 1913.
Bonhöffer, A. *Epiktet und die Stoa*, 1890.
Bonhöffer, A. *Die Ethik des Stoikers Epiktet*, 1894.
Botsford, G. W., and Sihler, E. G. *Hellenic Civilisation*, 1929.
Bréhier, E. *Histoire de la philosophie*, 1926.
Bréhier, E. *Chrysippe*, 1910.
Brochard, V. *Les Sceptiques grecs*, 1887.
Bury, J. B., Barber, E. A., Bevan, E., and Tarn, W. W. *The Hellenistic Age*, 1925.
Cary, M., and Haarhoff, T. G. *Life and Thought in the Greek and Roman World*, 1946.
Cochrane, C. N. *Christianity and Classical Culture*, 1940.
Cornford, F. M. *Plato's Cosmology*, 1937.
Cowell, F. R. *Cicero and the Roman Republic*, 1948.
Davidson, W. L. *The Stoic Creed*, 1907.
Doege, H. *Quae ratio intercedat inter Panaetium et Antiochum Ascalonitam*, 1896.
Dudley, D. R. *A History of Cynicism*, 1937.
Elorduy, E. 'Die Sozialphilosophie der Stoa', *Philologus Supp.*, xxviii (1936).
Foster, M. B. 'The Christian Doctrine of Creation and the Rise of Modern Natural Science', *Mind*, xliii (1934).
Foster, M. B. 'Christian Theology and Modern Science of Nature', *Mind*, xliv, xlv (1935-6).
Gierke, O. F. von. *Natural Law and the Theory of Society*, 1934.
Goedeckemeyer, A. *Geschichte des griechischen Skeptizismus*, 1905.
Gomperz, T. *Greek Thinkers*, 1906.
Goodenough, E. R. 'The Political Philosophy of the Hellenistic Kingship', *Yale Studies*, i (1928).
Heinemann, S. *Poseidonios metaphysische Schriften*, 1928.
Hicks, R. D. *Stoic and Epicurean*, 1910.
Hoyer, R. *De Antiocho Ascalonita*, 1883.

Labowsky, Lotte. *Die Ethik des Panaitios*, 1934.

Lebreton and Zeiller. *The History of the Primitive Church*, 1942.

Lewis, H. D. 'Some Observations on Natural Rights and the General Will', *Mind*, xlvii (1938).

Mahaffy, J. P. *Greek Life and Thought from the Age of Alexander to the Roman Conquest*, 1896.

Maritain, J. *True Humanism*, 1939.

Maritain, J. *Scholasticism and Politics*, 1940.

Martindale, Rev. Fr. C. C. *What are Saints?*, 1932.

Montaigne. *Essays*.

More, P. E. *Hellenistic Philosophies*, 1923.

Murray, G. G. A. *Stoic, Christian and Humanist*, 1940.

Murray, G. G. A. 'Posidonius and Hellenistic theology', *Five Stages of Greek Religion*, 1925.

Nebel, G. 'Der Begriff des καθῆκον in der alten Stoa', *Hermes*, lxx (1935), 439-60.

Nettleship, H. 'Ius Gentium', *Journ. Philol.*, xiii (1885).

Oates, W. J. *The Stoic and Epicurean Philosophers*, 1940.

Ogereau, F. *Essai sur le système philosophique des Stoiciens*, 1885.

Orton, W. A. *The Liberal Tradition*, 1946.

Patrick, Mary M. *The Greek Sceptics*, 1929.

Pauly-Wissowa. *Real Encyclopädie*, articles on Antiochus, Philo, etc.

Pohlenz, M. *Staatsgedanke und Staatslehre der Griechen*, 1923.

Pohlenz, M. *Grundfragen der stoischen Philosophie*, 1940.

Pohlenz, M. *Der Hellenische Mensch*, 1947.

Pohlenz, M. *Die Stoa*, 1948.

Reich, K. 'Kant and Greek Ethics', *Mind*, xlviii (1939).

Reinhardt, K. *Kosmos und Sympathie, neue Untersuchungen über Poseidonios*, 1926.

Reinhardt, K. *Poseidonios*, 1921.

Rieth, O. *Grundbegriffe der stoischen Ethik*, 1933.

Ritchie, D. G. *Natural Rights*, 1924.

Robin, L. *La Morale antique*, 1938.

Robin, L. *La Pensée grecque et les origines de l'esprit scientifique*, 1923.

Rostovtzeff. *Social and Economic History of the Hellenistic World*, vol. ii, 1941.

Schäfer, M. *Ein frühmittelstoisches System der Ethik bei Cicero*, 1934.

Schäfer, M. 'Diogenes als Mittelstoiker', *Philologus*, xci (1936), 174-96.

Schindler, K. *Die Stoische Lehre von den Seelenteilen und Seelenvermögen insbesondere bei Panaitios und Poseidonios und ihre Verwendung bei Cicero*, 1934.

Schmekel, A. *Die Philosophie der mittleren Stoa*, 1892.

Stein, L. *Die Psychologie der Stoa*, 1886.

Syme, R. *The Roman Revolution*, 1939.

Tarn, W. W. *Hellenistic Civilisation*, 1951.

Tatakis, B. N. *Panétius de Rhodes*, 1931.

Taylor, A. E. *Plato: Timaeus and Critias* (trans.), 1929.

Taylor, A. E. *A Commentary on Plato's Timaeus*, 1928.

Wendland, P. *Die Hellenistische-Römische Kultur*, 1912.

Wilamowitz-Moellendorf, U. von. 'Panaitios', *Reden und Vorträge*, vol. ii (1926), pp. 190-215.

Witt, R. E. *Albinus and the History of Middle Platonism*, 1937.

The following digests of papers read at the tenth international conference of philosophy (called 'the Amsterdam Conference, 1948') have been consulted. They, together with the many other papers on aspects of humanism read at that conference, indicate the importance of theories of humanism in contemporary philosophy.

Bréhier, E. 'Sur une des Origines de l'humanisme moderne, le *De Officiis* de Cicéron.'

Frère, H. 'Bases positives de la dignité humaine.'

Gibson, A. B. 'Dogmatism and Scepticism in Aesthetics.'

Hook, S. 'Nature and the Human Spirit.'

Kolman, A. 'The Tasks of Contemporary Philosophy in the Struggle for New Humanism.'

Král, J. 'Humanitisme ou humanisme?'

Novak, M. 'Esquisse d'une théorie de l'humanisme.'

Ramsay, I. T. 'Man and Religion: Individual and Community.'

Werner, C. 'Les Origines chrétiennes de l'humanisme.'

INDEX

Brown, Prior, Anderson Pty. Ltd., Melbourne